D1168497

le

UNMAILABLE

# UNMAILABLE

Dorothy Ganfield Fowler

The University of Georgia Press
Athens 30602

## Congress and the Post Office

Library of Congress Catalog Card Number: 75–36689
International Standard Book Number: 0–8203–0402–6

The University of Georgia Press, Athens 30602

Set in 10 on 13 point Primer type
Printed in the United States of America

To
Emmett Fowler
and
to the memory of my sister,
Jane Ganfield,
librarian

# Contents

# Introduction

The United States' postal system is purely a legislative creation. The Post Office has, during its existence, performed various functions: it has been a source of revenue, a political machine, a public service, and guardian of public morals. It has been part of the Treasury Department, an independent department with its head a member of the president's cabinet, and now it has become an independent establishment.

Congress set up the organization of the Post Office. At first it specified postal routes in detail, this function being considered one of the perquisites of congressmen. Later·this function was delegated to the postmaster general and congressmen became more interested in appointments of postal employees. Congress specified postal rates for mailable matter and then began to set up categories of nonmailable material. At first Congress limited the carriage by the postal service to written matter and then gradually broadened the mailable categories to include packages, finally establishing the parcel post system. Certain matter was declared nonmailable, at first in order to protect the mail bags and postal employees. Later Congress came to view the postal service as potentially dangerous since it was the main vehicle for the dissemination of information and opinion. The Congress gradually extended the nonmailable categories for the protection of the public.

Many congressmen wanted to expand the nonmailable classifications for regulatory purposes because the power "to establish post offices and post roads" seemed to be without constitutional limit at a time when Supreme Court decisions had limited the use of the power to tax and the power to regulate interstate commerce. Efforts to extend nonmailable categories were fought by powerful lobbies, states' rights defenders, and liberals intent on protecting rights of individuals.

The setting up of nonmailable categories gave rise to certain questions:

1. Does a citizen have a right to the use of the mails or is it a privilege conferred by Congress as it wishes?

2. Does the Fourth Amendment, establishing freedom from "unreasonable searches," apply to letters? (Congress in the United States has always given lip service to the inviolability of sealed letters, but from time to time there have been charges that mail has been tampered with. In England as late as 1845 mail could be opened by executive departments.)

3. Does freedom of the press include in addition to the right to publish the obligation that the Post Office circulate the publications?

4. Should the regular judicial proceedings apply to administrative regulations of the Post Office?

5. Are orders of the postmaster general subject to judicial review?

6. Does the doctrine of separation of powers prevent the courts from declaring illegal administrative activities of the postmaster general and from declaring unconstitutional acts of Congress regulating the postal service?

The answers to these and other constitutional questions differed in various periods of history in accordance with the mores of American history at the time. The purposes of this study will be to examine and record these changes and to describe the influences that brought them about.

UNMAILABLE

# Establishment of the Postal System

The War of Independence meant for the General Post Office not only a separation from the British postal system but also a revolution in purpose. The colonial post office had been expected to produce a profit but the emphasis during the Revolutionary and Confederation periods was on service.[1]

The colonial post office had been established by William III in 1691. The master of the mint, Thomas Neale, had been named postmaster general of the British possessions in America and had been given the exclusive privilege of carrying letters in the colonies. Thus at the beginning the postal service was a monopoly. In 1711 the whole colonial postal service was put under the direction of the postmaster general of England; one of the purposes of this change was to raise money to help pay the expenses of the War of the Spanish Succession.[2]

In 1753 Benjamin Franklin, postmaster in Philadelphia since 1739, was appointed postmaster general for the American colonies. He reorganized the whole system—straightened routes, shortened the time in transit, established a system of advertising dead letters in newspapers, reduced postal rates, and changed a deficit into a surplus. One significant change that was made was the requirement that riders had to carry all newspapers at a specific rate. Up to that time a local postmaster (who often was a newspaper publisher) not only made special arrangements with the mail carriers to have his paper carried but also got excluded from the mails papers published by others.[3]

On January 31, 1774, Benjamin Franklin received notice, as he wrote Thomas Cushing, "that his Majesty's postmaster-general *found it necessary* to dismiss me from my office of deputy postmaster-general in North America." Franklin's appearance before the Privy Council sponsoring the petition of the assembly of Massachusetts for the removal of Governor Hutchinson may have had something to do with his dismissal. Franklin pointed out that the British ministers intended to put their own appointees into all offices and since, by act of Parliament, postmasters under certain conditions could open letters, correspondence of patriotic colonists would hardly be safe.[4] An American citizen in London warned Lord North that the dismissal of Franklin as postmaster general for the colonies would lead to the establishment by Americans of a carrier system of their own, which would starve the British postal system.[5]

That is exactly what happened. Early in 1774, under the initiative of William Goddard, printer of the *Maryland Journal*, local committees of correspondence along the eastern seaboard began making arrangements for organizing an independent courier service.[6] Sam Adams urged towns to enter into plans to establish a post throughout America to replace the British system. Representing the Committee of Correspondence of Boston, he wrote the committee at Marblehead, March 24, 1774, that a colonial post was essential not only for the carrying of letters but even more for the conveyance of public intelligence from colony to colony to bring about a union of the colonies, which Britain was endeavoring to prevent. He also said that the British postal system was another example of Parliament's raising revenue without the consent of the colonists. The reason there had been little protest about this, he observed, was "because the office was thought to be a publick Utility." But now that the post office was being "made use of for the purpose of stopping the Channels of publick Intelligence and so in Effect of aiding the measures of Tyranny . . . the

2

necessity of substituting another office in its Stead must be obvious," he concluded.[7]

Before much could be accomplished on the local level delegates from the colonies met at Philadelphia in the First Continental Congress and prepared to establish a union government. A secretary (Charles Thomson of Philadelphia) and a president (Peyton Randolph of Virginia) were elected. The Congress recessed on October 22, 1774, to meet again May 10, 1775. In the interim momentous events took place; the battles of Lexington and Concord were fought and on the very day the Second Continental Congress convened Fort Ticonderoga on Lake Champlain was captured by colonial forces. The colonies were moving fast toward separation from Great Britain and the need for their own machinery of government was apparent.[8]

One of the first resolutions passed by this Congress declared that "the present critical situation of the colonies renders it highly necessary that ways and means should be devised for the speedy and secure conveyance of Intelligence from one end of the Continent to the other." A committee of five was elected to find means for setting up posts to convey letters throughout the colonies.[9] On July 26 a resolution establishing an American postal system, known as the Constitutional Post was adopted. A postmaster general, with power to appoint a secretary and comptroller, was authorized to set up headquarters in Philadelphia. Under his direction a line of posts was to be organized from Falmouth in New England to Savannah, Georgia, with as many crossroads as he saw fit. The postal rates were to be 20 percent less than those set by the act of Parliament. Of particular significance was the provision that any deficit should be made good by the united colonies.[10] By unanimous vote Benjamin Franklin was selected postmaster general for one year; Richard Bache, his son-in-law, was appointed comptroller.[11] William Goddard, who had taken the initiative in organizing a local postal service, was made surveyor of the posts to help organize the new system. The surveyor has been called the forerunner of the inspector in the United States Post Office.[12]

The Continental Congress kept close supervision over all governmental machinery, including the postal service. Some have called it meddling; others considered it a form of ministerial responsibility. Since this was wartime one of the problems was that of intercepted letters. General Washington sent many such letters to Congress; they were referred to a committee of seven with instructions to select which ones should be published and laid before Congress. Later another committee of three was set up to examine private letters; if they contained no information of public importance they were to be forwarded to the addressee. Much inconvenience to individuals was caused by local self-appointed committees who stopped and opened the mail. Congress finally ruled that only the committee of safety in each colony should be authorized to stop the Constitutional Post. There seemed to be no idea of the inviolability of letters.[13] Letters of prominent Americans were intercepted by the British and military information contained in some of these letters was published in London newspapers. General Washington finally refused to trust important dispatches to the Constitutional Post.[14]

Inadequate and irregular service, mail robberies, disloyal employees, the difficulty of obtaining new personnel because of inadequate compensation, and the continual deficit in the budget made the postal service a subject of frequent discussion in Congress. The postmaster general was directed to "endeavor, to the utmost of his power, to procure sober, diligent, and trusty persons." To help him secure postmasters and riders of undoubted loyalty the surveyor was directed to obtain recommendations from local committees and provincial congresses.[15] A resolution of Congress (August 30, 1776) stated that "the communication of intelligence with frequency and despatch, from one part to another of this extensive continent, is essentially requisite to its safety."[16] Thomas Jefferson, at that time a member of the Virginia House of Delegates, wrote John Adams, May 16, 1777, suggesting that riders travel night and day and that there be three trips a week. He wrote: "The speedy and frequent communication of intelligence is really of great consequence. So many falsehoods have been propagated that nothing now is believed unless coming from

# Establishment of the Postal System

Congress or camp. Our people merely for want of intelligence which they may rely on are become lethargick and insensible of the state they are in."[17] Adams explained that the post "from the North and South" was fairly regular, but the run was made only once a week as it was not easy to get faithful riders. He elaborated: "The expense is very high, and the Profits, (so dear is every thing, and so little Correspondence is carried on, except in franked letters), will not Support the office."[18]

Committee after committee was set up to study the postal service. Some of the most prominent men in Congress served on these committees, e.g., John and Samuel Adams and Elbridge Gerry of Massachusetts, Richard Henry Lee of Virginia, and Robert Morris of Pennsylvania.[19] In 1777 the post office organization was expanded to include two additional surveyors and an inspector of dead letters. The inspector was directed to examine all letters sent to the office and report to Congress those which contained any intelligence of any inimical schemes. He was cautioned against divulging any information contained in these letters except to Congress and "to preserve carefully all money, loan office certificates, lottery tickets, notes of hand, and other valuable papers."[20] Finally, in January, 1779, a standing committee on the post office was established.[21]

Not until the Articles of Confederation went into effect, March 1, 1781, was Congress recognized as having a monopoly over a postal service. Article nine of the Articles gave Congress "sole and exclusive right and power of . . . establishing or regulating post-offices from one state to another, throughout all the united states, and exacting such postage on the papers passing thro' the same as may be requisite to defray the expences of the said office."[22] For some time after that individuals continued to carry letters, and Maryland argued she had the right to carry on an intrastate postal service. By 1789, however, all states had discontinued local postal service except New Hampshire, which carried on a supplementary one for several years.[23]

On January 28, 1782, Ebenezer Hazard, nominated by Roger Sherman of Connecticut, was elected postmaster general. He had been commissioned postmaster of the Constitutional Post Office in New York City, October 5, 1775, surveyor for the eastern department in 1776, and then inspector of dead letters. At that time (1782) there was also appointed an assistant postmaster general, James Bryson.[24]

That year a complete reorganization of the postal service was made by Congress. The Post Office committee and Congress had been considering it off and on for over a year. This ordinance, adopted October 18, 1782, was the basic act governing the postal service for ten years. It began: "Whereas the communication of intelligence with regularity and despatch, from one part to another of these United States, is essentially requisite to the safety as well as the commercial interest thereof; and the United States in Congress assembled, being, by the Articles of Confederation, vested with the sole and exclusive right and power of establishing and regulating post offices throughout all these United States." The act provided for a postmaster general with authority to appoint an assistant and deputy postmasters "for whose fidelity he shall be accountable." Posts should be maintained throughout the United States from New Hampshire to Georgia as the postmaster general judged necessary or Congress should direct. Letter rates were established by the ordinance but the postmaster general was authorized to license every post rider to carry newspapers at moderate rates. The monopoly of the Post Office was emphasized, as the ordinance declared that only regular postal officials were to have the right of handling letters and packets for hire. The inviolability of private letters was to be protected; employees of the General Post Office were to be punished if, in time of peace, they "knowingly or willingly" opened or detained or destroyed letters or dispatches except by express warrant of the president or Congress.[25]

At the request of the secretary of the United States for the Department of Foreign Affairs a resolution was passed (1785) authorizing that officer to inspect any letters in any post office when he thought the safety and interest of the United States required such inspection. Excepted from this inspection, however, were letters franked by or addressed to members of Congress.[26]

However, prominent men continued to complain that their letters were being opened or delayed. General Washington charged that his mail was being tampered with and that the contents of his letters that passed through the Post Office became known to all. It was rumored that the Virginia trio, James Madison, Thomas Jefferson, and James Monroe, used a cipher to communicate with each other since the practice of opening mail was so notorious.[27] Postmaster General Hazard reported that state executives, accustomed to opening letters during wartime (permitted by the ordinance of 1782), were continuing to do so. He recommended that the inviolability of the mails be further protected. Congress then declared that that body had the sole power of regulating post offices and that not only had it not delegated to the executives of the states authority to open letters but that it was inexpedient to do so.[28]

From 1785 through 1788 Post Office committees of Congress discussed revising the ordinance of 1782. Many were the complaints of delay and inefficiency of mail delivery and of deficits in the postal service. Some congressmen suggested the use of stagecoaches for the transportation of mail, saying this would not only lead to better service but also would bring an increase in revenue; others declared stages would "rob it of all profit." In 1785 the postmaster general, under the direction of the Board of Treasury, was authorized to make contracts with owners of stagecoaches for the transportation of the mail.[29] A proposed revision of the Post Office ordinance was presented to Congress, February 14, 1787, but no action on it was taken.[30] There was difficulty keeping a quorum in Congress. This was particularly true after a convention convened in Philadelphia in May to amend the Articles of Confederation.

At the federal convention, considering the framing of a new constitution, there was almost no discussion of a postal system since it had been in existence for many years. Both the Pinckney and Patterson (New Jersey) plans provided for a post office as a source of revenue. The convention, however, adopted resolutions based on the Virginia plan, which merely stated the powers of the legislature in general terms. The listing of those powers was done by the committee on detail and among the powers delegated to

Congress was that of establishing post offices. In the convention (August 16) Elbridge Gerry of Massachusetts moved to add "and post roads." This, seconded by John Francis Mercer of Maryland, was adopted by a narrow vote of 6 to 5 (New Hampshire, Connecticut, New Jersey, Pennsylvania, and North Carolina).[31]

This postal power of Congress received little notice in the ratifying conventions in the states. In Massachusetts an amendment was proposed that that power should not "be construed to extend to the laying out, making, altering, or repairing highways, in any state, without the consent of the legislature of such state."[32] James Madison, commenting on that power in *The Federalist*, said that power to establish post roads was "a harmless power" although it might "become productive of great public conveniency."[33]

During the debate on the ratification of the Constitution, Postmaster General Hazard was accused of preventing the circulation through the mail of certain newspapers opposed to ratification. Printers in New York, Boston, and Baltimore complained they were no longer receiving papers from west of the Hudson, where there were reports of opposition to the Constitution, nor papers containing essays opposing the new government, nor any independent papers, but "the devoted vehicles of despotism pass uninterrupted." They claimed it was part of a "nefarious design" of the Post Office officials to enslave their countrymen by cutting off all communication between patriots. One correspondent who called himself "Centinel" wrote: "Attempts to prevent discussion by shackling the press ought to be a signal of alarm to freemen." The next day he declared, "every avenue to information is so far as possible cut off, the usual communication between the states through the medium of the press, is in a great measure destroyed by a new arrangement at the Post Office, scarcely a newspaper is suffered to pass by this conveyance." The riders of the postal system claimed that the circulation of the newspapers was not being curtailed for political reasons but because carrying them was not part of their contracts. The editor of the *New York Journal* retorted that no one could deny it was a political evil and that the public should be informed of it in order to demand a remedy.[34]

# Establishment of the Postal System

Postmaster General Hazard, in a letter to the *Journal*, replied to his critics. He stated that the Post Office had been established only "for the purpose of facilitating commercial correspondence" and had "no connection with newspapers," that the carriage of them had been merely "an indulgence granted to the post-riders, prior to the revolution." He maintained that the postmaster general had given no orders about newspapers to postmasters or riders nor had any change been made in postal policies regarding them. One who called himself "A True Federalist" wrote in reply to Hazard's letter: "*You have either wilfully misrepresented the established rules and customs of the post-office . . . or you are totally ignorant of the subject.*" One signing himself "Watchman" wrote: "*Ebenezer Hazard, Esq.* prohibited sending any papers in the mail. What must be the feeling of every freeman in America, on the conduct of this little despot in office?"[35] Samuel A. Otis, delegate to Congress from Massachusetts, wrote a friend that Hazard was "in a bad box." He said the federalists accused him of being opposed to the Constitution while the antifederalists charged him with stopping the papers and "muzzling the press." Otis expressed the hope that Congress would not oust him but give him "a little shaking." In spite of the criticism Hazard continued to hold the office for more than a year.[36]

The first Congress under the Constitution was too busy to make formal provision for the postal system and continued the establishment as it had been defined in the ordinance of 1782. Postmaster General Hazard had sent a letter to the speaker of the House in July, 1789, "submitting the propriety of some immediate provision, by law, for the arrangement of that department." It had been referred to a committee consisting of Elias Boudinet of New Jersey, Benjamin Goodhue of Massachusetts, and Richard Bland Lee of Virginia. An act for the temporary establishment of the Post Office was approved September 22. It provided merely for the appointment of a postmaster general who should have the same powers as under the ordinances of the late Congress. The postmaster general was to be subject to the direction of the president "in performing the duties of his office, and in forming contracts for the transportation of the mail."[37]

9

Four days after the approval of the act President Washington appointed Samuel Osgood postmaster general. There had been several contenders for the position, among them Richard Bache, Franklin's son-in-law and acting postmaster general from 1776 to 1782, and John Adams's son-in-law, Colonel William Smith. Osgood had seen service in the army, reaching the rank of colonel; he had had experience as a legislator both in Massachusetts and in the Continental Congress. He had been a director of the Bank of North America and had served three years as a member of the Treasury Board and later as one of the three commissioners in charge of the treasury. It would seem, therefore, that it was his financial experience that was more or less responsible for his selection as postmaster general.[38]

President Washington in his brief annual message to Congress, January 8, 1790, said: "I can not forbear intimating to you the expediency . . . of facilitating the intercourse between the distant parts of our country by a due attention to the post office and post roads."[39] The postmaster general presented to President Washington a long report and a draft of a bill containing suggested changes in the General Post Office, the official name of the system. Washington transmitted the report to Secretary of Treasury Hamilton, as the postal system was considered part of the revenue department and all communications were to be made through the secretary of the treasury.[40] This was in accordance with British practice.

Insufficient revenue seemed to be the chief concern of both the secretary of the treasury and the postmaster general. The former had wanted to apply the revenue of the postal system to the sinking fund for the public debt.[41] The postmaster general thought the system, if well regulated, could bring in annually a half-million dollars instead of twenty-five thousand. Too few letters were written, postal rates were not realistic, the franking privilege had been too far extended, and distances between communities were too great, he pointed out. He recommended that newspapers pay one or two cents postage instead of being carried free, that more crossroads be built, and that postage rates be readjusted. He emphasized particularly that the postal system should be a monopoly and stated that anyone who received and carried letters, whether for hire or not, should be punished. He even suggested that contractors who carried mail be given the exclusive privilege of driving stages on post roads.[42]

The first objection in the House to the postmaster general's report was that he had included with the communication a proposed bill. Thomas Fitzsimmons of Georgia said he "thought there was a degree of indelicacy, not to say impropriety, in permitting the Heads of Department to bring bills before the House. He thought it was sufficient for them to make reports of facts, with their opinions thereon, and leave the rest to the discretion of the Legislature." John Page of Virginia agreed with him and stated that "no bill ought to be read in the House that did not originate with its leave." A select committee, headed by Fitzsimmons, was appointed to prepare a bill.[43] Disagreement between the House and Senate over whether the post roads should be described in detail in the bill or whether the power of laying them out should be left to the president and postmaster general led to the defeat of the bill. Finally the act that was passed, August 4, 1790, merely continued in force the temporary measure of the preceding year.[44]

Samuel Osgood resigned as postmaster general in the summer of 1791. He had not wanted to move when the capital was shifted from New York to Philadelphia. Secretary of State Jefferson and Attorney General Randolph suggested for the position Thomas Paine, the pamphleteer of the American Revolution who had served as secretary for the Committee on Foreign Affairs, 1777–1778.[45] Instead Timothy Pickering, well versed in public affairs, was appointed. An authority on public administration said of him: "He was . . . one of the most prominent officials of his day. . . . The dominant characteristics of his mature personality were independence, combativeness, and courage, all harnessed to a strong and unswerving devotion to duty."[46] Pickering suggested to the secretary of the treasury that the General Post Office be located in two rooms in a house he had found for his large family. Not only could the family and public offices share the same building but also the services of a domestic. For the two rooms, the use of the servant, and storage space for wood, he proposed a charge of three hundred dollars. With the permission of Secretary Hamilton, Pickering hired such a house, one formerly occupied by Frederick Muhlenberg, first speaker of the House of Representatives.[47]

President Washington devoted a whole paragraph to the needs of the General Post Office in his third message to Congress (October 25, 1791). He stressed the importance of the post office and post roads and urged the establishment of more crossroads.[48] Again debate in the House revolved around the establishment of post roads. The committee bill designated in detail the post roads. Theodore Sedgwick of Massachusetts moved that the power to establish post roads be given to the president. Opponents maintained the power could not be delegated and that the government should be administered by representatives of the people and that an important function of the government was the establishing of post roads. One declared that if the House gave up this jurisdiction they might just as well say: "There shall be a Postmaster General, who shall have the whole government power of the post office, under such regulations as he from time to time shall be pleased to enact." Another pointed out that congressmen came from all parts of the country and collectively, therefore, possessed more information about local needs than an executive could obtain. There was also expressed fear that too great executive control over the postal system might turn it into a dangerous political instrument. In reality congressmen were reluctant to give up this important perquisite of their office, and one they often used in their claim for reelection. Sedgwick's motion was defeated and the bill describing in detail the post roads passed both houses of Congress. Congressmen were so jealous of this power that the Senate voted down a motion that would have given the postmaster general power to desist sending mail over a post road if the revenue did not amount to two-thirds of the expense.[49]

There was also considerable debate over a resolution that would permit proprietors of stages carrying mail to carry passengers "without being liable to molestation or impediment, on any of the post roads." The reason for this was that several states, notably Maryland and Virginia, had given exclusive privileges to specific companies to drive stages with passengers over certain roads.

# Establishment of the Postal System

Later these roads had been made post roads. Those in favor of the motion argued that the states should not grant such monopolies and that federal authority should be superior. Those opposed maintained that the clause giving Congress power to establish post offices and post roads was understood to extend only to the "conveyance of intelligence which is the proper object of the Post Office establishment; it gives no power to send men and baggage by post." Since state governments had always had the authority to make regulations concerning transportation of passengers in their state such an extension of the authority over post roads by Congress would leave the state legislatures lying "prostrate at the feet of the General Government." This resolution was defeated by a vote of 33 to 25.[50]

On February 20, 1792, the first act describing the postal system under the Constitution was passed; its operation, however, was limited to two years. At the seat of government there was to be the General Post Office, headed by a postmaster general. He was given authority to appoint an assistant, to make contracts for carrying the mail (only after advertising for bids and not to exceed eight years), and appoint deputy postmasters and make regulations for the conduct of their offices. He was required to make quarterly reports to the secretary of the treasury. Postmasters were to receive a commission (up to $1,800) based on the receipts of their offices and were exempt from militia duty (in 1799 also from jury duty).

Postage rates were set by the act; they were based on distances. Inviolability of letters was recognized, for any unauthorized employee of the General Post Office who unlawfully detained or opened any letter or packet was to be punished (maximum fine of $300 and/or imprisonment for six months). Deputy postmasters were instructed to publish in local newspapers lists of letters uncalled for; those not called for within a certain length of time were to be sent to the dead letter office where they could be opened. The act provided for punishment for anyone who conveyed mail "whereby the revenue of the General Post Office might be injured." Every printer of a newspaper was permitted to send one paper to every other newspaper printer free of postage. News-

13

papers had to have a cover that was open at one end and were to be conveyed in separate bags from letters; the postage was considerably less than on letters.[51] President Washington favored as widespread transmission of newspapers as possible, with "a full conviction of the importance of facilitating the circulation of political intelligence and information."[52]

In 1797 Congress enacted the first law putting a limitation on what could be sent through the mail. It was a mild regulation and was enacted merely to prevent damage to the rest of the mail, but it was the first of a long series of such acts in which matter was declared nonmailable. Complaints from patrons who had not received newspapers to which they had subscribed led to this first regulation concerning nonmailability. A committee of the House investigating the complaints discovered that some printers who wished to get their papers in the mail as quickly as possible did not take time to dry them completely so that the package became a wet mass with the addresses often indecipherable. Surprisingly, this proposed regulation on drying newspapers aroused heated debate in Congress and was passed by a very narrow vote. Some considered it an oppressive regulation on printers and said it would make newspapers more expensive, as they would have to be dried by a fire. Others feared the delegation of so much power to a postmaster, as he was the one who could decide which papers were wet and which were not. Sponsors of the regulation ridiculed the idea that a postmaster "would unnecessarily obstruct the circulation of newspapers" and pointed out that a postmaster who did so would be liable to punishment. Section 6 of the new Post Office act (March 3, 1797) read as follows: "That no newspapers shall be received by deputy postmasters, to be conveyed by post unless they be sufficiently dried and enclosed in proper wrappers, on which, besides the direction, shall be noted the number of papers which are enclosed for subscribers, and the number for printers." Deputy postmasters were not to allow packages of newspapers not directed to their offices to be opened.[53]

During the crisis of 1798–1799 the General Post Office came in for a great deal of criticism. The revolution in France had repercussions on American politics; the Republicans, followers of

# Establishment of the Postal System

Thomas Jefferson, favored the revolutionists while the Federalists, especially after the execution of Louis XVI and the outbreak of war, tended to be pro-British. The refusal of France to accept United States ministers, the notorious XYZ affair, and the undeclared war on France led to the passage of the Sedition Act, July 14, 1798. The act was directed mainly against Republican pamphleteers and editors. This act, in contrast to the acts passed during World War I, did not mention the mails but provided punishment for criticism of the United States government and governmental officials. There were, however, complaints that opposition newspapers were being suppressed by the Post Office or were obliged to have postage paid on them while Federalist newspapers went through the mails free.[54]

There were even more numerous complaints that letters were being delayed and opened by local postmasters. Most of the deputy postmasters were Federalists and it seemed that some, in spite of the act of 1792, had little compunction about opening letters. Jefferson wrote John Taylor on November 26, 1798, that he owed him a "political letter" but "the infidelities of the post office and the circumstances of the times are against my writing fully & freely." To another he sent an unsigned letter saying: "you will know from whom this comes without a signature; the omission of which has rendered almost habitual with me by the curiosity of the post offices." Elbridge Gerry claimed that for many years the seals on the letters he received had been tampered with, destroying his confidence in the postal system. He pointed out that only "one prostituted officer on each line, is sufficient to betray all the secrets of the chief magistrate; conveyed thro' this channel." Many of these prominent men sent letters by friends or by "bearers," as that gave them the "opportunity of writing more freely, than by the post."[55]

The provision against opening and detaining letters and packets was retained in the postal law of 1799. Postmaster General Habersham,[56] who had replaced Timothy Pickering when the latter became secretary of war, January 2, 1795, was asked by the House of Representatives to give his opinion on the draft of a new bill. He commented particularly on the section dealing with the

15

safety of correspondence. He pointed out that it had been copied without alteration from the previous act, except it had substituted corporal punishment in place of death for detaining packets containing money or securities. He favored the change for he felt the death penalty was "contrary to the present humane regulations." The section declaring wet newspapers nonmailable was also continued. The suggestion of Postmaster General Habersham that a postmaster be permitted to receive or reject packages that weighed more than three pounds was not included in the act. Habersham thought the postmaster general was not appreciated. He said in other countries the postal service was considered "an object of more importance, and its execution have been more liberally provided for." He maintained he needed a larger establishment to supervise nearly seven hundred post offices and the transportation of the mail over more than sixteen hundred miles of post roads. The act of 1799 made little improvement in the office. There was only one assistant who kept the accounts and dealt with theft and delays in the mail. A solicitor took care of legal matters, such as overseeing the making of contracts and the suing of delinquent postmasters. There was a chief clerk and five other clerks; one examined accounts, one acted as bookkeeper, one registered letters, and another had charge of the dead letter office.[57]

With the election of Thomas Jefferson in 1800 the administration of the federal government came into the hands of the Republicans for the first time. A Federalist anticipating this "revolution" wrote to the *Connecticut Courant* that the greatest difficulty the "Jacobins" had had with spreading their propaganda had been not the printing of the papers, notably the *Aurora*, but transporting them. Now he foresaw one thousand deputy postmasters, with the power of the frank, sending and receiving through the mail free of postage the *Press*, the *Aurora*, the *Age of Reason*, and "every other seditious, slanderous, demoralizing, atheistical publication, which the wickedness of Jacobins could collect, and disseminate."[58]

Jefferson appointed (November 28, 1801) Gideon Granger of Connecticut as his postmaster general. In contrast to his predecessor, who had been primarily a businessman and planter, Granger had, during most of his adult life, been a politician. Graduate of Yale, lawyer by profession, he had, at the age of twenty-five (1792), become a member of the Connecticut General Assembly where, with the exception of two years, he had remained until 1801. In 1798 he had associated himself with the Republicans, which meant an end to a political career in Federalist Connecticut. In the election of 1800 he had supported Thomas Jefferson and so had earned a political reward.[59]

One of Granger's first recommendations to Congress was the suggestion that the employment of Negroes by mail contractors be prohibited. He gave as the official reason the fact that Negroes could not be witnesses in some states and therefore men, being unafraid of conviction, might feel more free to rob the mail. To Senator James Jackson of Georgia he explained that colored mail carriers might become leaders of slave revolts, as their work as post riders gave them not only the opportunity to acquire information but also to establish a chain of intelligence and to organize a corps of brethren. He concluded that it was "easier to prevent the evil than to cure it."[60] The act of 1803 contained a provision that no other than "free white persons" could be employed in carrying the mail of the United States.[61]

In 1803 there was a debate over the importance of the office of postmaster general when a bill raising his salary from $3,000 to $4,000 (and that of his assistant from $1,700 to $2,000) passed the Senate. It was argued that Granger was the best man for the office and if he did not obtain the raise he might resign. The House, however, refused to go along with the proposed increases. One representative said: "All that is necessary in a postmaster general is mechanical talents, honest & constant industry. If the present officer has high talents they are *surplusage*, & for that surplusage we ought to make no allowance."[62]

In 1810 was passed the first comprehensive postal law to make any substantive changes in the law of 1792. This act, describing the "Post Office Establishment," provided for a second assistant postmaster general. It authorized the postmaster general to appoint special agents, not exceeding five. (He had been doing so by executive order since 1801.) There was some opposition in

17

Congress not only because of the additional expense but also because of the increase in patronage. An amendment to take away from deputy postmasters the franking privilege was defeated. The provision against detaining and opening letters was repeated. Service was to be somewhat more effective, for local mail was to be separated from the through mail. Previously the local postmaster had taken out of the mail sack letters for his office and put back the others; thus mail was handled by many postmasters. The provision asked for by Postmaster General Habersham that no postmaster should be required to receive a packet weighing more than three pounds was finally enacted into law.[63] Professor Rogers, who made a legal study of the postal power of Congress, stated: "Congress, therefore, very early exercised the right of determining what articles should be mailable and the conditions upon which they should be carried."[64]

From time to time there had been expressions of dissatisfaction with Gideon Granger as postmaster general. In 1806 a committee of the House of Representatives had been appointed to inquire into his conduct, whether he "hath so acted, in his capacity as Postmaster General, as to require the interposition of the constitutional powers of this House" (impeachment proceedings). Because of the shortness of the session the investigation was postponed and not revived.[65] Madison, when he became president in 1809, retained Granger in office. Five years later the postmaster general was summarily removed for political insubordination; he and the president had disagreed over the appointment of postmaster of Philadelphia. President Madison did not even notify Granger that he was removing him but merely sent into the Senate, April 11, 1814, the name of Return Jonathan Meigs of Ohio to be postmaster general.[66]

Postmaster General Meigs suggested to Congress that a law be passed prohibiting the transmission of books through the mail. In 1816 an act had set rates of postage for magazines and pamphlets; some postmasters construed books to be pamphlets. Meigs argued that books were not like letters and newspapers, which were valuable only if conveyed rapidly. Books could, he said, be sent by the routes used for articles of merchandise. He had instructed postmasters not to receive books at the low pamphlet rate but they had ignored this order, so he asked Congress for a law.[67] No attention was paid to this suggestion.

President Monroe, July 1, 1823, appointed John McLean of Ohio as postmaster general; he was one of the ablest men to hold that position. He had been a member of Congress, 1813–1816, and then a member of the Ohio Supreme Court; in 1822 he had become commissioner of the General Land Office. He served as commissioner less than ten months before being appointed postmaster general. Professor White says, "McLean infused new energy and vitality into the post office from 1823 to 1829."[68]

President Monroe in his annual message to Congress, December 2, 1823 (the message that contained the famous statements known as the Monroe Doctrine), discussed the Post Office. He was the first president since Washington to do so. He called Congress's attention to the report of the postmaster general. He pointed out that there were now 5,240 post offices and 88,600 miles of post roads, that the receipts amounted to $1,114,345.12 and the expenditures, $1,169,885.51.[69] From that time it has been customary for presidents to include with their messages to Congress reports from the postmasters general.

President John Quincy Adams, in December, 1825, pointed out that for the first time in many years the receipts from the postal system exceeded the expenditures. He said:

It hence appears that under judicious management the income from this establishment may be relied on as fully adequate to defray its expenses, and that by the discontinuance of post-roads altogether unproductive others of more useful character may be opened, till the circulation of the mail shall keep pace with the spread of our population, and the comforts of friendly correspondence, the exchanges of internal traffic, and the lights of the periodical press shall be distributed to the remotest corners of the Union, at a charge scarcely perceptible to any individual, and without the cost of a dollar to the public Treasury.[70]

Postmaster General McLean was anxious to limit the use of the postal system by organizers of lotteries. Lotteries were popular and were used even by churches and colleges to raise money.

Postmasters with their privilege of sending and receiving mail free, by frank, had a great advantage. McLean wrote one post-master that a paper full of lottery advertisements was not a news-paper. He removed one postmaster who was running a lottery agency. In 1827 he succeeded in obtaining a law that forbade postmasters from acting as agents for lotteries and prohibited them from using their frank to mail lottery tickets or circulars about lotteries.[71] Almost fifty years would elapse before lottery tickets and circulars would be declared nonmailable.

McLean's service was recognized as being of such high caliber that in 1827 his salary was raised from $4,000 (set in 1818) to $6,000, the same as that received by the four secretaries in the cabinet. Some objected to the postmaster general's receiving the same salary as cabinet members since the Post Office Department was not a separate department (although since 1823 it had been called the Post Office Department). Senator Van Buren of New York stated that he thought the postmaster general should be a member of the cabinet; the incumbent of the office agreed with him.[72]

It was not until the 1820s that Congress began to recognize the importance of the postmaster general and the postal system. The Post Office had been the first governmental organization established by the Continental Congress, but after that Congress seemed to have lost interest in it and little attention was paid to the recommendations of the postmasters general or the bills deal-ing with the postal system. Congressmen seemed to be primarily interested in only two things: the perquisite of specifying post roads and the inviolability of private correspondence. The postal system had a monopoly of the transportation of letters. After 1782 the carrying of newspapers was permitted and from time to time there were charges of political discrimination.

The presidents from Washington to Monroe also ignored the postal system in their messages to Congress. Postmasters general throughout this period were considered less important than other executive officers. This situation changed when Congressmen be-came interested in postmaster appointments and the postmaster general became a member of the president's cabinet.

# First Debate on
# Postal Censorship:
# Incendiary Matter

In 1829 the postmaster general became a member of the president's cabinet. This was done by executive action and aroused little comment. The change was proposed primarily to promote John McLean, to give him what he had long wanted, a seat in the cabinet. However, just a few days before President Jackson took office McLean was nominated for the Supreme Court and William T. Barry of Kentucky was appointed postmaster general. The latter had been promised the justiceship, so a switch in positions was made. Barry had deserted Henry Clay after the publication of the "bargain" story in 1825 (Clay was accused of throwing his support to John Quincy Adams for president in return for the appointment as secretary of state). Barry supported Andrew Jackson for the presidency in 1828. He had been a candidate for the position of governor in his state on the Jackson ticket and had been defeated, so was in line for an appointed position.[1]

Jackson in his first annual message to Congress said of the Post Office: "In a political point of view this Department is chiefly important as affording the means of diffusing knowledge. It is to the body politic what the veins and arteries are to the natural—conveying rapidly and regularly to the remotest parts of the system correct information of the operations of the Government, and bringing back to it the wishes and feelings of the people. Through its agency we have secured to ourselves the full enjoyment of the blessings of a free press."[2] It would appear that a Whig senator, George M. Bibb of Kentucky, was merely extending President Jackson's wishes for a free press when he proposed a repeal of law charging postage on newspapers. He estimated that the cost for postage per year of one daily newspaper amounted to five dollars, which naturally diminished its circulation. He said that his amendment would "diffuse valuable information over the United States to a greater extent than any proposition that had ever been laid before Congress, respecting this department of the Government."[3]

The real purpose of the proposal was to offset the advantages enjoyed by administration papers, which were not only often carried free by Democratic contractors but also received indirect government subsidies. The Post Office Department spent large sums of money for advertising of the mail contracts and also for the uncalled-for letters. It was the policy of the department that these advertisements appear in administration papers. For example, Postmaster General Barry wrote one postmaster: "You received the appt. of P. M. under the full impression you were ready and willing to take upon yourself the entire responsibility of cooperating with the administration in its measures. It appears, however, that you prefer advertising letters in an opposition newspaper while the *News Letter*, the supporter of the Administration is denied that little patronage."[4] Senator John M. Clayton of Delaware supported Bibb's amendment, stating it was essential for the freedom of the press "that it should be free from the shackles of Executive influence and Executive patronage." The chairman of the Committee on the Post Office and Post Roads, Felix Grundy of Tennessee, opposed it on the basis that it would decrease the revenue of the Post Office thus increasing its deficit. Bibb's amendment was defeated in the Senate, but only by one vote.[5]

The Post Office Department in 1830 was divided into three divisions. The first division, headed by a senior assistant postmaster general, had charge of finances, including the pay, bookkeeping, examiners, register, and solicitor offices. The second division, under the second assistant postmaster general, had charge of the establishment and regulation of post offices, appointments, mail routes, the dead letter office, and the Office of Instruction and Mail Depredations (forerunner of the inspection service). The third division was under a chief clerk and had charge of mail contracts and the transportation of mail. In 1833 Postmaster General Barry changed the organization to a geographical basis with northern and southern divisions.[6]

The department reached a new low under the administration of Major Barry, as he was called because of his service during the War of 1812. He had been well educated (at William and Mary), trained as a lawyer, and had held one government office after another since 1807. He was, however, a poor businessman with little administrative ability and was easily the dupe of less scrupulous men in the department.[7] As early as 1830 there was criticism of his management and in that year a committee was set up in the Senate to investigate his appointment policy.[8] In 1834 committees were set up in both houses of Congress to investigate the Post Office Department. In the Senate such prominent members as Daniel Webster of Massachusetts, Henry Clay of Kentucky, Thomas Ewing of Ohio, John M. Clayton of Delaware, and Felix Grundy of Tennessee were on the committee; the Whigs were in the majority. Their report was presented on June 9, 1834. It discussed in detail the department printing patronage, citing cases where party newspapermen had valuable mail contracts and received, instead of extra allowances, "the Newspaper Privilege," i.e., the "privilege of carrying and distributing newspapers at pleasure on his mail routes." It reported that "large sums of money appear to have been expended in such a manner that the obvious tendency of the expenditure is to extend the influence of the department over the public press, and through that press over the people."[9]

The House committee made its report February 13, 1835. The majority (Democrats) reported that the Post Office was in bad shape financially, although there had been a surplus in 1829. They stated that one of the most perplexing problems was the relation of the postmaster general to mail contracts. It was the system, however, that was to blame, not Postmaster General Barry.

Post roads were created by Congress but beyond that there was little direction for the postmaster general. The Whig minority attacked the postmaster general for his inefficiency and his partisanship. The report pointed out that postmasters with their franking privilege could be organized into a partisan corps and could facilitate the circulation of their party papers and prevent the distribution of papers of the opposition.[10]

Throughout the investigation there had been rumors that Postmaster General Barry would resign. His health was poor and his condition was no doubt aggravated by the investigations. Barry continued to insist that he was not going to leave the Post Office Department, but as he wrote his daughter (March 8, 1834): "The idea that I intend leaving it impairs the power and influence of my station. Contractors, Post Masters, and other agents, cease to respect the man who is about to quit, and look to the one who probably will succeed him in office." Finally, shortly after the presentation of the House report Barry resigned to become minister to Spain.[11]

Jackson appointed as postmaster general, May 1, 1835, one of the ablest members of his "kitchen cabinet," Amos Kendall. He had been, as had Barry, a friend of Henry Clay but had deserted him to support Jackson before the campaign of 1828. He had been a newspaperman and when he came to Washington in 1829 as fourth auditor in the Navy Department, he had become the president's speech writer and publicity man. He brought the Post Office Department back to the prestige it had enjoyed under Postmaster General McLean.[12]

Upon recommendation of Postmaster General Kendall an act reorganizing the Post Office Department was passed July 2, 1836. Up to that time there had been departmental unity and single-headed control. The postmaster general had been responsible for all functions, for the distribution of duties, and for all appointments. Now all postmasters whose commissions exceeded $1,000 a year (called presidential postmasters) were to be appointed by the president with the advice and consent of the Senate. They were to have a four-year term but could be removed by the president. The duties of the postmaster general were spelled out; he was required to report to Congress each year on contracts entered into, allowances granted contractors, and on the finances of the department. The revenues from the postal service were to be paid into the treasury and postal appropriations would be made by Congress upon estimates furnished by the postmaster general. There was also established a third assistant postmaster general; he was put in charge of the inspection office. In the field were the special agents. At that time the chief work of the agents was to investigate mail depredations and robberies, but later the agents would be involved in enforcement of the nonmailable statutes.[13]

The problem of transportation of mail by railroads came to the fore in Postmaster General Kendall's administration. President Jackson, in two of his messages, urged Congress to "fix by law the amounts which shall be offered to railroad companies for the conveyance of the mails, graduated according to their average weight, to be ascertained and declared by the Postmaster General." He expressed a fear that because of the monopolistic character of railroads they might boycott the postal service or charge exorbitant prices. In 1837 an act was passed stating that every railroad in the United States be considered a post road and the postmaster general was instructed to transport mail by railroad if it could be done on reasonable terms, not above 25 percent over what it would cost by stagecoach.[14] Thus successively roads, then navigable waters, then railroads were declared post roads.

At the end of his first year in office Postmaster General Kendall reported a surplus exceeding a half-million dollars and recommended a reduction of postages equal to 20 percent; this President Jackson endorsed. In 1840, when Kendall left office, there were 13,488 post offices, 155,739 miles of post roads, a gross revenue of $4,539,265 with expenses of $4,759,110. The postmaster general pointed out that loss of revenue was due in part to the fact that private expresses were allowed to carry items like packets on post roads. He argued: "If there is any grant of exclusive power to Congress upon which all unite in opinion, it is the power to establish post offices and post roads, and it may fairly be assumed as an admitted principle, that when Congress, in the exercise of that power, has established a post road, the right of a State, or the individual of a State, to establish lines of transportation for letters, packages and newspapers upon and over the same roads, for compensation, cannot be successfully maintained."[15]

The first real attempt at postal censorship came while Amos Kendall was postmaster general. The newly organized American Anti-Slavery Society (founded December, 1833) launched a vigorous propaganda campaign in 1835; over a million pieces of abolition literature were printed in the one year and $30,000 was appropriated for their distribution, chiefly through the mail.[16] Mailing lists were compiled from city directories and other public records and pamphlets were sent gratis to reputable citizens, especially clergymen, and whole bundles were sent to various post offices to be distributed by agents whose object, it was said, was to get the pamphlets into the hands of slaves. Riots broke out in many places, terrorizing the Southerners who were still apprehensive because of the Nat Turner revolt of 1831. Senator Forsyth of Georgia wrote that the tracts were "raising the devil through the whole Southern Country."[17]

The issue of the use of the mails was first raised by the postmaster of Charleston, South Carolina, Alfred Huger.[18] He wrote the postmaster of New York City, Samuel L. Gouverneur, that a steamer had arrived with thousands of abolition pamphlets and when this had been discovered a mob gathered outside the office and demanded the "incendiary publications" be handed over. This he refused to do but he did separate the "obnoxious papers" from the rest of the mail.[19] That night a mob broke into the post office and carried off the bag containing the tracts. Fear of mob rule led the Unionists and Nullifiers of Charleston to unite and a committee of twenty-one, headed by Judge Colcock and General Robert Y. Hayne, was set up to handle the situation. They announced that an arrangement had been made with the postmaster that no seditious pamphlets would be distributed from the post office until the civil authorities of the city had been informed. The committee also passed the following resolution:

*Resolved.* That the Post Office establishment cannot, consistently with the Constitution of the United States, and the objects of such an institution, be converted into an instrument for the dissemination of incendiary publications, and that it is the duty of the Federal Government to provide that it shall not be so prostituted; which can easily be effected by merely making it unlawful to transport by the public mail, through the limits of any State, any seditious papers forbidden by the laws of such State, to be introduced or circulated therein, and by adopting the necessary regulations to effect the object.[20]

Huger suggested to Gouverneur that the mail be separated in New York and that the bag containing letters be labeled "nothing but letters" and the bag containing the tracts be labeled "suspicious." A week later he begged the New York postmaster, if he could, to prevent "the transmission of these firebrands among us, for God's Sake do so; and let the question of Slavery be decided elsewhere than in the P.O. where the Post Master himself is a Slave holder, and cannot believe it sinful without convicting his own soul & his own ancestors for five generations." Gouverneur wrote the American Anti-Slavery Society enclosing Huger's letter and suggested that mail of that character be suspended until he had a ruling from the postmaster general. The executive committee of the organization, however, passed a resolution (August 8) stating that they could not "consent to surrender any of the rights or privileges which we possess in common with our fellow citizens in regard to the use of the U.S. mail." Gouverneur then announced that he would refuse to forward the objectionable mail.[21]

Huger had also appealed to Postmaster General Kendall; the latter gave a rather equivocal answer on August 4, 1835. He wrote to the postmaster at Charleston:

Upon a careful examination of the law, I am satisfied that the postmaster general has no legal authority to exclude newspapers from the mail, nor prohibit their carriage or delivery on account of their character or tendency, real or supposed. Probably it was not thought safe to confer on the head of an executive department a power over the press, which might be perverted or abused.

But I am not prepared to direct *you* to forward or deliver the papers of which you speak. The post office department was created to serve the people of *each* and *all* of the *United States*, and not to be used as the instrument of their *destruction*. None of the papers detained have been forwarded to me, and I cannot judge for myself of their character and tendency; but you inform me, that they are, in character, "the most inflammatory and incendiary"—and insurrectionary in the highest degree.

By no act, or direction of mine, official or private, could I be induced to aid, knowingly, in giving circulation to papers of this description, directly or indirectly. We owe an obligation to the laws, but a higher one to the communities in which we live, and if the *former* be perverted to destroy the *latter*, it is patriotism to disregard them. Entertaining these views, I cannot sanction, and will not condemn the step you have taken.[22]

President Jackson supported the stand taken by his postmaster general. He condemned the "monsters" who were attempting to stir up a servile war. He agreed that the law had to be carried out but thought postmasters could well be informed, verbally, they need not distribute such inflammatory papers except to those who subscribed to them and that the postmasters ought to take down the name of the subscribers and expose them in the public press. He hoped that this would bring them into such disrepute that they would stop subscribing to those papers.[23]

This position of the president and postmaster general was severely criticized by Northern newspapers. The editor of the *Evening Post* in New York called for the retirement from public office of Amos Kendall. Shortly after this editorial appeared the New York City postmaster was instructed to withdraw from the *Evening Post* the patronage of publishing the list of uncalled-for letters.[24]

Many Southern communities directed their postmasters to withhold abolitionist literature; some set up vigilante committees to look over such material in the mails, and some postmasters on their own initiative withheld antislavery papers even when addressed to individuals. One famous abolitionist, James Birney, complained when his papers were withheld that the postmaster at Danville, Kentucky, "has determined to become my intellectual caterer." Later he wrote: "The Post Office here has been put under the censorship of the P. Master, one of the most ignorant, unlettered and mobocratical of our citizens." Birney threatened to institute a suit; thereafter he received some papers but was sure he was not receiving all of them. Elizur Wright, corresponding secretary of the New York office of the American Anti-Slavery Society, wrote Birney that the organization was working to make the issue of abolition so important that it would become a matter of discussion not only in the state legislatures but also in Congress.[25]

In December, 1835, Kendall, in his annual report, described the work of the American Anti-Slavery Society and how it had tried to disseminate throughout the South "by the agency of the public mails" tracts to arouse the passions of colored men to bring about a slave war. He pointed out that slavery was a domestic institution under the protection of the states and that the general government had no power to pass laws protecting the states from domestic violence by prohibiting discussion. But he stated that the government could not be expected to help the circulation of "papers calculated to produce domestic violence." The department policy had been quite effective, he thought, but recommended that the whole matter be referred to Congress.[26]

President Jackson in his message to Congress, December 7, 1835, invited the attention of Congress to the "painful excitement" aroused in the South by the attempts to circulate the "inflammatory appeals addressed to the passion of the slaves." He recommended that Congress pass a law prohibiting the transmission through the mails of incendiary publications in the South.[27]

In the Senate John C. Calhoun of South Carolina moved that as much of the message of the president as related to the transmission through the mails of publications of a dangerous tendency be referred to a select committee instead of the Committee on the Post Office and Post Roads, for the latter had on it only one gentleman from the South. A big debate took place on this resolution. It was even suggested that part of the president's message be referred to the Judiciary Committee since constitutional issues were involved, namely: whether or not Congress had the power to regulate the Post Office Department and whether or not this power extended as far as suppression of circulation of matter through the mails. Calhoun's motion was finally adopted and a committee of five was elected. Calhoun was the chairman and the other members were John Davis of Massachusetts, John P. King of Georgia, Lewis F. Linn of Missouri, and Willie P. Mangum of North Carolina.[28]

On February 4, 1836, the select committee presented an eleven-page report; only Calhoun and Mangum concurred on the complete report, others approved parts of it. The report stated that committee members agreed with the president as to the character of the papers and the hope that the nonslaveholding states would be prompt to exercise their power to suppress the papers as far as they could. They agreed with the president as to the evil but not as to the way it should be suppressed, that is, a federal law prohibiting the transmission of incendiary publications. The report went on to say that Congress did not have the power to pass such a law and that it would subvert the reserved powers of the states. Such a law would also violate the First Amendment by limiting the freedom of the press. Since Congress's power over the Post Office was exclusive and since it could declare any road or navigable stream a post road and forbid any carrier on such road to carry newspapers and pamphlets (as had been so declared in regard to letters), it could "more effectually control the freedom of the press than any sedition law, however severe its penalties. The mandate of the Government alone would be sufficient to close the door against circulation through the mail, and thus, at its sole will and pleasure, might intercept all communication between the press and the people." But the states, which alone could regulate slavery, could pass laws to protect the institution. The federal government should cooperate with the states as far as possible in the execution of their laws.[29]

Calhoun then presented his bill which provided: "that it shall not be lawful for any Deputy Postmaster, knowingly, to receive and put into mail any pamphlet, newspaper, hand bill, or other printed, written, or pictorial representation touching the subject of slavery, directed to any person or post office where by the laws thereof their circulation is prohibited." According to this bill, matter touching on slavery would be nonmailable in certain states. Fines were to be imposed on those convicted of violating the act. The postmaster general was also authorized to dismiss the deputy postmaster thus convicted; he was to furnish deputies with the laws of the states. When deputies found such nonmailable matter in their offices they were to inform the postmaster general; the person who had deposited it might withdraw the matter, but if it were not withdrawn within one month the matter was to be destroyed.[30]

Debate on the bill occupied the Senate for a week in April and then two days in June, 1836. Several constitutional issues were brought up. One committee member, Davis of Massachusetts, expressed alarm at the tremendous power given a deputy postmaster, that he could decide what papers were incendiary and reject them; this was a judicial power and the person who deposited the papers would not only be denied the right of trial by jury but also would not even be present when the papers were rejected. He also asked how Congress could give to the states a power that the federal government did not possess. Another senator stressed the sanctity of the mail; he said Congress had the power to prescribe weight, bulk, and kind of material but the latter could be judged only by the outward appearance and not by breaking the seal or wrapper. He said that after a letter had been put in the mail, "It is then the property of the person to whom it is directed, and the United States has given him a solemn constitutional pledge that they will convey it to him, without permitting its contents to be inspected or suffering it in any degree or manner to be detained or injured beyond what must necessarily take place in its passage."[31]

John Milton Niles, newly appointed senator from Connecticut, who would succeed Kendall as postmaster general May 26, 1840, declared Calhoun's bill was unsound and dangerous for it would change the Post Office from a free institution into a legalized system of espionage. He continued: "The public mail, like the press, should be free, free as the air we breathe . . . . The public mail is the most important and beneficent of all the institutions of the Federal Government; it is one of unmeasured good, and brings its blessings to every man's door. It is one of those institutions that we must be careful how we touch."

Three prominent senators opposed Calhoun's bill: Thomas Hart

Benton, Democrat representing Missouri, 1821–1851, and two Whigs, Daniel Webster, senator from Massachusetts since 1827, and Henry Clay, Kentucky senator since 1831. Benton's biographer says that the Missouri senator was drifting away from the South and that this was the first time he voted against a bill desired by that region. Benton said that he was "not willing that the United States should be made a pack horse for the abolitionists; but it seemed to him to be going too far to invest ten thousand postmasters . . . with the authority invested in them by this bill."[32] Henry Clay denounced the bill with great vigor. He did not think Congress had the power to carry into effect the laws of the states or for that matter to regulate what should be carried in the mails. He said: "If such doctrine prevailed, the Government might designate the persons, or parties, or classes who should have the benefit of the mails, excluding all others."[33] Just before the vote was to be taken Webster addressed the Senate at length, devoting most of his speech to freedom of the press. What was the liberty of the press? he asked. It was the liberty of printing as well as the liberty of publishing, in all the ordinary modes of publication; and was not the circulation of papers through the mails an ordinary mode of publication?[34]

The only Northern senator of prominence who spoke in favor of Calhoun's bill was James Buchanan of Pennsylvania. He was an ambitious Democrat, long a supporter of President Jackson; he had served in the House for ten years and had just entered the Senate after representing the United States as minister to Russia since 1831. He discussed at length the power of Congress over the Post Office, which he said was complete and subject to "no limitation, no restriction." He stated that citizens should be entirely "free to print and publish and circulate what they pleased" but that the United States government did not have to provide for circulation through the Post Office.[35]

On April 30 Felix Grundy of Tennessee, friend of both President Jackson and Senator Calhoun, moved to amend the bill by striking out all but the enacting clause. His bill was not so dissimilar from Calhoun's except that it prohibited the delivery of such matter whereas Calhoun's bill made it unlawful for a post-master to receive or put such matter in the mail.[36]

Calhoun accepted the substitute but added an amendment that would permit the delivery of incendiary publications "to such persons as may be appointed to receive them"; his amendment was not adopted. Because the vote of Vice-President Van Buren broke a tie, Grundy's bill was ordered engrossed for the third reading. However, when the bill came up for a final vote on June 8 it was defeated by a vote of 19 to 25. Seven Southern senators, led by Clay of Kentucky, voted against the bill and only four Northern senators (Buchanan of Pennsylvania, John M. Robinson of Illinois, and the two New York senators) voted for it.[37]

In the House of Representatives the part of the president's message that dealt with the incendiary literature had been referred to the Committee on the Post Office and Post Roads. Samuel Beardsley of New York suggested that a bill in line with the message be prepared and this was referred to the same committee. The committee spent weeks discussing the bill but could not come to any agreement. Hiland Hall of Vermont submitted a minority report on March 25, but this was ruled out of order as no majority report had been presented. The question, however, came up for discussion in May during the debate on the Post Office reorganization bill. E. J. Shields of Tennessee presented an amendment incorporating the substance of Calhoun's bill. Hall made the leading speech against the amendment. He declared Congress not only had no power over slavery but also could not restrict publications from going through the mail; to do so would be a direct blow to freedom of the press. Congress had no power to become censors "or to erect a censorship of the press." The amendment was defeated without a count.[38]

Neither President Jackson's proposal for a federal law prohibiting the transportation of incendiary matter through the mail nor Senator Calhoun's bill, which would have made the delivery of such publications subject to state regulation, was adopted. There was in the Post Office Reorganization Act of that year the following provision:

That if any postmaster shall unlawfully detain in his office any letter, package, pamphlet, or newspaper with intent to prevent the arrival and delivery of same to the person or persons to whom such letter, package, pamphlet or newspaper may be addressed or directed in the usual course of the transportation of the mail along the route . . . he shall, on conviction thereof, be fined in a sum not exceeding five hundred dollars, and imprisonment for term not exceeding six months, and shall moreover, be for ever thereafter, incapable of holding the office of postmaster in the United States.[39]

This section was similar to provisions protecting the sanctity of the mail that had been in the Post Office ordinances since 1782. The question was whether or not that provision would be applied to postmasters in Southern states who held up what they considered incendiary publications.

Meanwhile the Southern states had either strengthened existing laws or passed new ones dealing with incendiary matter. South Carolina, the state where the commotion first occurred, had at the very time President Jackson was recommending legislation (December, 1835) passed eight resolutions by unanimous vote of both houses. The first resolution declared that the abolition societies had violated the obligations of the Union; the second, that the state could not acquiesce in the present state of affairs; the third requested the governors of nonslaveholding states to pass laws curbing abolition literature; the fourth declared that domestic slavery was a concern of the state; the fifth, that nonslaveholding states should declare they would not interfere with slavery; the sixth, that slavery in the District of Columbia would not be interfered with. The seventh expressed approbation of the measures adopted by the Post Office Department in regard to the transmission of incendiary tracts but called on the governor of the state to take immediate action if the policy was changed and such matter was again transmitted through the mail.[40]

The eighth resolution provided for transmission of the resolutions to the other states. North Carolina had, at the same time, been considering resolutions and agreed to cooperate with sister states in passing laws necessary to suppress the circulation of incendiary publications. These resolutions requested states to enact penal laws "prohibiting the printing within their respective limits, all such publications as may have a tendency to make our slaves discontented with their present condition, or incite them to insurrection." They also stated that they "confidently" relied on Congress to pass laws "to prevent the circulation of inflammatory publications through the Post Office Department."[41]

Several Northern states, both in the East (Maine, Massachusetts, New York) and in the Middle West (Ohio) passed resolutions recognizing the states' right to control slavery in their states and deplored anything that tended to disrupt good relations. The legislatures called on their citizens to abstain from public discussion of slavery that might render more oppressive the condition of slaves and could lead to a split in the Union.[42] Vermont, however, the only state that in 1798 during the debate on the Alien and Sedition laws had denied the compact of states theory, resolved "that neither Congress nor the State Governments have any constitutional right to abridge the free expression of opinions, or the transmission of them through the public mail."[43]

As months went by and no action was taken by Congress, laws rather than resolutions were passed by Southern states. The earlier resolutions had condemned abolition societies and literature, had called for cooperation among the Southern states, had asked Northern states to prevent the transmission of incendiary literature, and had urged action by the Post Office Department and Congress. In 1836 the states took more positive action. Maryland, April 2, 1836, passed an act providing punishment of from ten to twenty years' imprisonment for each offense for any person who circulated any papers of "an inflammatory character."[44] Virginia required postmasters to notify a justice of the peace that abolitionist literature had been received at his office. If the justice found the material to be antislavery in character he was directed to have it burned in his presence and to arrest the person to whom it was addressed. Postmasters who violated this provision were to be punished.[45]

Postmasters in Southern states were caught between Scylla and Charybdis. Southerners maintained that federal authority over the mail ceased when the mail reached its destination, so according to state laws postmasters could be fined and imprisoned if they distributed abolitionist papers. According to federal law they were subject to fine and imprisonment and loss of position if they intentionally and unlawfully delayed delivery of the mail. The latter law had, however, become a dead letter. John Quincy Adams, who in 1831 had been elected to the House of Representatives after his defeat for reelection to the presidency, brought the question up in debate in 1842. He declared that the freedom of the press was being infringed by the suppression in the South of all publications in any way connected with abolition. In this speech he called for the reading into the record of Postmaster General Kendall's letter to Postmaster Gouverneur, August 22, 1835. Adams said:

Here is an officer of the United States Government, who unequivocally admits that retaining papers in the post office without distribution is contrary to law, who expressly says that he does not and will not authorize it, and yet tells the postmaster who had applied to him for directions in the case that he must act in the matter upon his own discretion. I denounce it as a violation of the freedom of the press, as a violation of the sacred character of the post office, and of the rights and liberties of all the free people of the United States.[46]

A Whig postmaster general, Jacob Collamer (1849–1850) of Vermont, considered by many to be an abolitionist, insisted the law of 1836 was still in force and that he had no authority to substitute any new regulation. He claimed he had made no change in governmental policy, that no circular had ever been issued by a postmaster general intimating that a postmaster who withheld inflammatory matter would not be punished. He said the letter Postmaster General Kendall had written to the postmaster of New York was a private, "unofficial letter to a gentleman," that it had never been entered in the files or records of the department. However, there was no law which authorized a postmaster or the postmaster general to examine letters, and attempts in Congress to pass such a law had failed .The stringent law of 1836 was in force, and he had no authority to substitute any regulation in place of that law. He admitted, however, that if the local district attorney would not prosecute and the courts and juries would not sustain them, then the Post Office Department was helpless.[47]

# Postal Censorship: Incendiary Matter

In 1856 an official opinion on the situation was given. Jefferson Davis brought the issue before Postmaster General James Campbell (1853–1857). A postmaster in Mississippi refused to deliver a copy of the *Cincinnati Gazette* to a subscriber, claiming it was an abolition paper. The subscriber complained to the editor, who brought the matter to the attention of the Post Office Department. The first assistant postmaster general, on instructions from the postmaster general, told the postmaster he had no authority to withhold delivery of any mail. A citizens' committee wrote Davis: "We cannot believe that it is the object of the Federal Government, to become the Cooperators of abolitionism by making the officers and agents of the Post Office Department, in effect, the agents and abettors of the mad Fanatics of the North in the circulation of their incendiary and insurrectionary publications, in violation of the laws of our State, and to the danger of the peace and safety of our citizens." The postmaster, who under a Mississippi law of 1839 faced a penalty of imprisonment for ten years for circulating an incendiary publication, also wrote Senator Davis and said he would continue to refuse to deliver such abolitionist matter and if the Post Office Department ordered him to deliver it he would resign the office, "for I will not be made the instrument in the South, of distributing abolition newspapers—& that too in violation of the Laws of my State, and in violation of the rights of the Community in which I reside."[48]

Postmaster General Campbell, sympathetic to the plight of the Southern postmaster, sought the advice of Attorney General Caleb Cushing.[49] The latter, after reviewing the facts and laws involved, pointed out that there were two constitutional issues. The first was easily answered and that is that when there is conflict between a federal and a state law the federal law is supreme. The second was more complicated and that was the question of the constitutionality of the Post Office Law of 1836. If it were constitutional, then the postmaster general would be obliged to instruct the deputy postmaster to deliver all matter, for as deputy postmasters were merely deputies, it would not be fair to throw the burden of the decision on them. The main question was how much power over the Post Office was given to the federal government

37

by the Constitution; he thought, although the clause was imperfect, it was intended to give Congress entire power. But the United States also had the constitutional power to protect the states, so certainly the United States officials could not promote insurrection. Cushing decided that since the act of 1836 had said "unlawfully detain" that it did not apply to matter which it was unlawful to deliver under state laws. Of course a postmaster could not detain letters, but the Mississippi statute had specified printed publication. He ridiculed the idea that detention by a postmaster of papers meant censorship of the press; he called this charge "words of rhetorical exaggeration." He concluded: "A deputy postmaster or other officer of the United States is not required by law to become, knowingly, the enforced agent or instrument of enemies of the public peace, to disseminate, in their behalf, within the limits of anyone of the States of the Union, printed matter, the design and tendency of which are to promote insurrection in such State."[50]

Postmaster General Holt (1859–1861) was even more specific in his instructions as to incendiary publications. He had been made postmaster general after the unexpected death of Aaron V. Brown (1857–1859), in March, 1859. He had been commissioner of patents and was an able administrator.[51] One postmaster in Virginia refused to deliver to a subscriber the *New York Herald*; the postmaster general upheld his action telling him that the laws of his state not only forbade the introduction into Virginia of incendiary documents but also authorized their destruction after appropriate legal proceedings had taken place. The editor of the *New York Tribune* was scathing in his denunciation of Holt: "It has been very flippantly determined by the autocrat of the National Post-Office—who, in our estimation, has as much right to say what kind of printed matter shall, and what shall not, be transported by the United States mail, as he has to determine what sort of fish Catholics may eat in Lent—that his Virginia Postmasters may exclude all incendiary matter from the mails." He went on to say that the South had to take the New York newspapers, that they could not "lock themselves up in utter exclusion and silence." Then he raised the question: "What we particularly desire to know is whether the South and Mr. Postmaster Holt are in earnest in this contest; or whether it is only the intention of the parties concerned to reduce the Post Office Department to be a mere instrument of partisan politics."[52]

The postmaster at Lynchburg, Virginia, wrote Horace Greeley that his post office would not distribute copies of the *New York Tribune* because of its incendiary character. The postmaster was Robert H. Glass, editor of the *Lynchburg Republican* and father of Carter Glass, who was representative from 1902 to 1918 and senator from 1920 until his death. The editor of a small Wisconsin county paper wrote:

It is amazing to see the insolent boldness of usurpation and the blind, servile submission of party zeal. The P.[ost] M.[aster] Gen.[eral] has already authorized his deputies scattered through the Country, to judge whether the mail matter coming to their offices is fit or unfit to be circulated, and, to that end, to commit a *felony* (as defined by the post office law) by breaking packages and examining their contents. And this little postmaster Glass does but act out of the spirit of his master, when he undertakes to decide that a public journal, in all its numbers, present and future, is incendiary and must be suppressed. Its circulation is forbidden by the *laws of the land*, he says; and lest the *laws* should fail to uphold his partizan tyranny, he asserts that it is forbidden also, by a *proper regard for the safety of society*. He is the judge it would seem not only of *the laws* of the Land, but also of the "higher law" of *Salus Populi*.[53]

Holt's instructions were modified slightly when the issue of the nondelivery of the *Religious Telescope* by the postmaster at Lundy's Creek, Virginia, was brought to the attention of the postmaster general by Congressman Vallandigham of Ohio. Postmaster General Holt told Assistant Postmaster General Horatio King to inform the postmaster that he had misconstrued the laws of Virginia, that a paper could not be condemned just because one issue had in it incendiary matter; each issue had to be judged independently by the authorities.[54] This foreshadows decisions made in regard to nonmailability of obscene matter.

The issue was taken up in Congress early in 1860. A resolution was introduced by R. Holland Duell of New York in February asking the postmaster general to send copies of regulations, instructions, and correspondence authorizing postmasters to open and destroy letters and newspapers considered to contain incendiary matter. It was referred to the Committee on the Post Office and Post Roads and there buried. In the Senate bills introduced "to punish and prevent the unlawful detention of mail matter" were also buried in committee.[55]

By the end of December, 1860, South Carolina and some other Southern states had seceded from the Union and many of the postmasters resigned or ignored their obligations to the Union government. Postmaster General Holt wrote many of them, including Alfred Huger, postmaster at Charleston, South Carolina, asking whether he would continue to hold himself responsible to the United States government for the postal revenue collected.[56]

Schuyler Colfax of Indiana, in January, 1861, introduced a bill in the House to discontinue postal service in certain districts since the revenue could not be collected. A substitute bill gave authority to the postmaster general to discontinue postal service when he thought it could not be safely continued. There was some objection to the delegation of so much power to one officer; others said it would destroy the rights of the states. Senator Lazarus W. Powell of Kentucky claimed that one of the main objects of the bill was to make it possible for the postmaster general to stop the postal service in a district if the postmaster, in obedience to the laws of his state, refused to distribute incendiary tracts. After a debate on the legality of slavery and of secession the bill became a law just before the end of President Buchanan's administration.[57]

The first major debate in Congress over the relation of the Post Office to freedom of the press foreshadows many issues that later came up in Congress and the courts in connection with the nonmailable statutes. Did the First Amendment guarantee circulation as well as publication of newspapers? The question was widely discussed in the 1830s, since newspapers were by then considered as much a part of the mails as letters, although the inviolability of letters was stressed. Also there was raised the question of whether future issues of a paper could be denied access to the mails because of the character of one issue. Whether freedom of the press included the right to send through the mails matter that might cause harm to members of a community was a matter of concern. Many Southerners were afraid that the abolitionist literature might bring about slave riots.

Another issue prominent in this period was the relation of federal laws concerning the Post Office to state laws. The big difference was that during the pre-Civil War period state laws conflicted with distribution of the mails whereas in a later period Congress would use its power over the Post Office to bolster up state laws. Abolitionists' insistence on sending through the mails incendiary literature in spite of state laws was one factor in bringing about the War between the States.

# Postal Censorship during the Civil War

"The mails, unless repelled, will continue to be furnished to all parts of the Union," said President Abraham Lincoln in his inaugural address, March 4, 1861.[1] He was still in hope that the Southern states would return to the Union and that mail communication between the two sections might help bring this about. He had appointed as his postmaster general, Montgomery Blair, an ex-Democrat and a citizen of a border state, Maryland. He was the son of Frank Blair, the editor of the *Globe*, the official Democratic paper during Jackson's administration. Montgomery, at President Jackson's insistence, had been sent to West Point and then had served briefly in the war against the Seminoles. He had left the army to study law and had entered the office of Senator Thomas Hart Benton of St. Louis. Montgomery had been United States attorney for Missouri (1841), mayor of St. Louis (1842–1843), and judge of the court of common pleas in that city (1845–1849). He had joined his father in Washington in 1853 and had later been appointed solicitor of the United States in the court of claims. His father had helped form the Republican party in 1856 when Thomas Hart Benton's son-in-law, John C. Frémont, received the presidential nomination. Montgomery joined the party two years later, represented his district at the Republican National Convention in 1860, and on the third ballot voted

# Censorship during the Civil War

for Lincoln for president. He had campaigned and had been able to carry his state for the Illinois politician.[2]

The first issue that faced the new postmaster general was what should be done about the postal system in the seceded states. Although the postmaster general had the power, under the act passed by Congress just before the inauguration of President Lincoln, to discontinue service whenever he thought it could not be safely continued on a postal route or at a post office, he was reluctant to do so. He wanted to keep the lines of communication with the South open, hoping that when the people became aware of the implications of the rebellion they would repudiate the "revolutionary despotism temporarily established there." He felt the Southern authorities were suppressing all correct information and that the postal service was the best means of communication. He even wanted to reestablish offices that had been discontinued.[3]

His efforts were in vain, for the seven deep Southern states that had seceded had united into a confederacy and organized an army. With the firing on Fort Sumter, Lincoln's call for volunteers, the secession of four more states, and finally the blockade of the South, April 19, a recognition that a state of war existed, the situation became impossible, and on May 27 Blair ordered service discontinued in the seceded states except in western Virginia. As directed by an act of Congress he so informed that body on July 12, 1861.[4]

Letters from the South were intercepted and opened. Southerners then began to send mail by express companies; their agents would post the letters from some border city in the North. Postmaster General Blair stated that since there were no postal arrangements in the Southern states the law of 1825 which forbade the carrying of mail by express agents on post roads was not violated, but he insisted that the stamps be purchased in the Union. He instructed postmasters at border cities "to send all letters coming from States in which the postal service has been discontinued with our stamps upon them to the Dead Letter office, for the reason that we do not recognize stamps and stamped envelopes obtained from offices in such States which like other mail property has been fraudulently seized." On August 10, however,

President Lincoln issued a proclamation interdicting all corre-spondence with the Confederate states, and Postmaster General Blair directed that any express agent or other person receiving letters or papers to be carried from those states be arrested and the letters be seized and forwarded to the department.[5] The inter-cepting of correspondence necessitated the addition of many extra clerks in the division responsible for that work.[6]

At the request of the State or War departments postmasters were directed to detain mail addressed to certain persons, sup-posed to be agents for the "insurgents." William L. Yancey, who had been sent to England as commissioner of the Confederacy to obtain its recognition, directed his correspondents to address their letters to a certain Arthur Dare in London. The State Depart-ment, when this ruse was discovered, asked the postmaster gen-eral to alert the postmasters at key ports on the Atlantic to detain all letters addressed to Dare and to forward them either to the Post Office or the State Department. "It is presumed that this course will be approved by you," wrote F. W. Seward, assistant secretary of state (and son of the secretary of state), to Mont-gomery Blair. The order was put into effect without delay.[7]

The military was faced with the problem of preventing news of troop movements from reaching the enemy. Newspaper editors had entered into a gentlemen's agreement not to print news of that sort, but the agreement was not always kept. General Scott then issued an order prohibiting correspondents from sending any information about troop movements from the capital by tele-graph. The *New York Times* complained about the order and could see no reason for it when people living in Washington sent relatives military information.[8] News correspondents, resentful at the censorship of the telegraph, began sending their dispatches by mail. An authority on the press during the Civil War claimed that never did the government open letters "mailed from any military district to an address on loyal soil."[9] The well-known re-porter for the London *Times*, however, wrote that he had sent off his letters by an individual who was taking dispatches to England "as the post-office is becoming a dangerous institution. We hear of letters being tampered with on both sides."[10]

# Censorship during the Civil War

Postmaster General Blair stated that he thought it was his duty during time of war to prevent seditious matter from reaching the enemy and to close the mails to matter which might instigate others to aid the rebels.[11] He therefore denied to papers called traitorous the use of the mails. This was first done in the summer of 1861, shortly after the rout of the Union troops at Bull Run. A grand jury in New York on August 16 handed down a presentment that stated that there were certain newspapers "which are in the frequent practice of encouraging rebels now in arms against the Federal Government, by expressing sympathy and agreement with them, the duty of acceding to their demands, and dissatisfaction with the employment of force to overcome them." The papers were the *Journal of Commerce*, *Day Book*, *Freeman's Journal*, *News*, and the *Brooklyn Daily Eagle*. The jury accused the *Journal* of referring to the conflict as "the present unholy war." The presentment concluded: "The conduct of these disloyal presses is, of course, condemned and abhorred by all loyal men; but the Grand Jury will be glad to learn from the Court that it is also subject to indictment and condign punishment." The judge merely turned the matter over to the October court and dismissed the jury. The action of the jury, however, was universally accepted as an indictment.[12]

The Post Office Department interpreted it as such and immediately (August 22) issued an order to the postmaster in New York that "none of the newspapers published in New York City, which were presented by the Grand Jury as dangerous from their disloyalty, shall be forwarded in the mails." The New York postmaster then informed the papers that thereafter all issues would be refused by the Post Office for transmission in the mails. The *Journal of Commerce*, on receipt of the notice, did not publish its Saturday edition and published the Monday edition for only those subscribers who did not receive the paper through the mail.[13] The editor stated: "The ingenious device of forbidding the conveyance of obnoxious papers by the mails, is just as effective for their destruction as their forcible suppression would be. For, without the use of the mails, there is not a newspaper in the land that could long exist. Thus the 'third estate', according to this theory,

45

is entirely subject to the will of the Postmaster General. We know of no law authorizing such a procedure, on the contrary, the law seems to explicitly condemn it." He suggested the president appoint a censor for the city of New York and that his salary be paid by the newspapers he supervised and that they all promise to abide by his decision "until the return of the happy days when the liberty of the press shall again be enjoyed." That suggestion was not followed. Gerald Hallock, proprietor of the *Journal of Commerce*, resigned saying there was "no fun in editing a paper in such times as these, when men are so patriotic that they see traitors, secessionists and conspirators everywhere, and suspect treason, secessionism, and conspiracy in every line they read." The Post Office Department then rescinded the order excluding the paper from the mails.[14]

The suspension of mailing privileges was more effective in the other cases. The *Freeman's Journal* changed its name and *Day Book* ceased publication; the latter had lost its corporation advertising and subscriptions of Southerners. The *Daily News* lasted a little longer; it had been owned by the brother of Mayor Fernando Wood, the mayor who early in the war had suggested that New York City, tied by commercial interests and friendly relations with the seceded states, separate from New York State. The paper, when indicted, lost the city printing patronage that had been such a valuable asset. It finally (September 14) "hari-karied itself out of existence." On its closed doors was posted a notice that the paper was suspended until freedom of the press was restored.[15]

The papers in the border states were a particular source of trouble to the administration. Maryland, a crucial state since one had to pass through it in order to reach the capital from the North, had in it a great number of Southern sympathizers and had been prevented from seceding only through such drastic measures as the suspension of the writ of habeas corpus and the arrest by the military of some prominent secessionists. Several of the Baltimore papers were considered by the administration to be traitorous and incendiary journals; the editor of the *World* thought that the suspension of the mailing privileges of the New York papers might serve as a warning to them to mend their ways.

# Censorship during the Civil War

When it did not, the government in Washington decided that something would have to be done; it was suggested that the military commander in Baltimore take some action, but he was reluctant to do so without a direct order from the federal government. Finally, on September 10 Postmaster General Blair barred from the mails the three antiadministration newspapers of Baltimore.[16]

Kentucky had, at the outbreak of the war, declared itself neutral in the struggle between the South and the North. President Lincoln tacitly recognized its neutral status. In the August election the Unionists won control of the legislature, and when Jefferson Davis, president of the Confederacy, sent "alien troops" to Columbus, Kentucky, to defend the Mississippi River, the state legislature invited General Anderson (formerly of Fort Sumter) to take command of the troops of the state in order to repel the Confederate invasion. The outstanding paper in the state, the Louisville *Courier-Journal*, denounced the neutrality of the legislature, so Postmaster General Blair issued an order stating that the paper, "found to be an advocate of treasonable hostility to the government and authority of the United States, be excluded from the mails and post-offices of the United States." This was done at the suggestion of Secretary of State Seward.[17]

During 1861 the initiative for postal censorship came from the State Department. Secretary Seward received issues of newspapers that contained attacks on the Lincoln administration or seemed to have secessionist tendencies from super-patriots, from local chiefs of police, from United States marshals, from congressmen; then his office suggested to the postmaster general that any such newspaper be denied transmission through the mails. The postmaster where the paper was published was then ordered not to accept any issues of that paper for circulation in the mail. Being denied the facilities of the Post Office seems to have been the most effective method of suppressing a paper considered traitorous. If a newspaper office was destroyed by a mob, the printer after a short delay resumed publication; when closed by a United States marshal the proprietor appealed to the court; when the editor was jailed his wife took over the paper and continued

47

the attacks on the administration. When the Post Office Department barred a paper there was no redress.[18]

By the end of 1861 Postmaster General Blair had suspended mailing privileges of twelve newspapers accused of being treasonable or incendiary. The editor of the *National Intelligencer* compared Blair's exclusion from the mails of these papers with the actions of Postmaster General Campbell in the administration of President Pierce, in whose cabinet Jefferson Davis had been the "acknowledged chief." He pointed out that the issue had been brought up by a protest of Davis because of the plight of the postmaster at Yazoo, Mississippi. He said: "It was during this Administration that the question as to the right of the Postmaster General or his deputies to prohibit the circulation of printed matter 'the design and tendency of which are to promote insurrection,' was distinctly raised and authoritatively decided by the Executive Department of the Government." This decision had been received by universal commendation in the Southern states.[19]

The postmaster general in his annual report on December 2, 1861, had a section entitled "Disloyal Publications Excluded from the Mails." He explained in detail the actions of the department; he stated that various influential newspapers were advancing the cause of the enemy and thwarting the administration's effort to preserve the Union. Since judicial processes were so slow other methods were necessary to block their treasonable activities. Exclusion from the mails was one way. He continued:

The freedom of the press is secured by a high constitutional sanction. But it is freedom and not license that is guaranteed. It is to be used only for lawful purposes. It cannot aim blows at the existence of the government, the Constitution, and the Union, and at the same time claim its protection . . . . While, therefore, this department neither enjoyed nor claimed the power to suppress such treasonable publications, but left them free to publish what they please, it could not be called upon to give them circulation. It could not and would not interfere with the freedom secured by law, but it could and did obstruct the dissemination of that license which was without the pale of the Constitution and law. The mails established by the United States government could not, upon any known principle of law or public right, be used for its own destruction.

He went on to cite as his authority Joseph Story, associate justice of the Supreme Court from 1811 to 1845 and author of *Commentaries of the Constitution.*[20]

Censorship was tightened early in 1862. In January Congress passed an act authorizing the president when he thought public safety demanded it to take possession of all the telegraph and railroad lines "so that they shall be considered as a post road and a part of the military establishment of the United States, subject to all the restrictions imposed by the rules and articles of war." Postmaster General Blair stated that eventually the telegraph system would be taken over by the government. He declared that the clause giving Congress power to establish post offices and post roads was intended to give Congress "a monopoly in the conveyance of intelligence for hire."[21]

During 1862 newspaper censorship was taken over by the War Department. On February 25 Secretary Stanton issued an order taking military possession of all telegraph lines and proclaiming that all telegraphic communications about military operations were forbidden and that all newspapers that published unauthorized military news could be excluded from receiving information by telegraph or from transmitting their papers by railroad. There was, of course, considerable grumbling by the press at this order, but the *New York Times* thought the restriction was a necessary military measure to prevent knowledge of troop movements from reaching the enemy, now that Union troops seemed to be moving.[22] The Post Office Department cooperated and at Secretary Stanton's instigation on March 25 Postmaster General Blair issued an order to the postmasters that the secretary of war thought it was necessary to put restrictions on the publication of military news not only by telegraph but also by other means of transportation and had requested the cooperation of the Post Office Department. Postmasters were therefore ordered to notify publishers that they were not to publish any fact that had been excluded from the telegraph and that the paper would be excluded from the mails if this order was disregarded.[23]

Now requests or orders for the banning of "treasonable" newspapers from the mails came from army commanders rather than

49

from the State Department. Major General Blunt, commander of the Department of Kansas, branded as incendiary the New York *Caucasian*, New York *World*, Chicago *Times*, Columbus (Ohio) *Crisis*, and the *Cincinnati Enquirer*, and ordered postmasters within his district not to deliver those papers to their subscribers but to destroy them immediately.[24] The New York *World* was also banned in Ohio because of the tendency of its articles and editorials "to cast reproach upon the Government, and to weaken its efforts to suppress the rebellion, by creating distrust in its war policy." Postmasters were to "govern themselves by this order"; if they did not they would be promptly arrested and tried.[25]

Brigadier General Wright, commander of the Army of the Pacific, was particularly active in trying to suppress incendiary papers and sent orders to his subordinates to look out for papers in that area which abused the president and government of the United States. They were to send him copies and he would see that circulation through the mail was prohibited.[26]

A resolution was introduced in the House of Representatives in December, 1862, instructing the Judiciary Committee to "inquire and report to the House, at an early day, by what authority of Constitution and law, if any, the Postmaster General undertakes to decide what newspapers, and what shall not, be transmitted through the mails of the United States." The postmaster general replied at length to their request for information, quoting from his annual report of the previous year. He reviewed the action of the grand jury in New York that had resulted in the exclusion from the mails of the four city papers in the summer of 1861. He then reviewed the actions of Postmasters General Kendall, Campbell, and Holt and quoted at length the opinion of Attorney General Cushing. He said that for twenty-five years the department had excluded from the mails printed matter considered by postal officials to be treasonable or incendiary. Neither Congress nor the Supreme Court had made any attempt to restrain this practice. In fact, if the department allowed such matter to circulate it would be a party to treason and rebellion. He went on to say that he disagreed with some of the precedents, especially the giving to the postmasters authority to use their own judgment in deciding which papers were lawful or unlawful; he thought that power should rest with the postmaster general alone. The committee upheld the actions of the head of the Post Office Department, stating that he not only had the authority but also the obligation to exclude from the mails "all treasonable matter."[27]

In the Senate (January 15, 1863), Senator John S. Carlile of Wheeling, Virginia, introduced a resolution asking about the order Postmaster General Blair had issued in December of 1862. He inquired if this order applied to papers suppressed by military authorities. He also wanted to know by what law military commanders could exclude matter theretofore transmitted through the mails.[28] The postmaster general's answer of January 19 was equivocal. He said that the order rescinded only former orders excluding certain papers from the mail and did not interfere with any order of the military authorities. In reply to the second question he said: "The law or authority by which a commanding officer . . . suppresses the circulation, by postmasters or others, of objectionable printed matter, is, I presume, the law of public safety." He added that postmasters had to obey the order of the military and that postmasters had asked him for instructions and he had so informed them, but it was the military order, not his instructions, "which relieved him from the responsibility of delivering the mail matter in question."[29]

Not only were papers banned from the mails but their publication was suspended and property confiscated on orders of the secretary of war. Editors were jailed, tried by military tribunals, and imprisoned in government forts; letters of reporters were taken from the post offices, perused, and then sent on or sometimes destroyed.[30] One of the most famous cases was that of the Chicago *Times*; throughout the war it had been antiadministration and its criticism of Lincoln and the conduct of the war reached a peak in 1863. "On account of the repeated expression of disloyal and incendiary sentiments," the paper was ordered suppressed by General Ambrose E. Burnside on June 1, 1863. The proprietor attempted to obtain an injunction; the legislature of Illinois passed a resolution condemning the action and mass meetings were held calling on the president to respect the freedom of the press. Three days later (June 4) the order was revoked by President Lincoln.[31]

Another prominent newspaper suspended by the military was the New York *World*. During the early part of the war it had not been unfriendly to the administration and had even supported the banning from the mails of the *Journal of Commerce*. By 1862–1863 it had become more critical and its circulation had been prohibited in several military areas. It was a Democratic paper and in 1864, an election year, it was an irritant to the administration. On May 18 there appeared in the *World* and in the *Journal of Commerce* a copy of a proclamation allegedly signed by President Lincoln. This described the military situation in Virginia as very grave and called for a day of fasting on May 26. The proclamation asked for 400,000 more troops and stated that if quotas could not be obtained by volunteers a draft would be imposed. On the morning of the eighteenth it was discovered that the proclamation was a forgery, and that night the military took possession of the editorial and composing rooms and suspended publication of the two papers that had printed the proclamation. The forger, veteran newspaperman Joseph Howard, had been very clever; he had written the proclamation on the thin paper characteristically used by the Associated Press and had had it delivered by messenger to newspaper offices, between three and four in the morning, just as the papers were ready to be printed. In the office of the *World* the proclamation had been put into the box with other Associated Press dispatches and thus inserted in the paper; it appeared on page four in an inconspicuous position with no heading.[32]

Other papers were more fortunate; the messenger sent to the *Tribune* could not find the printing office and the editorial office was closed. The editor of the *New York Times* saw the proclamation and doubted its authenticity as the handwriting was different; he checked with the offices of the Associated Press and discovered that it was a forgery. Both the *Times* and *Tribune* editors thought the action of the military in summarily suspending publication of the *World* and the *Journal of Commerce* premature and unjust, as such a mistake could have been made by the most loyal of papers. The *Times*, however, took issue with the *Evening Post*, which declared the suspension of the two papers was a violation of the freedom of the press. The *Times* editor thought the papers had some responsibility and should have checked more carefully before publishing a proclamation of the president that might result in great harm to the government. On the other hand he pointed out that the suspension was a heavy penalty, costing the papers thousands of dollars. He suggested that the rules of common justice should have been followed; the editors should have been arrested first and after trial and conviction the papers might then be suspended.[33] The editor of the *World*, after publication had been resumed on May 23, stated that Lincoln, annoyed at the way the *World* had "exposed his imbecility and denounced his mal-administration," had long been "watching for a pretext to pounce on the opposition press" and took advantage of this trap to suppress the paper and "destroy freedom of discussion" during the presidential contest.[34]

The Post Office Department was denounced for playing politics, and it was asserted that postmasters were delaying the transmission of Democratic papers. The editor of the *World* claimed to have letters from subscribers complaining that issues of that paper failed to reach them as promptly as Republican papers mailed at the same time and place reached their subscribers. The editor asked for fair play from postmasters especially during the presidential campaign.[35]

During the summer when the campaign was at its height the *World* also had a series of editorials entitled "The Post Office Espionage." The editor maintained that letters of Democratic leaders were opened, read, sealed up, and then forwarded. Postmaster General Blair denied the charge in a public letter to the postmaster of New York. He offered a reward for any proof that any postal official had opened letters. He declared that the department permitted no tampering with letters at any time. He claimed that he was not so interested in the political effect of the charge but that the lies would injure his business as "carrier of letters for pay." The editor of the *World* replied that he was not accusing the postmaster general of ordering the interception of letters; in fact he may have protested the practice, but he could not deny that the mail had been tampered with on orders of the secretary of state and secretary of war, and although he may have protested he was still responsible since he was in charge of the Post Office Department. His protests should have been followed by his resignation.[36]

The following month the postmaster general did suddenly announce his resignation, but not because of the controversy over the interception of letters; instead it was offered at the urgent solicitation of President Lincoln. Montgomery Blair, because he favored a liberal reconstruction policy, was persona non grata to the more radical members in the Republican party. A group of them had held a separate convention, had adopted a plank in their platform which called for the punishment of rebels and condemned the leaders who did not agree with that principle, and had nominated General Frémont for president. In August some of the radical leaders made overtures to President Lincoln intimating that General Frémont might be induced to withdraw from the contest if Lincoln would get rid of the obnoxious postmaster general.

Accordingly on September 1 the president wired Blair, who was on vacation in New Hampshire, to return to the capital immediately, and on September 23 Blair formally presented his resignation.[37] He had waited until his successor was ready to take over the job. William Dennison, Cincinnati lawyer and businessman, was much more acceptable to the "radical" element in the Republican party. He had been a Whig (whereas Blair had been a Democrat), had been one of the first of the Ohio party leaders to join the Republican party, and had been a delegate to the first Republican party convention in 1856. He had been governor of Ohio, 1859–1861, had served as chairman of the National Union convention in 1864, the convention which had nominated Lincoln for president. He remained postmaster general until July, 1866.[38]

# Nonmailable Matter
# Defined by
# Congress and Court

After the Civil War Congress began to set up categories of matter that could not be sent through the mail. Previously it had excluded from the mail newspapers that had not been thoroughly dried and had authorized postmasters to refuse packages that weighed more than three (later four) pounds. Congress had specified from time to time what was mailable and the rates of postage for each class. Mailable matter in 1864 was defined as: first class—all correspondence; second class—printed matter "regularly issued at stated periods"; and third class—pamphlets, occasional publications, books, maps, photographs, seeds, bulbs, and scions.[1]

From 1865 to 1876 Congress set up three major categories of matter that were labeled nonmailable. Several reasons might be given for Congress's willingness at that time to ban certain things from the mail. During the Civil War the postmaster general had assumed the power of withholding from the mail papers which he considered treasonable or which contained information that might aid the enemy. Congress had upheld him and in doing so had recognized that it had the power to instruct the postmaster general to declare certain matter nonmailable. States' rights had given way to centralization, so there was little political opposition to federal as opposed to state regulation of the mail (as there had been in 1836). Some writers suggest that the nonmailable legislation was the result of a new puritanism, a reaction against the scandals of the war and of the Reconstruction era.[2]

The first type of mail to be declared nonmailable was obscene matter. Postmaster General Blair, in 1863, admitted that he had "at different times, excluded from the mails obscene and scandalous printed matter on exhibition of its criminal immorality." He added that he did not approve of the individual postmasters' deciding on what printed matter should be excluded from the mails (as had been done during the prewar period). He felt the postmaster general alone should have that responsibility; he received his authority from the Constitution and from "the definition of mailable matter given in the postal law."[3]

In his annual report of 1864 the postmaster general had recommended many revisions in the postal laws and had worked the recommendations into a bill that was introduced (February 8, 1865) in the Senate by Jacob Collamer of Vermont, postmaster general in the administration of President Taylor. One section provided that postmasters might take out of the mail obscene publications; another part provided penalty for those who put such matter in the mail. Collamer pointed out that the department felt something like that was necessary as the mails had been made "the vehicle for the conveyance of great numbers and quantities of obscene books and pictures, which are sent to the Army, and sent here and there and everywhere, and that it is getting to be a very great evil."[4]

One senator asked how a postmaster would know the material was obscene without breaking the seal. Collamer answered that most periodicals were open at one end and that no one had proposed a postmaster be allowed to break seals on letters.[5] Collamer said some feared such a bill as he presented might lead to political censorship, that postmasters might discard literature of an organization or party as before the war some had destroyed abolition papers. He was therefore willing to have the first section of the bill eliminated. Senator John Sherman of Ohio supported the suggested change in the bill; however, he thought the prohibition against sending obscene publications in the mail ought to stand. He pointed out that most of such matter came from New York

# Nonmailable Matter Defined

City and had on the back of it the name of the sender; postmasters, without opening mail, would thus recognize it as offensive matter not to be conveyed in the mails. Later the provision that all "obscene publications discovered in the mails shall be seized and destroyed . . . as the Postmaster General shall direct" was eliminated. The bill passed the Senate on February 8 and was passed by the House with no debate, February 21, 1865.[6]

Section 16 of the act, dated March 3, 1865, read as follows:

> That no obscene book, pamphlet, picture, print, or other publication of a vulgar and indecent character, shall be admitted into the mails of the United States; any person or persons who shall deposit or cause to be deposited, in any post-office or branch post-office of the United States, for mailing or for delivery, an obscene book, pamphlet, picture-print, or other publication, knowing the same to be of a vulgar and indecent character, shall be deemed guilty of a misdemeanor, and, being duly convicted thereof, shall for every such offense be fined not more than five hundred dollars, or imprisoned not more than one year, or both, according to the circumstances and aggravations of the offense.[7]

In the following Congress (February 19, 1866) Senator James Dixon of Connecticut presented a bill (S. 148) to prevent "the perversion of the mails to fraudulent and illegal purposes." This bill was buried in committee,[8] but the issue began to receive considerable public attention. Mayor J. Hoffman of New York City, agitated because of the number of letters complaining of swindles which poured into his office, wrote Postmaster General Dennison calling his attention to the "fraudulent practices carried on in this City though the medium of Post-Offices." A popular fraud at that time was the gift enterprise. Organizations having respectable-sounding names (for example, one was called the National Protective Union) and an impressive list of officers sent out circulars advertising a monthly program at which distribution of prizes among ticket holders would take place. Unwary persons sent money for tickets and then discovered the organization and even the town where the drawing was to take place were fictitious. Although the victims were trying to get something for nothing, they were indignant that they had been defrauded. They complained to the postmaster because such schemes could not exist except for the agency of the Post Office. The mayor suggested that Post Office agents have letters from businesses of this type sent at once to the dead letter office to be returned to the senders. The postmaster general replied that he would do everything he could to prevent the "prostitution of the postal service to purposes of fraud" but that he lacked the necessary authority to attack the problem as the mayor suggested.[9]

In 1868 Congress took up the problem of fraudulent gift enterprises and included in the law lotteries of all kinds. This was the year the notorious Louisiana State Lottery Company was chartered. As in the case of the discussion over the obscenity bill, there was disagreement over the clause authorizing a postmaster to remove from the mail letters or circulars if he suspected they concerned a lottery. It was not thought "wise to give postmasters this extraordinary power to be exercised upon a mere suspicion."[10] Section 13 of the act as signed by the president, July 27, 1868, provided: "That it shall not be lawful to deposit in a post office, to be sent by mail, any letters or circulars concerning lotteries, so-called gift concerts, or other similar enterprises offering prizes of any kind on any pretext whatever."[11] This law differed from the 1865 one in that it included letters and used the phrase "deposit in a post office, to be sent by mail." The law did not, however, provide any penalties for its violation; it merely set up a nonmailable category.

The vagueness of this law caused difficulties. The postmaster at Cincinnati detained letters sent to a box belonging to Murray Eddy, and Co., as it appeared that they were carrying on a lottery. The company instituted legal proceedings. Postmaster General Randall (1866–1869) appealed to Attorney General Browning for a ruling. Browning stated that the postmaster general was obligated to protect the public against fraud and that it was within his administrative duties to define the course to be pursued by the local postmaster but that no action should be taken unless it was wholly clear the scheme was dishonest. Later the postmaster general wrote Attorney General Evarts that he had found it impossible to define rules for the enforcement of the act of 1868. He felt it conflicted with the law of 1836, which imposed heavy penalties for unlawful detention of letters by employees of the Post Office Department. The later law had not repealed the former. The attorney general suggested that more stringent legislation was needed and that it was within the competence of Congress to "confer further authority upon postmasters that it may deem necessary to carry out the policy of the act of 1868."[12]

The question of additional legislation was taken under consideration during the next Congress when a bill to revise and consolidate the statutes relating to the Post Office Department was reported out of committee by Representative John F. Farnsworth of Illinois. Commissioners under the supervision of the Post Office Department had been authorized to review all the statutes concerning the Post Office that had been passed since 1789. The rules had never been codified. The bill passed the House that December and was brought up in the Senate in January, 1871, but Congress adjourned before action on it was taken. It was the first bill (H.R. 1) introduced in the House in the new Congress (March 4); it passed the House and Senate with very little debate and received the president's signature on June 8, 1872.[13]

This was the basic law in which Congress defined nonmailable matter, although the phrase was not used in the law. Excluded from the mail was matter that might do physical damage to Post Office equipment or personnel as well as written matter that might hurt, financially or morally, the clients of the Post Office. Penalties for depositing such matter in the mail were provided for in the law and became part of the criminal code. The law also incorporated in it the provision for penalties for employees of the Post Office who "unlawfully" detained any letter or packet.

The law of 1872 (section 149) declared it would not be lawful to deposit in a post office "any letters or circulars concerning illegal lotteries, so-called gift-concerts, or other similar enterprizes, offering prizes, or concerning schemes devised and intended to deceive and defraud the public for the purpose of obtaining money under false pretenses." Penalties of from $100 to $500 plus costs of prosecution were provided for those convicted of violating this provision. The postmaster general was also given the power, when he was convinced that a firm was engaged in a fraudulent scheme or lottery, to issue a fraud order directing the local postmaster to forbid payments on money orders drawn to such a firm and to return to the original post office registered letters addressed to that firm with the word "Fraudulent" on the envelope. The secrecy of the mail was protected by the provision that this act did not authorize any person to open a letter not addressed to himself. Any person using the mails with intent to defraud was to be punished by a fine of not more than $500 and/or imprisonment not to exceed eighteen months.

Section 148 of the act incorporated into the postal code the law of 1865 on obscene matter with two significant changes: after "indecent character" was added "or any letter upon the envelope of which, or postal card upon which scurrilous epithets may have been written or printed, or disloyal devices printed or engraved." This matter should not be *carried* in the mails.

The act also included in the section (sec. 133) defining third-class mail matter a clause stating that articles "liable to destroy, deface, or otherwise injure the contents of the mailbag, or harm the person of anyone engaged in the postal service" should be excluded from the mail and that should also be true of all "liquids, poisons, glass, explosive materials, and obscene books."[14]

Practically no attention had been paid by congressmen, during the debate on the revision of the postal laws, 1870–1872, to the section concerning obscene matter. The following year, however, the issue was again taken up. Credit for this was claimed by a young New Englander, Anthony Comstock, who said he had seen several young men "ruined" by pornographic publications. He represented a committee for the suppression of vice of the New York chapter of the Young Men's Christian Association. He claimed to have seized over 180,000 obscene pictures and five tons of books. He had tried, under the 1872 law, to obtain indictments against *Woodhull & Chaflin's Weekly*, for a story of a broker's seduction of two young maidens at a ball, and against Frank Leslie's *Day's Doings*, which advertised fancy books, gambling materials, and contraceptives. Judge Samuel Blatchford of the Second Judicial Circuit had ruled that the law did not apply to newspapers.[15]

Declaring the law of 1872 too narrow and too mild, Comstock,

# Nonmailable Matter Defined

loaded with books and pictures which he considered obscene, carried his campaign against obscenity to the capital. He set up an exhibit of obscene matter in the vice-president's office in the capitol. He furnished congressmen material for debate. Letters of his were read into the *Record*. He declared that six thousand persons were daily employed in this business of distributing obscene matter; in New York City, headquarters for this business, over one hundred and forty-four firms were engaged in producing obscene publications. Circulating libraries were organized in schools where boys were paid by dealers to sell copies of obscene books to their classmates at ten cents a copy. "Rubber articles for masturbation or for the professed prevention of conception" were disseminated through advertisements in magazines. Comstock pointed out that the business of selling obscene matter and rubber goods was carried on chiefly through the United States mails.[16]

Comstock won the support of Representative Clinton L. Merriam of New York and Senator William A. Buckingham of Connecticut. On the latter's motion a bill (really a composite of several bills drawn up by Comstock and his lawyer friends) was reported out from the Senate Committee on Post-Offices and Post-Roads, February 18, 1873. The bill dealt not only with the mails but also with the importation and sale of contraceptives in places under the jurisdiction of the United States. Senator Conkling of New York noted that senators were all so indignant and disgusted with obscenity that they were apt to act hastily. He asked that the bill be printed so they would know exactly what was in it; he urged deliberation. Section 2, dealing with the mails, was not even discussed, and the bill passed the Senate on February 21. It was near the end of the short session and it was early Sunday morning before the bill came up on the floor of the House. It is said that Comstock had a battle with his conscience whether or not he should appear on the Hill on the Lord's day. He went home and prayed. The bill was read and passed with no discussion at 2 A.M. and became law March 3, 1873.[17]

The act added to the one of June 8, 1872, the descriptive words "lewd and lascivious" before "book" and included in the banned categories "paper" and "any article or thing designed or intended for the prevention of conception or procuring of abortion" or "any article or thing intended or adapted for any indecent or immoral use or nature" or any publication giving information about such articles. Any person who knowingly deposited in the mail "any of the hereinbefore mentioned articles or things" or information where they could be obtained would be subject to a maximum fine of $5,000 and/or imprisonment at hard labor for from one to ten years.[18] The *New York Times* stated that the attempt to suppress obscene advertisements would now be successful since it was backed by a law of Congress. The writer of the *Times* article went on to say that the *Herald* would now have to cease printing its disgusting "medical notices" which "have brought ruin to the soul and bodies of countless human beings."[19]

Anthony Comstock got himself commissioned, March 6, 1873, as a special agent of the Post Office Department to see that the law was enforced. He served without pay and was zealous in his attempts to stamp out the dissemination of obscene matter. By the end of 1873 Comstock had made fifty-five arrests under the new law and had procured twenty convictions.[20]

The first test case of the 1873 law was in the federal district court in New York in *United States* v. *Bott.* John Bott was charged with sending through the mail a powder intended to produce an abortion. He then declared that in reality the powder was harmless. The judge declared that was no defense. He stated that although regulation of abortion was a state function Congress had "exclusive jurisdiction over the mails" and could prohibit the "use of the mails for the transmission of any article." In summary he said: "Any article of any description, whether harmless or not, may, therefore, be declared contraband in the mail, by Act of Congress, and its deposit there be made a crime."[21]

Dealers in obscenity quickly spotted a loophole in the law of 1873; penalties had been provided only for the mailing of articles sold for the purpose of preventing conception but not for the circulation of obscene literature. A bill to remedy this defect was sponsored by Representative Joseph Cannon of Illinois (later speaker) and passed with practically no debate. The bill differed from the other laws dealing with obscene matter in that it was stated in positive rather than negative terms. It read in part as follows:

Every obscene, lewd, or lascivious book, pamphlet, picture, paper, print, or other publication of an indecent character, and every article or thing designed or intended for the prevention of conception or pro- curing of abortion . . . are hereby declared to be nonmailable matter, and shall not be conveyed in the mails, nor delivered from any post office nor by any letter carrier; and any person who shall knowingly deposit, or cause to be deposited, for mailing or delivery, anything declared in this section to be non-mailable matter . . . shall be deemed guilty of a misdemeanor . . . .

This is the first time that the word "nonmailable" was used in a postal act. There was no debate on the phrase "non-mailable mat- ter" and it was probably used so that all the items in the act would be covered.[22]

Section 2 of the bill provided that the word "illegal" before "lot- teries" in the 1872 law be struck out so that circulars concerning any lottery would be nonmailable. The word "illegal" had not been used in the 1868 law. Senator Hannibal Hamlin of Maine, when he called up the bill that had passed the House, explained that the Post Office Department thought it better and wiser to treat all lotteries alike. The House had not debated this section at all but the Senate discussed it at length, ignoring section 1, dealing with obscenity. Two Southern senators raised the issue of states' rights. They declared a state had the authority to charter a lottery, even though it might be considered legalized gambling, and Congress had no right to prevent the Post Office from carrying its circulars. Senator West from Louisiana said that lotteries did not offend public morals as did obscenity and that once Congress gave the Post Office jurisdiction over such things as lotteries, legalized by a state, there could be no limit to the authority of postal officials.

This section of the bill was defended by several senators, among them John A. Logan of Illinois (Republican vice-presidential can- didate in 1884). He declared that a community "so demoralized" as to favor gambling would legalize lotteries, but it was the duty of Congress to prevent anything pertaining to a lottery from going through the mails into other communities. Senator Morrill of Vermont pointed out that if but one state had legalized lotteries the laws of all other states against lotteries would be null and void if the mails did not prevent the circulation of lottery tickets. The motion to strike out section 2 was defeated and the bill with some minor changes in section 1 (adding "writing" to the list of nonmailable obscene matter) passed the Senate. The House acquiesced and it became a law on July 12, 1876.[23]

The Post Office Appropriation Act of 1879 made several changes dealing with nonmailable matter. One section added to the nonmailable category "any publication which violates any copyright granted by the United States." The law established four classes of mail matter and stated that the fourth class would include all matter not in the other three classes "which is not in its form or nature liable to destroy, deface, or damage the contents of the mail bag, or harm the person of anyone engaged in the postal service, and is not above the weight provided by law." The second class included newspapers and magazines, which were given a low rate.[24]

Special rates had always been given newspapers, as they had been recognized "as an agency of the greatest importance in the promotion of the public good." In 1874 newspapers had been given the benefit of bulk rates, whereby, without regard to distance, papers that were issued weekly or oftener paid two cents a pound. Difficulties arose as people began to send advertising matter under this provision.[25] At the suggestion of the Post Office Department a conference of businessmen and publishers was held in New York City to discuss the classification of mail matter. They adopted resolutions suggesting that matter tending to promote the public good should be carried at as cheap a rate as possible but that the Post Office Department should absolutely refuse its facilities for the distribution of matter "deemed injurious to the public morals." They endorsed a pending bill but suggested a revision that would "prevent the Post Office Department from unjustly refusing registration."[26] The bill provided for a flat rate of two cents a pound for newspapers and magazines, but a certificate of registration had to be obtained from the local postmaster. If he refused it, appeal could be made to the courts. Charges that this would mean postal censorship of the press resulted in the bill's being dropped.[27]

Instead there was added to the Post Office Appropriation bill a provision authorizing the postmaster general to grant very low second-class rates to newspapers and magazines that fulfilled four requirements: they must be printed and issued at regular intervals (at least four times a year), have a known office of publication, a list of subscribers, and be published "for the dissemination · of information of a public character, or devoted to literature, the sciences, arts, or some special industry."[28] It was the latter clause that postmasters general in the twentieth century used to effect a form of postal censorship.

The first Supreme Court decision (*In the Matter of A. Orlando Jackson*) concerning Congress's power to declare certain things nonmailable was handed down May 13, 1878. The petitioner, A. Orlando Jackson, had been sentenced to fine and imprisonment (until the fine was paid) for sending a circular concerning a lottery through the mails. His lawyers claimed that the law was unconstitutional, that Congress had no power to declare any written matter nonmailable and prohibit its transmission through the mail. They maintained that Congress could make changes in types of things admitted to the mails such as postal cards, money orders, merchandise, and the like, but they could not declare nonmailable any letters or newspapers, irrespective of information they carried. The defendant's attorneys also declared that the Constitution had not conferred upon Congress authority to regulate public morals, that every state had the right to determine for itself whether or not lotteries should be regarded as immoral or legitimate and that correspondence about lotteries in states where they were legal could not be abridged.

Justice Stephen J. Field delivered the unanimous decision of the Court. He pointed out that the act of 1876 had eliminated the word "illegal" in connection with lotteries. He then discussed the constitutionality of the acts declaring matter nonmailable. He said:

The power vested in Congress "To establish post offices and post-roads" has been practically construed, since the foundation of the government to authorize not merely the designation of the routes over which the mail shall be carried and the offices where letters and other documents shall be received to be distributed or forwarded, but the carriage of the mail, and all measures necessary to secure its safe and speedy transit, and the prompt delivery of its contents. . . . The power possessed by Congress embraces the regulation of the entire postal system of the country. The right to designate what shall be carried necessarily involves the right to determine what shall be excluded.

There were, however, a few limitations, he added. All regulations concerning mail matter had to be in accord with the Fourth Amendment, the right of people to be secure against unreasonable searches and seizures. This, the justice said, also applied to their papers, thus closing them to inspection. He laid down the dictum: "No law of Congress can place in the hands of officials connected with the postal service any authority to invade the secrecy of letters." Nor could the Post Office Department make regulations concerning the mailability of printed matter which would interfere with the freedom of the press and he considered the "liberty of circulating . . . as essential to that freedom as liberty of publishing." In summary he cited the various postal acts and stated that Congress, in declaring certain articles nonmailable, had merely refused the postal facilities for the distribution of things considered injurious to the public morals and had provided for punishment for those who used the postal system for that purpose. He concluded that there was no doubt as to the constitutionality of the act of 1876.[29]

The postmaster general's power to issue fraud orders was also challenged in the courts by lottery companies. The act of 1872 had authorized nondelivery of registered letters and money orders to firms engaged in a fraudulent scheme or lottery. Thus, when the postmaster general was informed that a certain firm was engaged in conducting a scheme to obtain money through the mails by means of fraud, he instructed the local postmaster to forbid payments of any postal money order drawn to the order of that firm and to return all registered letters with "fraudulent" stamped on the outside. From 1875 to 1880, 134 such orders had been issued. In only three cases had the firms seriously questioned the order.[30]

# Nonmailable Matter Defined

A suit was begun by the Commonwealth Distribution Company to restrain the postmaster at Louisville, Kentucky, from obeying the orders of the postmaster general directing him not to deliver letters to them. The assistant attorney general for the Post Office Department pointed out that the policy of Congress had always been to preserve the inviolability of letters but to exclude improper matter altogether. The law made unmailable a letter concerning a lottery, so it was presumed a letter addressed to a lottery company concerned a lottery and was thus nonmailable. This suit was decided in favor of the department and was dismissed by the circuit court. The fraud order, denying to the company reception of money-orders and registered letters, was continued.[31]

The president of the Louisiana State Lottery,[32] in order to test the constitutionality of the statutes, filed a bill of complaint against Postmaster General Key (1877–1880) in the Supreme Court of the District of Columbia. The postmaster general, November 12, 1879, had issued an order that registered mail and postal money orders were not to be delivered to M. A. Dauphin of New Orleans. Dauphin claimed he was not engaged in a fraudulent business and that the act of Congress and the actions of the postmaster general violated his rights and privileges guaranteed by the Constitution. Justice Cox, in his decision, first discussed the privileges of citizens and stated that the use of the mails certainly could not be a privilege of state citizenship and "privileges and immunities" of national citizenship had been mentioned first in the Fourteenth Amendment. He then examined in detail the power given to Congress by the Constitution to establish post offices but asserted that it was a power not a duty, so the use of the mails was a legislative grant and subject to legislative destruction. Therefore citizens of the United States did not have the constitutional right to mail service. He stated: "The right of every citizen to the benefit of the discretionary legislation of Congress must be subject to the necessities of public health, morals, order, and the general welfare, and the efficient execution of the powers expressly conferred by the Constitution." The complainant could not claim he was being deprived of property if money orders and registered mail that should not have been deposited in the mail were not delivered to him. He pointed out there were two sections dealing with lotteries, one that imposed a fine on anyone depositing matter dealing with lotteries in the mail and another that was merely preventive—"to preserve the mail from misuse." The law and the actions of the postmaster general were declared legal.[33]

Dauphin brought suit in the United States Supreme Court and Postmaster General Key permitted the delivery of postal money orders pending the outcome of the case. Shortly after this Key resigned to become United States judge for the Eastern District of Tennessee. It was not until September, 1883, that the order against Dauphin was renewed by Postmaster General Gresham. Gresham was a lawyer and had been a federal district judge from 1869 until his appointment in April, 1883, as postmaster general after the death of Timothy O. Howe (1882–1883). Gresham, before issuing the order, had consulted Supreme Court Justice John Marshall Harlan, who had assured him there was sufficient warrant for the postmaster general to exclude letters of a lottery company from the mail. Gresham's instructions to the postmaster at New Orleans were to refuse to deliver mail either to the Louisiana Lottery Company or the First National Bank, its agent. Gresham's attempt to curb the activities of the Louisiana Lottery Company was blocked by Federal District Judge Billings at New Orleans; he declared that Gresham's order was of doubtful validity since it was based on Key's order, which had been revoked. Gresham was incensed at the idea of a court's "attempting to control the discretion of one of the departments of the executive branch." He immediately began to agitate for a broadening of the power of the postmaster general to deal with lotteries.[34]

The first decision of the United States Supreme Court concerning the nonmailable character of obscene matter was not made until 1890. The power of Congress to exclude such publications from the mail was never seriously challenged in that Court.[35] What constituted obscenity, however, was discussed in many lower courts. The first case to receive considerable publicity was *United States* v. *Bennett* (1878). Bennett, editor of the *Truth Seeker*, an agnostic publication, had been brought up on charges in 1877 for depositing in the mails two tracts, but there had been no indictments. He then sponsored a petition to Congress for the repeal of the Comstock law. The author of that law, Anthony Comstock, now a postal agent, was determined to prosecute Bennett for violation of the law of 1873. The opportunity came when Bennett distributed a pamphlet through the mails entitled *Cupid's Yokes: or the Binding Force of Conjugal Life*, written by Ezra Hervey Heywood.[36]

Heywood, a pamphleteer in Boston and organizer of the New England Free Love League, had been convicted in June, 1878, for sending obscene matter (*Cupid's Yokes*) through the mail and had been sentenced to two years at hard labor. He had been pardoned by President Hayes on the grounds that his health was being undermined by his imprisonment. The president, also, had not thought the law had been violated by Heywood, for although the pamphlet advocated "wrong ideas" of marriage it was not really "obscene, lascivious, lewd, or corrupting in the criminal sense." The president had been severely critized for his pardon of Heywood and was on the defensive about it.[37]

It was in answer to a letter sent by Comstock under the name of G. Brachett that Bennett had sent the copy of *Cupid's Yokes* through the mail. He was brought up on charges in March, 1879, in the federal district court in New York. The issue was whether or not the book was obscene because certain passages were obscene. The district attorney said the general character of the book was not in question but only certain portions of it. These portions he read to the jury. The jury was told to apply to these passages the test of obscenity, "whether the tendency of the matter is to deprave and corrupt the morals of those whose minds are open to such influences, and into whose hands a publication of this sort may fall." The judge told the jury that the act did not violate freedom of the press for it did not prevent publishing or dissemination of the book but merely prevented the use of the mails for the distribution of obscene matter. He added: "The necessity of such a statute is obvious to any person who has paid attention to the facts. If you think what the United States mails are, how they are protected by the law, where they go, the secrecy attending their operations, you will at once see, that, for the distribution of matter of any kind upon paper, there is no other engine of equal power. It is the machine best adapted to the dissemination of obscene literature." It made no difference that the pamphlet was sent in answer to a decoy letter, said the judge; the mailing was the important factor, not the motive in mailing it. Bennett was sentenced to thirteen months of hard labor. The decision was upheld by Judge Blatchford for the circuit court. He cited as precedent the British case *Regina* v. *Hicklin* (1868).[38]

The insertion in the postal law of 1876 of the word "writing" led to many and conflicting court decisions. At first, decisions of the lower courts held that "writing" did not include a communication between two persons. One man, arrested on complaint of Anthony Comstock, was charged with sending an obscene letter through the mails. United States Commissioner Allen of the Eastern District of New York in *United States* v. *Williams* (1880) defined obscene writing as "one offensive to decency, indelicate, impure, and an indecent one, as one unbecoming, immodest, unfit to be seen." He said there was no doubt that the letter in question was both obscene and indecent and the postmark on the envelope was proof it had been deposited in the mail. But he declared "writing" did not apply to private letters, as the act of 1876 was merely an amendment to the act of 1873 and therefore did not make nonmailable anything that had not been made so by the previous act. Congress had declared many times that its object was to refuse the facilities of the mails for the "distribution of matter deemed injurious to the public morals" which, therefore, would mean publications.[39]

Judge Deady, of the district court of Oregon, in *United States* v. *Loftis* (1882) agreed emphatically with Commissioner Allen that a sealed letter addressed to someone was not prohibited by the law regardless of how indecent and obscene it was. He said: "It never was the intention of the law to take cognizance of what passes between individuals in private communications under sanctity and security of a seal. . . . It could not well do so without establishing an espionage over private correspondence, which would never be thought of in a free country."[40]

In the federal circuit court in Illinois, in *United States* v. *Gay-*

*lord* (1883), however, Judge Drummond, with Justice Harlan concurring, held that "writing" did not mean a publication, for such had already been included in the listing of book, pamphlet, print; it therefore meant a letter. It did not make any difference whether or not it was sealed although, of course, postal authorities could not open a sealed letter. The justices declared Congress intended to "purge the mails" of obscene matter and it was immaterial whether it was inside an envelope or outside it.[41] Justice Drummond's interpretation was followed by others, including Judge Deady. The latter in *United States* v. *Morris* (1884) said he had changed his mind because he had heard that the word "writing" had been added by Congress "apparently because Judge Blatchford had held that, without it, a letter containing obscene matter was not included therein."[42]

The issue finally reached the Supreme Court in 1890. Leslie G. Chase had been found guilty in the Massachusetts district court of mailing an obscene letter so "grossly obscene" it was not even printed in the court record. The issue before the Court was whether or not the term "writing" included a letter. Justice Lamar, giving the opinion of the Court, in *United States* v. *Leslie G. Chase*, declared that the statute meant a published writing and not a private letter, that "writing" was listed in the same series with book, pamphlet, etc., and that the word "letter" was used further on in the law. Therefore, an obscene letter knowingly deposited in the mails and enclosed in an envelope on which was written nothing but the name and address of the person was not in the category of nonmailable.[43]

By the 1880s the postmaster general had been given tremendous power by Congress. He could give or withhold substantial subsidies in the form of second-class mailing privileges to newspapers and magazines. Such withholding might even bankrupt a publisher. He had the power not only to protect the mail from matter that might damage other mail or hurt a postal employee but also to shield citizens from matter that might impair their morals. He could prevent them from receiving through the mail obscene literature, contraceptive devices, lottery tickets, or information about them. He had been given the power to protect an individual's copyright and to prevent him from being robbed by fraudulent schemes that used the mails. His extensive powers had been upheld by the Supreme Court. In only one decision was there a minor setback, when the Supreme Court limited his dominion over communications between two individuals by means of letters.

There had been few protests against postal censorship by congressmen. In fact, many wished to extend the power of the federal government in many fields and one of the easiest methods, from a constitutional standpoint, was by means of the postal power.

# Buttressing the Postal Laws, 1888-1900

In almost every Congress during the last decade of the nineteenth century the question of extending the nonmailable categories was discussed. Congressmen, however, were reluctant to apply this weapon against a business unless it was very clear that that business was injurious to public morals.[1] Therefore the only laws that were passed were ones to strengthen the basic laws already on the statute books, those dealing with obscenity, lotteries, and fraud.

The postmasters general were zealous in enforcing the nonmailable statutes and met little rebuff from the courts. Although the courts during this period were protecting private property by a narrow interpretation of Congress's power to regulate interstate commerce, there was no hesitation about upholding Congress's power over the post office. At least a dozen cases concerning the nonmailable statutes were decided by the Supreme Court during the last decade of the nineteenth century, while only one such case had been decided by that Court before 1890. In no case was the plenary power of Congress over the Post Office denied and in only one decision was the ruling of the postmaster general reversed.

Because of conflicting interpretations of the laws dealing with obscenity, which enabled dealers in obscene matter to continue their activities, congressmen acted to close the loopholes in the law. An act of June 18, 1888, clarified the part of the law that pertained to what was written on the outside of an envelope. Changes were made in the law of 1876 as follows (indicated by italics): "And *all matter otherwise mailable by law* upon the envelope *or outside cover or wrapper* of which, or postal card, upon which indecent, lewd, lascivious, obscene, *libelous, scurrilous, or threatening* delineations, epithets, terms, or language, or *reflecting injuriously upon the character or conduct of another*, may be written or printed, are hereby declared to be non-mailable matter."[2]

The act had barely gone into effect when Senator Vest of Missouri introduced (July 10) a new bill, which was speedily passed by both houses and received the president's signature on September 26, 1888. It had been introduced at the request of the postmaster general to improve the law of June because some people, in order to injure the character of another, used transparent envelopes instead of writing on the outside. In large letters printed on the inside sheet was the following: "Collecting bad debt" and "If it is necessary to send another notice it will come in an envelope like this." Such a species of blackmail could be disastrous for a businessman. Also, since the law specified "written or printed," some used stylographic process to impress on the envelopes obscene epithets.[3]

The new act added the word "defamatory" to the list of epithets and then stated *"or calculated by the terms or manner or style of display* and obviously intended to reflect injuriously upon the character or conduct of another may be written or printed, or *otherwise impressed or apparent*, are hereby declared non-mailable matter." The act also provided that such matter "shall be withdrawn from the mails under such regulations as the Postmaster General shall prescribe." Senator Hawley of Connecticut had objected to this provision as giving too much power to local postmasters as he said some of them were not capable of judging what was libelous or indecent and therefore ought not to have the power to discard such material. Senator Vest said that the regulations of the postmaster general provided that the matter be sent to the

Post Office Department. This was a new power, included for the first time in an act dealing with nonmailable matter.[4]

Penalties for mailing such matter were also reduced from a maximum of ten to five years' imprisonment at hard labor and the minimum penalty was eliminated, as Senator Hoar of Massachusetts pointed out that sometimes the crimes might be committed by children or by feeble-minded persons. Those changes were vehemently opposed by the sponsor of the bill, who thought no penalty was too severe for dealers in obscenity. He said he had in his possession material with which a female academy had been deluged but which was too dirty to be read in the Senate. There is no worse crime than this, not even murder, he declared for, "It saps the very foundations of society. It poisons the minds of the young; it outrages the sensibilities of the old."[5]

The second section of the act inserted the word "letter," as the courts had disagreed on whether the word "writing" included private letters. The act of 1876 was amended to read: "Every obscene, lewd, or lascivious book, pamphlet, picture, paper, letter, writing . . . ." It also made information concerning contraceptives "whether sealed as first-class matter or not" nonmailable matter. To be sure that this provision would not be interpreted to give a postmaster the power to open letters, there was added at the end: "That nothing in this act shall authorize any person to open any letter or sealed matter of the first-class not addressed to himself."[6]

John Wanamaker, postmaster general, 1889–1893, former department store owner and elder in the Presbyterian church, brought to the Post Office business experience and a zeal for reform. He was determined to suppress the traffic in obscenity and lotteries. Under the act of September 26, 1888, he ordered Tolstoi's *Kreutzer Sonata* banned from the mails on grounds of indecency. The story was, however, appearing in some newspapers in installments, so Wanamaker wanted to exclude the newspapers also from the mail. Attorney General Miller, however, declared he did not think the order was sufficient to justify exclusion of all copies of the newspapers publishing installments of the book, as some installments might not be obscene.[7]

An officer of the department wrote that nearly every day orders were issued to throw out pictures and pamphlets considered obscene, that hundreds of indictments were obtained and many convictions secured. Ezra H. Heywood, who had been convicted of mailing obscene matter in 1876 but had been pardoned by President Hayes, was again convicted in 1890 and sentenced to two years of hard labor. Assistant Attorney General Tyner thought the laws in regard to obscenity not stringent enough and urged further legislation.[8] In response to this suggestion a Senate report stated that it was Congress and not the postmaster general that had the power to determine what was nonmailable and that it was questionable whether it should go further in delegating any general authority to postal authorities.[9]

The Supreme Court, in a series of decisions, upheld the Post Office Department in its efforts to enforce the postal laws declaring obscene matter nonmailable and making it a crime to deposit such matter in the mail. All of the cases were criminal cases and in most cases the accused was brought to trial by means of a decoy letter sent by a postal agent. The Court in *Grimm* v. *United States* (1894) authoritatively declared that the fact the letter had been sent in answer to a request by a government agent was not an excuse, as the purpose of the agent was not to induce the commission of a crime but to ascertain if the defendant was engaged in an unlawful business, which the agent suspected. In this case Grimm was accused not of sending through the mail obscene matter but sending information as to where obscene pictures might be obtained. Atterman Huntress (a fictitious name taken by Robert W. McAfee, a Post Office inspector) had written Grimm that he traveled a lot and was sure he could sell fancy photographs, which he had heard Grimm had. The latter had answered that he had some eight hundred lascivious pictures and they could be obtained for two dollars a dozen. Justice David J. Brewer ruled that the indictment of Grimm was correct, that he had been indicted not because he possessed obscene pictures but because he had mailed a letter giving information as to where they could be obtained. It was not necessary that the pictures be displayed.[10]

Four of the cases concerned the definition of obscenity. In one case (*Swearingen* v. *United States*, 1896) the Supreme Court reversed the decision of the lower court. Dan K. Swearingen had been convicted of depositing in the mails an issue of the *Burlington Courier* that contained an article calling a politician names, which the jury claimed were "obscene, lewd, and lascivious." Justice George Shiras said the lower court had erred in that the judge had declared the articles obscene and nonmailable and had left to the jury only the question of whether or not the papers had been deposited in the mails. He stated he did not think the articles obscene, that the words of the statute referred only to "sexual impurity." The language used in the article was coarse and vulgar and "plainly libelous" but not "obscene, lewd, or lascivious." He asserted, "As the statute is highly penal, it should not be held to embrace language unless it is fairly within its letter and spirit." Justices Harlan, Gray, Brown, and White dissented.[11] Attorney General Griggs, in light of this decision, suggested that Congress add the words "indecent, filthy, or vulgar" to the statute declaring nonmailable obscene matter,[12] but no new descriptive terms were added until 1909.

In the three other cases the postmaster general was upheld. In two of the cases the paper was sent in response to a decoy letter. Lew Rosen (*Rosen* v. *United States*, 1896) was sentenced to thirteen months of hard labor for mailing a paper, *Broadway*, which contained pictures of females partially covered with lamp black that was easily erasable by rubbing bread over it. He appealed on the basis that the indictment had not charged that he knew the content of the paper deposited in the mail was obscene. The court declared that since the paper bore his name he undoubtedly knew of the content. In this case the jury had been given the job of deciding if the paper was obscene and was told "the test of obscenity is whether the tendency is to deprave and corrupt the morals of those whose minds are open to such influence and into whose hands a publication of this sort may fall." Justice John Marshall Harlan declared that Congress's efforts to purge the mails of obscenity would be in vain if Rosen's views of what was obscene were accepted. He stated: "Everyone who uses the mails of the United States for carrying papers or publications must take notice of what, in this enlightened age, is meant by decency, puri-

77

ty, chastity in social life, and what must be deemed obscene, lewd, and lascivious." Justices White and Shiras dissented on the basis that the indictment had been incorrect.[13]

In another case (*Dunlop* v. *United States*, 1897) the Court declared that although the jury had been charged to consider obscene any matter that "tended to deprave the morals in any way whatever" it was obvious that the matter in the paper was in the direction of impure sexual relations. The paper contained advertisements by women soliciting visits by men to their rooms. The publisher of the paper claimed he seldom saw the advertisements, although he did not deny general knowledge of the contents of the paper. The Supreme Court affirmed the sentence of the lower court to two years of hard labor and a fine of $2,000.[14]

In the other obscenity case (*Price* v. *United States*, 1897) decided by the Court that year the publication was so offensive that it had not been set forth in the indictment. Justice Rufus Peckham declared there were degrees of obscenity, "but when a book is stated to be so obscene that it would be offensive if set forth in full in an indictment, such allegation imports a sufficient degree of obscenity to render the production nonmailable under the statute." In this case the publication had been sent to a government inspector, and again the Court declared that it was no defense that the publications had been sent to a postal agent who had written decoy letters asking for them.[15] In all the cases the Court gave a broad definition of obscenity if the material was connected with impure sexual relations.

The Court, in *Andrews* v. *United States* (1896), on the basis of the law of September 26, 1888, which had added "letter" to the list of obscene categories, declared obscene letters enclosed in a sealed envelope nonmailable. A Post Office inspector had seen an advertisement in the newspaper and had answered it under the name of Susan H. Budlong and in reply had received a very obscene letter. The inspector had used this expedient because of the provision in the law that only a person to whom a letter was addressed could open it. Again the Court declared it was "no defense to the crime of mailing obscene letters . . . that they were sent in answer to letters written under an assumed name by a government detective."[16]

So much of the obscene matter was sent first class in sealed envelopes and since the offender could not always be caught by means of a fictitious letter the postmaster general asked Congress to grant him authority to use the fraud order against those dealing in obscene matter. By use of the fraud order the department could return letters and money orders to the sender, marking the envelopes with the word "fraudulent," when it was convinced that firms were dealing in obscene matter. These fraud orders had been quite effective in dealing with lotteries and gift enterprises.[17] This power was not granted the postmaster general until the middle of the twentieth century.

Efforts to prevent the use of the mails for fraudulent schemes occupied the attention of the Post Office Department and Congress even more than the efforts to curb obscenity. The green goods swindle was the "most extensive one 'worked' through the medium of the mails," said one historian of the Post Office Department. He described how a large gang in New York City flooded the mails with circulars offering for sale counterfeit money "so perfect that it cannot be told from the genuine." The circulars, however, seldom used the terms "counterfeit bills" or "coins" but described their merchandise as "green goods," "green articles," "queer coins," "bills," "paper goods," or just "goods." The person who received the circular was cautioned not to write but to send a telegram and make an appointment for a conference. At the meeting the buyer would be shown a real bill, but if he bought some he would later discover that the package he had received contained loose papers or bricks. The postmaster general was powerless to deal with this racket and the laws providing for punishment of persons conducting fraudulent businesses were inadequate.[18] The selling of counterfeit money through the mail had been discussed in Congress when the revision of the postal laws was being debated in 1872, but it was not specifically mentioned in the provisions dealing with the use of the mails to defraud.

The question was brought up in the Fiftieth Congress. The well-known postal agent Anthony Comstock urged the passage of a very stringent bill. He said he had received 1,500 complaints of this kind of fraud during the preceding eighteen months. He pointed out that the success of the business depended on the use of the mails, that the businesses were "headed by some of the sharpest, shrewdest, and most unscrupulous tricksters." They used fictitious names and arranged to have their mail received at some saloon or public place, the proprietor of which, if approached, would deny knowing the person to whom the letters were addressed.[19]

Comstock criticized the bill that had been presented in the House of Representatives by Benjamin A. Enloe of Tennessee on January 10, 1888. A new bill prepared by the Post Office Department was substituted and passed with no real debate. The first bill dealing with this type of fraud became a law on March 2, 1889.[20] The first section of the act listed in detail the various schemes used to defraud by selling counterfeit money or government securities. It provided for punishment of anyone trying to use the Post Office for such a purpose ($500 and/or eighteen months' imprisonment for each offense). Section 2 prohibited the use of fictitious names for such schemes; section 3 stated that the postmaster general might direct that mail be withheld from those who used fictitious names, that the party claiming such mail would have to appear at the post office, be identified, and prove his claim to the letters. If he could not prove his claim the packages were to be sent to the dead letter office. Section 4 stated: "That all matter the deposit of which in the mails is by this act made punishable is hereby declared non-mailable; but nothing in this act shall be so construed as to authorize any person other than any employee of the dead-letter office, duly authorized thereto, to open any letter not addressed to himself."[21]

The issue of lotteries and proposals as to how their use of the mails could be prevented were brought before Congress in almost every report of the postmasters general during this period. Letters and circulars concerning lotteries had been declared nonmailable and persons mailing them were subject to a fine. Also when the postmaster general was convinced that a firm was engaged in a fraudulent lottery or scheme he could direct the local postmaster to refuse payment of money orders or to deliver registered letters to the firm. The law of 1876 had eliminated the word "illegal" in the section of the law dealing with the nonmailability of lottery circulars but had not done so in the case of the issuance of fraud orders. Postmaster General Gresham, thwarted by the court in his attempt to break the Louisiana State Lottery Company, had recommended strengthening the laws. He had suggested that the word "fraudulent" be eliminated in all sections of the postal codes that dealt with lotteries. He also urged that newspapers containing advertisements of lotteries be excluded from the mails.[22]

When bills to prohibit the mailing of newspapers containing advertisements of lotteries were introduced in both houses of Congress there was a great outcry. There were protests that this meant too much centralization and would also be a violation of freedom of the press. Congressional reports pointed out that the states could suppress lotteries, and all but three (Louisiana, Delaware, and Vermont) had done so. Congressmen opposed a federal law, fearing that the central government by use of the public welfare principle would gradually absorb all the functions of the states. Closing the mails to the distribution of lottery circulars was different from closing them to newspapers carrying lottery advertisements. The former dealt with that one topic, but to compel newspapers to exclude lottery advertisements would violate freedom of the press. The First Amendment would be a dead letter if Congress through its power over the Post Office could "exclude *both* from the *mails* and *post routes* newspapers that may be deemed objectionable because of the publications contained therein. The freedom of circulation by the ordinary channels of communication is the very essence of the press's freedom," congressmen declared.[23]

The argument that such a law would violate freedom of the press was answered by Senator James F. Wilson of Iowa. He pointed out that "nothing is allowed to enter the mail except in pursuance of law," that the Constitution did not "even by implication" say Congress had to provide for transportation of news-

papers through the mail. Congress could have limited postal facilities to sealed letters and no one would have raised the issue of
the free press. He reminded congressmen that the pamphlet had
been an important form for discussion at the time of the framing
of the Constitution and yet no one now expressed doubts as to
the right of Congress to exclude from the mail an obscene pamphlet. He defended the bill for it would "tend to protect the people
against the frauds now practiced on them through conscienceless
lottery schemes."[24]

All bills concerning lotteries in the Forty-eighth, Forty-ninth,
and Fiftieth Congresses were pigeonholed.[25] The Louisiana State
Lottery Company had a powerful lobby in Washington. One authority on the Post Office said that the company "jingled their
money bags in the very corridor of the Capitol." The company
was dependent on the Post Office; it sent out an average of 11,000
letters daily, received 5,800 letters, 2,800 registered letters, and
1,600 postal orders a day. Forty-five percent of the business of the
New Orleans post office was connected with the lottery.[26]

The new Republican administration brought pressure to bear
on Congress. President Harrison, in a special message to Congress, July 29, 1890, declared: "Severe and effective legislation
should be promptly enacted to enable the Post-Office Department
to purge the mails of all letters, newspapers, and circulars relating to this business."[27] He sent with his message a letter from
Postmaster General Wanamaker. The latter said it was humiliat-
ing to think that the whole postal system was the principal agent
of the Louisiana lottery. He pointed out that Congress had intended to prevent that but that the laws were inadequate. He enclosed a draft of a bill. The bill defined the offense for depositing
letters relating to lotteries in the mail and provided for the prosecution in any district court into which the letter might pass, thus
removing the trial from local influence. It also authorized withholding of registered letters and payment of money orders to
agents of lottery companies and also prohibited the use of the
mails to newspapers containing lottery advertisements.[28]

In this Congress (Fifty-first) a great number of memorials and
petitions against lotteries were presented and several bills were

introduced in each house.[29] On July 28, 1890, the House Committee on the Post-Office and Post-Roads reported out its own bill (H.R. 11569) with a strong report in favor of its passage. The majority report explained that the bill was necessary for several reasons: first, that the former laws had been declared penal statutes, enforceable by the courts only, and that the postmaster general had no power to detain any letter or packet not *known* by him to relate to lotteries; he could seize only unsealed circulars. Second, this law made the mailing of lottery letters a continuous offense, triable in any court through which the circulars might pass. It had been almost impossible to obtain convictions in the state of Louisiana because of the power of the Louisiana State Lottery Company. Third, of great benefit would be the closing of the mails to advertisements giving lists of prizes, thus partially cutting off communication between the lottery and its customers. Also, the bill gave the postmaster general power to cut off delivery of registered letters from agents of lottery companies. The report ended with a statement that it was no longer necessary to discuss the immorality of lotteries for the day had passed for that type of discussion and Congress was willing "to provide any correction of these evils, within the letter and spirit of the Constitution." There was considerable debate in the House; Walter I. Hayes of Iowa presented a minority report that made the usual objections that the bill was unconstitutional, that it was unnecessary as there were enough laws, that it was dangerous in its tendency toward centralization, that it abridged freedom of the press and gave power of espionage to public officials. The bill, however, passed with only minor amendments on August 16, 1890. In the Senate the House bill was reported out by Senator Philetus Sawyer of Wisconsin and was passed with no debate on September 16.[30]

The act of September 19, 1890, represented Congress's attempt to block up all loopholes. The first section declared nonmailable letters, postal cards, circulars, list of drawings, lottery tickets, drafts, money orders, and newspapers or publications carrying advertisements of lotteries, gift concerns, or similar enterprises offering prizes dependent on chance. None of these things should be carried in the mail or be delivered by a carrier. It further stated that anyone who knowingly deposited or sent or caused to be delivered by mail anything forbidden would be guilty of a misdemeanor and punishable by fine of not more than $500 and/or one year imprisonment for each offense. Trial could be in the district where unlawful publication was mailed or where it was delivered. Sections 2 and 3 eliminated the word "fraudulent" from before "lottery" and also provided that registered letters and money orders could be withheld from an agent of a lottery company. The advertisement by a company that remittances could be sent to a certain firm or bank would be *prima facie* evidence that the bank was the agent, "but the Postmaster-General shall not be precluded from ascertaining the existence of such agency in any other legal way satisfactory to himself."[31]

One student of the American Constitution declared: "Never until the passage of the act known as the anti-lottery law, approved Sept. 19, 1890, did Congress ever venture to assert that it possessed the power to exclude newspapers and other publications from the mail by reason of their contents. That act, although designed to destroy the Louisiana State Lottery Company, operates directly upon the publishers of all American newspapers who claim the right to print what they please, subject to the limitations which the First Amendment embodies."[32]

Postmaster General Wanamaker in his annual report for that year hailed the passage of the act. The day after the president signed it the department officially notified the 62,401 postmasters and sent out regulations as to the procedures to enforce the act. Wanamaker said the department would not apply the law harshly to local schemes, especially those connected with charitable and religious organizations. He had asked the opinion of Attorney General Miller about a guessing contest sponsored by the *Cincinnati Enquirer*. The paper offered to give a prize to the first person to submit by mail the correct guess as to the number of votes the Republican and Democratic candidates for secretary of state in Ohio would receive in the next election. The guesses had to be sent in on blanks clipped from the newspaper. The attorney general replied that since the statute was penal in character it should be strictly construed. He stated that this contest was not a lottery

84

because it was not dependent entirely on lot; a person could win by making a reasonable estimate.[33]

The target of the law was, of course, the Louisiana lottery. Chief Inspector Rathbone was put in charge of operations and he sent the inspector from the St. Louis division to New Orleans to help the local postmaster, a newly appointed antilottery Republican. The business of the New Orleans post office fell off by one-third in the two months after the passage of the act. The first arrest took place on November 5, 1890, that of J. Pinckney Smith, business manager of the *Daily States*; he was accused of mailing an edition of the paper carrying advertisements of the lottery. It was discovered that Smith had been out of town at the time of the mailing so the case was dropped. During the first year that the act was in effect there were 202 arrests, 653 indictments, and 59 convictions.[34]

The first decision concerning the constitutionality of the act handed down by the Supreme Court (*Ex parte John L. Rapier*) was in February, 1892. It involved George W. Dupre, one of the editors of *Daily States*, and John L. Rapier, publisher of *Mobile Daily and Weekly Register*. The former mailed to the latter a letter containing a lottery ticket and a newspaper containing lottery advertisements. Lawyers for both Dupre and Rapier claimed that the powers of Congress were limited to those specified in the Constitution and that all other powers had been reserved to the states by the Tenth Amendment. Lotteries, they declared, were neither *mala prohibita* or *mala in se*. They also claimed that the law was a violation of freedom of the press. Attorney General Miller replied: "They totally ignore the fact that the sole effect of the Act of Congress is that the General Government, its officers, employes, and agencies shall in no way aid or abet this business; that its mail-bags and the hands of its servants shall not be used in spreading and manipulating snares for its unwary victims; that it simply says to federal officials hands off."

Chief Justice Melville E. Fuller, in a brief opinion, merely analyzed the power of Congress over the establishment of the postal service, pointing out that it was a complete power. He also denied the act abridged freedom of the press, saying that neither the circulation nor the publication of newspapers was forbidden but that governmental agencies should not assist in the dissemination of matter Congress considered injurious to the people.[35] It was this decision that led Hannis Taylor to write the article, "A Blow at the Freedom of the Press." He stated that this was the first case in which the "rights of the press under the federal constitution were ever presented for adjudication." He criticized not only the decision but also the brevity of the opinion, for the Court had made merely a brief statement declaring that the power of Congress over the Post Office had been settled in *ex parte Jackson*. Taylor pointed out that the first case concerned the deposit of a circular letter by a person but this dealt with newspapers, not in the law at the time of the Jackson decision. He reviewed the issue of freedom of the press in modern times and discussed at length the debate in Congress in 1836. He stated that this decision "held that Congress possesses the power to establish and maintain, as to the contents of the mails, an *Index Expurgatorius*, once vested in the Star Chamber."[36]

Postmaster General Wanamaker took credit for destroying the Louisiana State Lottery Company. He pointed out in 1892 that lottery companies had practically ceased using the mails for distribution of tickets or for advertising. As evidence he cited notices sent to the employees of both the Louisiana State Lottery Company and the Gran Loteria Juarez of Mexico directing them not to mail letters that had anything to do with the lottery business.[37] Because of the stringent lottery law in Louisiana (January 1, 1894) the Louisiana State Lottery Company set up as a Florida institution and went out to sea or to Cuba or to a West Indian island to have their drawings. The Court, however, declared that circulars containing lists of prizes at a drawing in a foreign country was as much a violation of the law as if it had taken place in the United States. The Court also declared that an offender could be tried in the district where the circular was delivered.[38]

Lottery operators turned to the use of express companies for transportation of lottery tickets. They also used the regular first-class mail rather than registered letters because the postmaster general's power to return letters marked "fraudulent" applied only to registered letters. Senator Hoar of Massachusetts took the lead in pushing through a bill to suppress the lottery traffic through interstate commerce and the postal system. In defense of the bill reported out (April 17, 1894) from the Judiciary Committee, of which he was chairman, he stated he could see no reason why the postmaster general's power should be confined to registered letters. Every day Hoar presented petitions from various groups, churches, colleges, and business firms to keep the topic alive. The bill with a few minor amendments became law on March 2, 1895.[39]

Section 1 of the act provided for punishment for anyone bringing tickets from abroad to be deposited in the mails to be transported from one state to another. Section 4 made applicable to all letters and matter sent by mail the powers of the postmaster general that he had received under the act of 1890.[40] This act of 1895 gave the postmaster general power to issue a fraud order when he had reason to think a firm was running a lottery or trying to obtain money by fraud. Thereafter all mail directed to the person or firm would be returned to the sender with the word "fraudulent" stamped on the envelope. The fraudulent promoter, therefore, would be unable to receive any mail. Often a firm had a legitimate business as well as the illegal one. The department therefore tried to have a *prima facie* case before the accused was summoned to appear at the office to answer why such an order should not be issued against him. Most of them appeared and the hearing sometimes lasted as long as two weeks.[41]

The courts sustained the department in almost every case of the issuance of fraud orders. Three cases came up before the Supreme Court under the act of 1872 (sections 300–301) as amended March 2, 1889. Jay T. Stokes and eight others were convicted for conspiracy of using the mail for fraudulent purposes. Stokes and the others had represented themselves as dealers in various kinds of merchandise and each had certified the others as being financially responsible. Stokes had ordered shoes from several parties and enclosed in his letters checks in payment, but there was no money on deposit in the bank on which the checks were drawn. Justice Henry B. Brown agreed that the persons charged had devised a scheme to defraud and that they had intended to carry out this scheme by means of the postal system.[42] In the second case (*Streep* v. *United States*, 1895) the Court declared proof of intent to defraud unnecessary in this instance, for it was a scheme to sell counterfeit securities of the United States government by means of circulars sent through the mail.[43] The third case was that of *John H. Durland* v. *United States* (1896). The Provident Bond and Investment Company had sent out circulars stating that upon payment of a certain amount per month the investor would receive a bond. On the face of it the proposition seemed to be all right, but there was sufficient evidence to show that the sponsor of the scheme had no intention of permitting the bonds to mature and he had merely expropriated the money for his own use. Justice David Brewer stated: "Some schemes may be promoted through mere representations and promises as to the future may constitute a scheme or artifice to defraud" and an unlawful use of the mails.[44]

In the first test case (*American School of Magnetic Healing* v. *McAnnulty*, 1902) of the act of March 2, 1895, the Court upheld the authority of the postmaster general to deny postal privileges in a case of fraud as Congress had given him that power and Congress had "full and absolute jurisdiction over the mails." The justices, however, did not agree with the postmaster general that the American School of Magnetic Healing was necessarily carrying on a fraud. The school, incorporated under the laws of Missouri, claimed it could heal diseases through the influence of the mind. Much of its business was done through the mails; the school received on the average $1,000 to $1,600 in checks a day. The Post Office Department claimed the school was not engaged in a legitimate business but in a scheme to obtain money by false and fraudulent pretense. Postmaster General Smith (1898–1901) had on May 15, 1900, ordered the postmaster at Nevada, Missouri, to pay no more money orders and to return to the senders all letters addressed to the school. Money orders amounting to $10,000 and 25,000 letters had accumulated in the post office. Kelly, head of the school, complained that his business was being wrecked and that the order violated the Fourth, Fifth, and Four-teenth Amendments. He claimed the fraud order statutes were void as there was no provision for a court or tribunal to hear violations of the statute, that it vested absolute authority in the postmaster general. The latter, he said, had the power "to interdict and absolutely prohibit the carrying on of all commercial and business transactions of the country done through the mailing system, if they see fit to do so, and make the postmasters and Post Office Department the sole judges in their own cases."

Justice Rufus Peckham, delivering the majority decision, November 17, 1902, conceded that the postmaster general had the authority to determine the relevant questions of fact arising in the administration of the statutes but also the courts had the power to grant relief when the postmaster general has exercised jurisdiction in a case not covered by the statutes. In this case he thought the postmaster general had gone too far, that the efficacy of healing by mind was not a matter for his decision. "Unless the question may be reduced to one of fact, as distinguished from mere opinion," he said, "we think these statutes cannot be invoked for the purpose of stopping the delivery of mail matter."[45]

Two years later the postmaster general was completely upheld in his order denying the use of the mails to a firm which called itself the Public Clearing House (*Public Clearing House* v. *Coyne*). It was an organization acting as fiscal agent for the League of Equity, which was a voluntary association of unmarried people. Each person paid three dollars as an enrollment fee and one dollar per month for sixty months. If the person had not become married within a year he or she received a certificate with a full realization value of $500. There was, however, no reserve fund and no investment of money. The department became convinced this was a lottery and as such not entitled to the use of the mails. In accordance with the act of 1895 the department issued an order that no letters were to be delivered to the Public Clearing House. The company asked for an injunction against the local postmaster to prevent him from enforcing the order denying it the right to receive any mail. This was denied and the decision was affirmed by the Circuit Court for the Northern District of

Illinois. Public Clearing House appealed to the Supreme Court.

The appellant challenged first the constitutionality of the statutes authorizing the postmaster general to deny the use of the mails to a firm without a hearing or trial. He then declared the postmaster general had acted beyond his authority as this was not a lottery. Justice Henry Brown handed down the decision in which Justices Brewer, White, and Holmes concurred. He said:

We find no difficulty in sustaining the constitutionality of these sections. The postal service is by no means an indispensable adjunct to a civil government, and for hundreds, if not for thousands, of years the transmission of private letters was either entrusted to the hands of friends or to private enterprises. Indeed, it is only within the last three hundred years that governments have undertaken the work of transmitting intelligence as a branch of their general administration.

Justice Brown went on to say that Congress established the postal system and could annex to it such conditions as it pleased and it had set up a long list of nonmailable categories. This in no way denied citizens of any rights. Of course the party who thought he was injured could appeal to the courts, but the Executive branch of government would be paralyzed if before taking action the administrative officers had to obtain the sanction of the court. He concluded: "Every executive department has certain public functions and duties, the performance of which is absolutely necessary to the existence of the government, but it may temporarily, at least, operate with seeming harshness upon individuals. But it is wisely indicated that the rights of the public must, in these particulars, override the rights of individuals, provided there be reserved to them an ultimate recourse to the judiciary."[46]

By 1900 the Post Office Department had received almost plenary power for dealing with attempts to use the mails to defraud. Administratively the department could refuse to deliver to a firm all letters and refuse to cash money orders drawn on their behalf. The laws against lotteries had been so effective that by the end of the century there were no organized lotteries doing business through the mails. There had sprung up hundreds of so-called bond investment companies. An assistant attorney general for the department expressed his amazement at the gullibility of some people. "It is a strange freak of human nature that makes people believe that *strangers* are going to *give* them something," he wrote. The department, therefore, watched such companies constantly. The postmaster general reported that frauds of serious kinds were still being carried on through the mails, but as soon as the concerns came to the attention of a postal agent they were promptly suppressed. The chief impediment in enforcing the laws was the lack of a large enough force of inspectors; there were at that time only two hundred. The postmaster general suggested that Congress authorize the inspectors to take out search warrants whenever necessary for carrying out their duties.[47]

One reform that had helped the Post Office Department in its enforcement of the laws against lotteries was that the cases could be tried in the districts where the letters were received as well as where they were deposited. Postmasters general urged that this be permitted in cases involving dealers in "green goods" and those selling obscene matter. These dealers were centered in New York City and there the courts were crowded with cases and the climate of opinion was less unfriendly to the dealers. They also wanted the power to use fraud orders against sellers of obscene matter.[48] Those powers were granted to the Post Office Department in the twentieth century.

# A New Postal Code

The beginning of the new century was marked by an effort to revise and codify the laws relating to the Post Office Department. Thirty years had elapsed since the last codification in 1872. The attorney general of the Post Office Department, with a commission assisting him, had prepared a summary of all laws passed since then; he expressed the hope that Congress would whip them into shape. Two different bills were introduced on January 20, 1900, in each house; ones dealing with the categories of nonmailable matter were referred to the committees on the Post-Office and Post-Roads and the others, providing criminal penalties for misuse of the mail, were referred to the judiciary committees. This indicates the twofold character of most of the nonmailable statutes. A bill to recodify the postal laws passed the House on January 28, 1901, but was blocked in the Senate.[1]

On April 1, 1902, the Post Office Department, however, codified the postal laws and regulations that were in effect. The new code described the machinery of the department. The officer in charge of enforcing the nonmailable statutes was the chief inspector under the fourth assistant postmaster general. There were fifteen inspectors in charge of geographical districts. Responsible directly to the postmaster general was the superintendent of the dead letter office. Third- and fourth-class mail which was nonmailable was sent here and was destroyed if the person who deposited it in the mail could not be determined or unless the postmaster general directed it be retained.[2]

Ten classes of nonmailable matter were listed and their disposal described; four of these were merely routine: matter having insufficient postage, misdirected, of excess weight, or mutilated. The other classes were more specifically described and what was to be done with them was explained. Category three, entitled "destructive," matter liable to damage the mail or injure the person handling it, was subject to regulations of the general superintendent of Railway Mail Service. Under no circumstances were the following to be admitted into the mail: "Intoxicating liquor (ardent, vinous, spiritous or malt), poisons, explosive or inflammable articles, live or dead (and not stuffed) animals, insects and reptiles (. . .), guano, or any article exhaling a bad odor."[3] Other matter to be withdrawn from the mail included lottery and fraudulent matter, "green goods," and matter addressed to fictitious persons; these were to be sent to the dead letter office. Scurrilous and obscene matter was to be sent to the first assistant postmaster general. If matter was known to be nonmailable it was to be refused; postmasters were held responsible for failure to exclude such matter from the mails.[4] Postmasters were alerted to watch especially for obscene matter from foreign countries; if sealed letters or packages were suspected to contain any matter of that type it was to be so indicated on the outside and the package was to be sent to its destination. There the postmaster was to notify the addressee and he was to open it in the presence of a customs officer. Postmasters were cautioned that under no circumstances were they to "break or permit to be broken the seal of any letter or any other matter." Only officers of the dead letter office could do so.[5]

There seemed to be developing some consciousness that the powers granted by Congress to the postmaster general might be too extensive, that the rights of the individual were not being fully protected, and that the traditional safeguards of judicial procedure were not being observed. At the suggestion of Assistant Attorney General Tyner, Postmaster General Payne (1901–1904) urged that reform be made in the procedure for dealing with mail frauds. He pointed out that the authority given to the postmaster general to issue fraud orders, which meant that a firm against whom such an order had been issued would receive no mail nor payment on money orders, was very broad and discretionary. He suggested, therefore, that provision be made for a summary appeal to the courts from the action of the postmaster general and that provision be made for a speedy hearing. Tyner said he thought such a law would fully "safeguard the privilege of the citizen to use the mails in a proper and legitimate way, while continuing in the Postmaster General the authority to exclude from the mails fraudulent matter and matter relating to lottery enterprises."[6]

Payne's successor, George B. Cortelyou (1904–1907), however, was vehemently opposed to any legislation that would delay operation of fraud orders. Representative Edgar Crumpacker of Indiana had introduced a bill (March 12, 1906) that would require the postmaster general, when he was convinced a person was using the mails to defraud, to give him notice citing the charges against him; this was to be done by the marshal of the district. Fifteen days were to elapse before a fraud order was to be issued in order to give the accused a chance to object. To curb fly-by-night firms, provision was made for the postmaster general to order mail impounded pending the investigation, although the individual could commence legal proceedings and have a summary investigation by the court both of facts and law. Crumpacker, in support of his bill, said the practice of fraud orders had been introduced because of "the peculiar adaptability of the mails to the purposes of the criminal and the perpetrator of frauds." If its use had been confined to "green goods" concerns and get-rich-quick establishments, as originally contemplated by Congress, there would be little objection, he said, but this vast power of the postmaster general had grown until it reached almost every class of business. He reported that the number of fraud orders issued in the preceding two years were 630, 71 more than during any other four years. During the preceding year every application to courts to enjoin the enforcement of the orders had been denied, he stated.[7]

The bill received the unanimous support of the Judiciary Committee; Henry D. Clayton of Alabama, in reporting out the bill, criticized the procedure used by the Post Office Department in issuing fraud orders. The authority conferred on the postmaster general was only incidental to postal matters and properly belonged to the judicial rather than the administrative branch. He pointed out that investigations by the inspectors were secret, that usually there was a hearing but it was held in Washington. Also, the person accused was often at a loss as to how to reply since he had not been informed of the evidence against him. Although there was provision for judicial review the court had held that questions of fact were not reviewable. The bill passed the House in January, 1907.[8]

Postmaster General Cortelyou opposed the bill. In a long article in the *North American Review*, April, 1907, he defended fraud orders. He said: "Few governmental functions exercised by the great Executive Departments at Washington operate so widely or generally to conserve the interests of all classes of citizens, or so directly and effectively to discourage dishonest practices." He admitted that sometimes legitimate business enterprises were caught in misleading advertisements, but if they were not intentionally trying to defraud they were allowed to continue their business. He pointed out that the value of the fraud orders was that they could stop the scheme to defraud immediately. For that reason he opposed legislation pending in Congress that could delay putting into effect the order. He claimed that this proposed legislation was due to the agitation by those who had been hampered in their "nefarious undertakings through the issuance of fraud orders." He went on: "It is not the law, but the law's delay, which the operators of fraudulent methods would be glad to obtain. For it must be borne in mind that many, if not most, of the schemes to defraud are of the fly-by-night order." He pointed out that many firms used a dozen or so different names and changed from one to another when they came to the attention of the Post Office Department.

He also said the activities of the department would be greatly hampered if it were necessary before a fraud order could be issued to have evidence acceptable in a court of law in a criminal procedure. He was successful in getting the bill buried in the Senate committee.[9]

Congress also inquired into the power of the postmaster general to deny or grant second-class mailing privileges. The authority of the postmaster general under the law of 1879 to refuse admission to the mails under those rates had been upheld by the Supreme Court in *Bates and Guild Co.* v. *Payne* (1904). In that case the postmaster general had denied second-class mailing privileges to the publication *Masters of Music* because each issue was complete in itself, treating the works of a single master musician. It was not, therefore, in the view of Postmaster General Payne, a periodical. Justice Henry Brown upheld the discretionary power of the postmaster general and stated that "where the decision of questions of fact is committed by Congress to the judgment and discretion of the head of a department, his decision thereon is conclusive" and that even upon questions of law or mixed questions the courts would not ordinarily review the decision although they had the power to do so.[10]

Earlier that year Senator Boies Penrose of Pennsylvania had introduced a bill that would cause a magazine to lose its second-class mailing privileges if one issue of the paper had been declared nonmailable. Postmaster General Payne had opposed the bill, as he said it would work hardship on publishers and cause unnecessary expense for the department. He related a recent case when an issue of the *Ladies Home Journal* contained an advertisement in violation of the lottery law. Ordinarily the whole issue would have been withdrawn but the publisher had been able to enclose a supplement withdrawing the offer made in the advertisements. If that arrangement had not been worked out and if the proposed law had been in force the publisher then would have forfeited his second-class maling privileges, which would have been very unfair, Payne said. The bill received an adverse report from the Senate Committee on Post-Offices and Post-Roads.[11]

In the Fifty-ninth Congress Representative Charles Bartlett of

# A New Postal Code

Georgia introduced a resolution asking why a certain paper, the *Union News*, had been denied second-class mailing privileges. He said it was published by the Farmers' Union of the State of Georgia and was the official organ of 40,000 farmers. It had been a semiweekly with second-class mailing privileges; it proposed to become a weekly and when it applied for the reduced rates it was denied. The Post Office Department declared the paper was largely devoted to advertising and dealt only with business relations of members of the Farmers' Union. Bartlett made a very partisan speech that was interrupted repeatedly by enthusiastic applause. He said it was time "that the United States Congress should wake up to the proposition and realize that we are being ruled not by ourselves as much as by the bureaus in the various Departments of this Government." He introduced a bill to provide for mandamus proceedings against the postmaster general if he denied an application for second-class mailing privileges, but it was tabled.[12] Bills to prevent exclusion of newspapers from the mails without due process of law were also pigeonholed.[13]

President Theodore Roosevelt, on the other hand, would have liked to have excluded from the mail papers advocating anarchy and those that published sensational news items. In 1906, incensed by an article of the Socialist leader Eugene V. Debs, which had appeared in *Appeal to Reason*, a syndicalist weekly published by J. S. Wayland at Girard, Kansas, Roosevelt wrote Attorney General Moody to notify the Post Office Department to bar the paper from the mails, if that could legally be done. He also asked if it were possible to institute criminal proceedings against Debs and the proprietor of the magazine. No action was taken.[14]

Two years later the president wrote Attorney General Bonaparte about *La Questione Sociale* of Paterson, New Jersey. He said articles in that paper recommended the use of dynamite and advocated the murder of enlisted men in the United States army and officers of the police force. The postmaster general had been directed to exclude the paper from the mails under the law declaring obscene matter nonmailable. Roosevelt stated he thought the preaching of murder and arson as done in this paper was certainly as immoral as the circulation of obscene and lascivious litera-

97

ture and was on a level with the use of the mails for the distribution of poison. He declared: "No law should require the Postmaster General to become an accessory to murder by circulating literature of this kind."[15]

The president asked the attorney general to find a law under
which those "enemies of mankind" could be prosecuted. Charles
J. Bonaparte replied that the articles might constitute an offense
against common law but they did not constitute a federal offense
since there was no statute making it so. The attorney general
stated, however, that the Post Office Department had authority to
exclude the paper from the mail and had already done so, since it
did not come within the class as mailable matter under second-
class mailing privileges. However, there was no statute making
mailing of such articles a criminal offense. Bonaparte cited the
law of 1876 which made it a criminal offense to mail matter considered indecent, but *La Questione Sociale* was not indecent in the
sense in which the word was used in the law. Congress had the
authority to declare such matter nonmailable and to make it a
criminal offense to deposit it in the mails, and the attorney general thought Congress would probably be willing to pass such a
law since it had passed a law excluding persons who opposed organized government from entering the United States.[16]

On April 9, 1908, President Roosevelt sent a special message to
Congress enclosing the opinion of the attorney general. He explained that the president had the power to prevent the "use of
the mails for the advocacy of murder, arson, and treason" and
that he had acted on that premise. He described the anarchist as
"the enemy of humanity, the enemy of all mankind" who was not
allowed to enter this country as an immigrant. He recommended
legislation that would prevent the circulation of a paper that
"propagates anarchistic opinions." In response to this message the
Senate Committee on Post-Offices and Post-Roads added to the
Post Office appropriation bill, which had just passed the House,
an amendment that would authorize the postmaster general to
exclude from second-class mailing privileges anarchistic publications. The only protest to this amendment was made by Senator
Eugene Hale of Maine, and he merely cautioned that the effect of

this would amount "to a practical censorship of the press by the Post-Office Department." This amendment was changed by the conferees and their report was accepted without debate. The obscenity statute was changed to read, "the term 'indecent' within the intendment of this section shall include matter of a character tending to incite arson, murder, or assassination."[17] Although the Post Office Department now had authority to bar Debs's paper from the mails it did not do so. Roosevelt said that although the paper really ought to be kept out of the mails as it was "an appeal, not to reason but to hatred and malice" and contained "open incitement to murder," the banning would "work more mischief than the paper itself does."[18]

President Roosevelt also favored excluding from the mails papers that printed disgusting details of murder trials, divorce suits, and the like. The cause for this recommendation was the trial of Harry K. Thaw. The latter, on the night of June 25, 1906, had shot and killed the well-known architect Stanford White during the opening performance of *Mamzelle Champagne* on the Roof Garden of the old Madison Square Garden, designed by White. Thaw's wife, a former Charles Dana Gibson model and Floradora showgirl, had been a "friend" of White's and had continued to see him after her marriage. Thaw was said to have shouted as he fired three bullets into White: "I did it because he ruined my wife."[19]

The trial opened at the end of January, 1907, and continued to occupy the front pages of the papers throughout February. When the examination of witnesses began February 6, the judge warned women spectators that "some of the evidence might be highly colored"; a few left the courtroom but most remained and, according to one reporter, "risked embarrassment to satisfy their curiosity." Mrs. Thaw took the stand and related how White, when she was a sixteen-year-old chorus girl, had lured her to his private studio on West 24th Street and had plied her with champagne and had seduced her. She said she had told the story to Thaw when he first proposed to her and at which time she refused him. Finally she gave in to Thaw's pleading and they were married, but White continued to "pursue" her.[20]

The public was incensed at the explicit details published in the papers. Mass meetings were held in various cities to protest the publication of the testimony in the papers. The postmaster general in Canada said, "Any newspaper publishing offensive evidence of a trial in court . . . would be guilty of a misdemeanor under the Canadian law." United States District Attorney Stimson in New York sent a letter (February 11) to newspaper publishers in the city warning them that "portions of the testimony of Evelyn Nesbit Thaw had violated the postal regulations." He threatened criminal prosecution. President Roosevelt, after having read an unexpurgated edition of a newspaper that had printed in full a stenographic report of the testimony of Mrs. Thaw, and in response to letters and telegrams from all over the country, asked Postmaster General Cortelyou if he had the power to bar from the mails the newspapers that published the disgusting details of the trial. His proposal was discussed in cabinet meeting (February 13) and the papers were turned over to the attorney general to see what action could be taken. The officials of the Post Office Department thought it was too late to take any action that would affect the Thaw trial, as it was nearing an end. They also thought it difficult to make "any fixed regulation on the subject for future application."[21]

Congressmen, under pressure from constituents, introduced many resolutions and bills. The *New York Times* called the bills "Silly Cries for a Censorship," introduced by legislators trying for "an extremely cheap reputation for virtue." The editor claimed the paper was performing a public service by publishing the full account of the judicial proceedings because it was the first time a man had been indicted for murder in the first degree who had millions of dollars available for defense. It was so often charged that rich criminals escaped punishment that the public had the right "to know whether the proceedings tend to support or to demolish an accusation so injurious to the reputation of the courts." He went on to say that the public also should be informed on how much a part the "unwritten law" plays in criminal jurisprudence so they can decide whether or not it ought to be incorporated into statutory law. The papers themselves should decide where the line of good taste should be drawn; of course papers would differ on where that line would be drawn, but citizens could select the paper of their choice. The editor cynically concluded by speculating whether the ones raising the greatest outcry against the printing of details did not try to find out which paper was most reckless in their treatment, "not to avoid, but to buy and read it."[22]

The codification of the postal laws was finally taken up seriously in January, 1908, when a Joint Committee on Revision and Codification of Laws made a report simultaneously in both houses. Not many changes in the postal code were proposed; most of them dealt with grammar and with a reorganization of sections. Senator Heyburn of Idaho, in presenting the section dealing with obscene matter, said that he was sure no senator would object to its "being made as broad as language could make it."[23] Congressmen favored increasing the descriptive terms in that section because of the narrow definitions of obscenity given by some district and circuit judges (there were no Supreme Court decisions on this issue during the first decade of the twentieth century). A district judge had reluctantly declared that a pamphlet, which in coarse and vulgar language ridiculed the concept of the Virgin birth, was not lewd or lascivious and therefore entitled to circulate in the mails.[24] Publications describing cures for sexual debility and syphilis were declared by another court to be repulsive reading, but since they did not "pander to lascivious curiosity" they could not be banned from the mails.[25]

The debate in Congress centered on adding the words "vile, filthy, and indecent." One senator suggested including the word "disgusting" and said it was needed, as the Post Office Department had captured several tons of postal cards in Chicago that could not be called lascivious or vile but were not the thing that should go through the mails. The Senate finally compromised on the phrase "and every filthy" and stated that "filthy" was synonymous with nasty, dirty, polluted, foul, impure, and obscene.[26] Section 211 then read: "Every obscene, lewd, or lascivious, and every filthy, book, pamphlet, picture, paper, letter, writing, print, or other publication of an indecent character . . . is hereby declared to be nonmailable matter."[27]

This section also spelled out in great detail contraceptive devices, such as any instrument, substance, drug, and medicine, and used the words "advertised or described in a manner calculated to lead another to use or apply it for preventing conception or producing abortion, or for any indecent or immoral purpose" instead of just the words "thing designed or intended for the prevention of conception or procuring of abortion."[28] No changes were made in the section dealing with libelous and indecent matter on wrappers or envelopes.[29]

In the House of Representatives a small group attempted to broaden the section concerning lotteries to have circulars relating to bucket shop gambling and futures dealing declared nonmailable. They wanted any notice or record of a contract providing for future delivery of any commodities or stocks to be declared nonmailable and punishment provided for mailing such matter. The author of the amendment explained that lotteries had practically disappeared because they had been denied the use of the mails and the same thing could be done to any illegitimate gambling transaction. This amendment was an excuse for an intemperate attack on Wall Street and its brokers and bankers by representatives from Tennessee, Kansas, Texas, and Mississippi. Walter Humphreys from Mississippi said that speculation in futures had the same appeal to many as lotteries had had, but that buying lottery tickets meant only a financial loss for the individual but "in stock gambling the rights and interests of the great toiling masses are involved and hazarded without their volition and positively against their consent." The amendment, however, was rejected by a vote of 89 to 103.[30]

There were few changes made in section 213 dealing with lotteries. This section had been interpreted by the attorney general and the Post Office Department, following decisions in state courts, to include guessing contests and horse-racing pools.[31] The maximum punishment for knowingly mailing circulars concerning a lottery was increased from a fine of $500 and/or one year's imprisonment to a fine of $1,000 and/or imprisonment of two years for the first offense, and for any subsequent offense, imprisonment of not more than five years. Also the phrase "concerning schemes devised for the purpose of obtaining money or property under false pretenses" was omitted, as these schemes could come under the fraud section.[32] Section 214 provided for punishment of no more than $100 fine (previously $50) and/or one year's imprisonment for an employee of the postal system (not just postmasters, as before) who acted as agent or vendor for a lottery company or who knowingly delivered lottery circulars. The statute of 1889, dealing with counterfeit coins, paper money, and government obligations, was incorporated into section 215, but the section was changed to read (new part in italics): "*Whoever*, having devised or intending to devise any scheme or artifice to defraud, or *for obtaining money or property by means of false or fraudulent pretenses, representations, or promises . . . shall, for the purpose of executing such scheme or artifice, or attempt to do so*, place or cause to be placed, any letter . . . in any post office . . . shall be fined not more than one thousand dollars or imprisoned not more than five years, or both."[33] This became the basis for the department's attack on those using the mails to defraud.

During the debate Thetus Sims of Tennessee objected to section 217, declaring it was almost entirely new. In this section were grouped all kinds of things that might be considered "destructive." Such articles as poison, poisonous animals, insects, reptiles, explosives, inflammable materials, infernal machines, disease germs, were declared nonmailable. The postmaster general, however, might permit, if properly packed, the transmission in the mails of such articles that were not dangerous or injurious. Penalties were provided for mailing such articles in violation of the postal rules; maximum fine of $1,000 and/or imprisonment of two years were to be imposed, but if this action were taken with design to kill or hurt anyone or to injure the mails then the fine was $5,000 and/or imprisonment for ten years.[34]

Representative Sims objected because the word "liquids," which had been in the law of 1872, had been omitted. He charged that the omission had been brought about by the liquor interests and that if the bill was not amended the postmaster general would have to receive intoxicating liquors in the mail and every mail route would become converted "into a whiskey carrying route." An amendment was added: "*Provided*, That all spiritous, vinous, malted, fermented, or other intoxicating liquors of any kind, are hereby declared to be nonmailable and shall not be deposited in or carried through the mails."[35]

In 1912 the power of the postmaster general over mailability of matter was further extended. One law declared nonmailable any "film or other pictorial representation of any prize fight or encounter of pugilists under whatever name, which is designed to be used or may be used for purposes of public exhibition." Maximum punishment for violation was set at $1,000 fine and/or one year of imprisonment at hard labor. The incident that seems to have triggered action on this bill was a fight between a Negro and a white man held in New Mexico on July 4, 1912. Some senators objected to the bill, saying that the obscenity law was certainly broad enough to cover pictures of prize fights. It was pointed out that the bill was more similar to the lottery law but it did not go so far as to prevent newspaper accounts and reports of contests, although Senator Heyburn of Idaho would have limited references to prize fights to three lines and not allowed in the mails any newspaper that published more than three lines. The phrase "or any record or account of the same" was struck out of the bill because it would have subjected to penalties any reporter who sent an account of the fight through the mails to his newspaper. H. Robert Fowler of Illinois tried unsuccessfully to have the bill include fights between men and animals or between animals. He thought bull fighting was as demoralizing as prize fighting. There was only one protest as to constitutionality. Representative Murray of Massachusetts said prize fighting was a matter of state jurisdiction and nearly all states had outlawed them. He taunted the Southern representatives who were urging such legislation in spite of their usual devotion to states' rights.[36]

A section in the Post Office Appropriation Act of 1912 required newspapers to file with the postmaster general the names of editor, publisher, business manager, owners, stockholders, and approximate number of copies of each issue sold. Any reading matter that had been paid for had to be plainly marked "advertisement." Any paper not complying would be denied the privilege of the mail. Henry A. Barnhart of Indiana, author of the amendment, stated that his purpose was to make clear what was the inspiration behind news items and editorials, for he was sure that the ownership of a paper affected the policies of the paper. He cited, as an example, the ownership of the *New York Mail* by George W. Perkins, who was connected with the harvester and steel trusts. The amendment was adopted with little debate and by an overwhelming vote.[37]

The requirement of registration was challenged by the Lewis Publishing Company. E. G. Lewis had been in trouble with the Post Office Department several times. Fraud orders had been issued against him and the People's United States Bank in 1906. In 1911 the *Woman's National Weekly*, of which he was editor and publisher, had had its second-class mailing privileges curtailed.[38] The Lewis Publishing Company claimed the law of 1912 abridged the freedom of the press, for any paper that did not obtain a blank from the Post Office Department and file the requested information before the first of April each year would be denied mailing privileges. Lewis claimed that this was not a law to regulate the mails *"but to regulate journalism."* He said there was no reference to the mails except exclusion from the mails, which is used "as a means of enforcing this censorship of the press." He claimed publicity as to ownership and the like, was not a proper concern of the Post Office, that its only function was to carry the mail. Chief Justice Edward D. White in *Lewis Publishing Co.* v. *Morgan* (1913) reviewed legislation governing newspapers and stated that they had received special privileges but that there were certain conditions in order to obtain these privileges. Since 1888 publications desiring these privileges had had to file answers to certain questions. The provision in the 1912 act merely supplemented existing legislation. Congress, "in exerting its power concerning the mails" and "in the interest of the dissemination of current intelligence," had the power to define conditons for admission of a privileged class of mail. The law, he said, was not enacted to regulate the press or to curtail its freedom. The injunction suit of the publishers was denied.[39]

The Supreme Court during this period upheld the quasi-judicial power exercised by the postmaster general, in many cases overruling the lower courts. Most of the cases that reached the highest court concerned postal frauds. Postmaster General Frank Hitchcock (1909–1913) made war on swindlers by using both the fraud order and criminal prosecution simultaneously. The fraud order was often ineffective, as the swindler would merely reorganize the same scheme under a different name, using his same mailing lists and sometimes even the same address. If he was arrested, indicted, and his tools confiscated he would be out of business. The postmaster general recommended that the law be changed so postal officials would be required simply to prove the mailing of the advertisements rather than the intent to defraud. If that was done he predicted that the department could "easily stamp every fraud operator in America out of business within the period of a year." Congress ignored his recommendation.⁴⁰

The Supreme Court, however, upheld the postmaster general in both the criminal and fraud order cases. In *United States* v. *Young* (1914) the justices stressed that it was not necessary to prove the scheme was one to defraud; the placing of a letter concerning a project in the post office was the important point. The object of the statute was to protect the United States mails from being used to effect a fraud.⁴¹ The Court interpreted "cause to be placed . . . in any post-office" very broadly. In *United States* v. *Kenofsky* (1917) a life insurance agent delivered to his superior a fraudulent death claim with false proofs, although he knew the allegedly deceased man was alive. He was aware that such a claim would be mailed to the head office for approval before payment. The Court said the defendant "deliberately calculated the effect of giving false proofs to his superior officer" and was therefore responsible for fraudulent use of the mails.⁴²

Section 215 of the postal code was the only federal law protecting the public against fraudulent land and mining deals, which were particularly prevalent at this time. The fraudulent scheme itself might be outside the jurisdiction of Congress (as the powers of Congress were interpreted at that time) but the use of the mails to commit such a fraud could be made a criminal offense. Misrepresentation of property exaggerating the climate, productivity, improvements if sent through the mail was "a scheme or artifice to defraud" even though the purchase price of the property might be a fair one.[43] Using the mails to carry out a scheme by making promises which it would be impossible to perform or which the defendant had no intention of performing was also using the mails to defraud.[44]

One defendant claimed section 215 was beyond the power of Congress, for the mailing was a "mere incident of a fraudulent scheme that itself is outside jurisdiction of Congress to deal with"; he also claimed that making the deposit of each letter a separate offense, with the penalty imposed for each offense, violated the Eighth Amendment in that it imposed cruel and unusual punishment and excessive fines. The Court in *Badders* v. *United States* (1916) denied his claims and declared, "The overt act of putting a letter in the post office of the United States is a matter that Congress may regulate." The law made each deposit of a letter in the mails a separate offense.[45]

The quasi-judicial power the postmaster general used when issuing fraud orders was upheld in broad terms. The Court in *Deggs* v. *Hitchcock* (1913) denied a writ of certiorari to review a ruling of the postmaster general ordering the local postmaster not to deliver mail to a company accused of using the mails to defraud. The petitioner claimed that citizens had a "common right" to use the mails. The postmaster general claimed the Court could determine whether or not he misconstrued the law but could not review the facts. Justice Joseph Lamar agreed with him. He stated the action of the postmaster general was administrative and not judicial and therefore the writ could not be used. The issuance of such a writ "would be an invasion of the Executive by the Judicial branch of the Government," he concluded.[46]

During the last decade of the nineteenth century there had been many attempts to limit the postmaster general's enforcement of the obscenity statutes. In the early twentieth century, although there were many cases in the lower courts on this issue, no decision was handed down by the Supreme Court. There was practically no opposition either in Congress or in the Court to a broad definition of obscenity in the nonmailable statutes.

This was not true as far as use of the mails to defraud was concerned. Before 1890 attention had been centered on lotteries and counterfeit money schemes, but shortly before the end of the nineteenth century the Post Office Department began to take cognizance of more sophisticated schemes, such as fraudulent investment houses and land and mining companies issuing false advertisements. The power of the postmaster general to issue fraud orders was also broadened at that time. Because the usual judicial safeguards were not observed in these Post Office Department procedures, the use of that power was challenged in Congress and in the courts. After 1895 many cases dealing with the use of the mails to defraud reached the Supreme Court, but in practically every case the actions of the Post Office Department were upheld. There were no other federal laws to protect the public from swindlers, although the Court had at that time given a broad interpretation of the commerce clause (*Champion* v. *Ames*). In their decisions the justices stressed separation of powers, rejecting judicial encroachment on Executive departments.

The postmaster general's power over granting second-class mailing privileges also was challenged during the early twentieth century, both in Congress and in the courts, but in every instance he was upheld. Postmasters general in annual reports as late as 1914 stressed that it had never been the policy of the Post Office Department to exclude from the mails a publication just because a certain issue or issues had been found to contain matter prohibited by law. During World War I the postmaster general was criticized for following a contrary policy, i.e., barring newspapers from the mails because certain issues had what he considered treasonable matter in them.

# Unamerican
# Political Doctrines
# Declared Nonmailable

On the same day, February 5, 1917, that the Senate passed a resolution endorsing President Wilson's breaking of diplomatic relations with Germany, Senator Lee S. Overman of North Carolina introduced a bill to define and punish espionage. When he reported it out from the Committee on Judiciary a week later he said it was a composite of fourteen bills before the committee. One paragraph of the bill provided punishment for anyone who sent by post any letter or document "containing any matter written in any medium which is not visible unless subjected to heat, chemicals or some other treatment." Albert Baird Cummins of Iowa thought this a "remarkable proposal." The offense seems to be the sending through the mails of an invisible message, no matter what the message, he said. It might be one between two lovers. He added: "Seemingly, so great is the fear that the people of this country will communicate with each other in a secret way that we have here attempted to make it a crime for one person to write to another unless the writing is plain and visible." The session came to an end before the bill could be acted on.[1]

Congress was called to meet in special session April 2; President Wilson delivered his message that evening recommending a declaration of war. On Friday, April 6, Congress passed a joint resolution declaring a state of war existed between the United

States and Germany. Meanwhile bills to punish espionage had been introduced in both houses.[2] Debate on them began in earnest April 25. A provision that caused vehement opposition was one empowering the president to prohibit "the publishing or communicating of ... any information relating to the national defense which, in his judgment, is of such character that it is or might be useful to the enemy." The secretaries of war and navy would be empowered to suspend for thirty days a newspaper publishing military or defense information useful to the enemy. The Newspaper Publishers Association formally asked Congress to eliminate any provision that might provide for censorship of the press. They maintained that they had been observing the voluntary censorship agreement and had cooperated with the Committee on Public Information set up by executive order on April 14. They pointed out that any newspaper editor who wilfully published information of military value could be punished under the law of treason and that control of messages by mail, telegraph, and cable would accomplish the desired object. This section, which had been advocated by the administration, was eliminated in the House by a vote of 220 to 167 on May 4, 1917. A milder censorship provision was substituted, however, after many of the opponents of censorship had left the chamber.[3]

Another provision that aroused considerable debate in the House dealt with the use of the mails:

Sec. 1100. Every letter, writing, circular, postal card, picture, print, engraving, photograph, newspaper, pamphlet, book or other publication, matter, or thing of any kind in violation of any of the provisions of this act, or of a treasonable or anarchistic character, is hereby declared to be nonmailable matter and shall not be conveyed in the mails or delivered from any post office or by any letter carrier.

Sec. 1101. Whoever uses or attempts to use the mails or Postal Service of the United States for the transmission of any matter declared by this title to be nonmailable shall be fined not more than $5,000 or imprisoned not more than five years or both. Any person violating any provision of this title may be tried and punished either in the district in which the unlawful matter was mailed, or to which it was carried by mail for delivery according to the direction thereon, or in which it was caused to be delivered by mail to the person to whom it was addressed.

# Unamerican Doctrines Nonmailable

Representative Webb, reporter of the bill, explained to the House that the bill's sponsors had intended to use only the word "treasonable" but had received from the Post Office Department some mail matter that was so horrible but not treasonable that the word "anarchistic" was inserted. The matter was too shocking to be printed in the *Congressional Record.* There then developed a long debate on the meaning of the word "anarchist" and the undesirability of allowing the postmaster general to decide what was an anarchist paper. James R. Mann, minority leader, questioned whether the postmaster general should be given such "autocratic power—greater power than the Czar of Russia." William H. Stafford of Wisconsin said that decisions of the Supreme Court invariably held that Congress had "plenary power" over the postal service and that under the clause in the Constitution "to establish post offices" Congress had the power, if it wished, "to exclude from the mails whatever it determines to exclude." He claimed that if the word "anarchistic" was kept the postmaster general could "pass upon the character of a publication without the right of resort to the courts to review his decision." One member expressed the fear that the postmaster general might have the right to censor the mail of members of Congress. Finally an amendment was adopted to strike out "or anarchistic" and insert "of a character advocating the destruction of or injury to the Government by violence." The bill then passed the House on May 4 by a vote of 260 to 106 (62 not voting).[4]

The Senate was discussing S. 2 when it received word of the passage of H.R. 291. The House bill was amended by substituting for it the Senate bill, leaving only the enacting clause of H.R. 291. The chapter of the Senate bill dealing with nonmailable matter consisted of five sections. The first section was similar to section 1100 of the House bill except in place of "treasonable or anarchistic character" it had "or intended or calculated to induce, promote, or further any of the acts or things by any provisions of this act declared unlawful." Section 2 declared matter "of a seditious, anarchistic, or treasonable character" nonmailable, and section 3 gave the postmaster general the authority to forbid the use of the mails to any one circulating matter declared by this act to be nonmailable. Section 4 stipulated punishments and section 5 provided for review by injunction proceedings in the District of Columbia Supreme Court.[5]

The progressive senators led the opposition to granting so much power to the postmaster general. Senator Cummins of Iowa said that they were creating a postal system that would not only have the power to judge infractions of the law but also the authority to decide whether matter to be carried in the mail might bring about a violation of the law. He pointed out that the proceedings were entirely *ex parte*, that the administrative official carried on the investigation, examination, hearing, and then gave the judgment. Senator La Follette of Wisconsin opposed enlarging the powers of the Post Office officials, "thus permitting them to suppress publication through arbitrary denial of mailing rights." He also charged that his mail had been tampered with in spite of the law stating clearly that letters could not be opened.[6]

The bill passed the Senate May 14 and went to conference committee.[7] There was almost no disagreement over Title XII, which dealt with the mails. The House conferees insisted on the elimination of the phrase "or intended or calculated to induce, promote, or further any of the acts or things by any provision of this act declared unlawful." Section 1 was therefore identical with section 1100 in the original House bill except for the omission of "or of a treasonable or anarchistic character" and a statement at the end that nothing in the act authorized the opening of letters, added by the Senate. Section 2 read as follows: "Every letter, writing, circular, postal card, picture, print, engraving, photograph, newspaper, pamphlet, book or other publication, matter or thing, of any kind, containing any matter advocating or urging treason, insurrection, or forcible resistance to any law of the United States, is hereby declared to be nonmailable."

Section 1101 of the House bill was substituted for section 4 of the Senate bill and sections 3 and 5 were eliminated. The main discussion in the conference committee was over the press censorship clause. In spite of pressure from the White House the bill was agreed to without provision for censorship of newspapers. Senator Borah said that with the postmaster general's power to bar from the mails newspapers he considered seditious "there is no use to worry about the censorship of the press for that will be lodged absolutely in the hands of the Postmaster General."[8]

Postmaster General Burleson (1913–1921) lost no time in carrying out the provisions of Title XII of the Espionage Act of June 15, 1917. The department issued "Rules of Procedure for Exclusion of Illegal Publications from the Mails under the Espionage Act." It stated that no publication would be barred from the mails because of the general tone of the paper but only if specific articles violated the act. The postmaster general was to be informed if there were articles in a paper that were traitorous or impeded the war effort. He would then tell the publisher to show cause why his publication should not thereafter be excluded from the mails. A hearing would be held as promptly as possible and a decision would be given immediately after the conclusion of the hearing. The postmaster at the place of publication would be informed of the result by telegraph and he would notify the publisher. Several issues of newspapers and periodicals were declared nonmailable for having in them articles that might impede recruiting or enlistments.[9]

In both houses of Congress resolutions were introduced asking the postmaster general to furnish information as to what newspapers and periodicals had been denied the privileges of the mail under the Espionage Act, when, if reasons for the denial had been furnished the papers, and what instructions had been issued local postmasters. The House resolution, introduced by Representative London of New York, a Socialist, was reported out adversely from the Committee on the Post-Office and Post-Roads by John A. Moon of Tennessee on July 23. He said the postmaster general had given all the information he deemed compatible with the public interest and that Congress had no right to ask more from a coordinate branch of the government. Burleson had said that although certain issues had been barred from the mail no newspapers had been denied the privileges of the mail and that the department had not suppressed "free criticism, right or wrong, of the Government," or had it "attempted in any way to interfere with the legitimate expression of views which do not coincide with those of the Government in the matter of the war with Germany or any other matter." He refused to disclose his correspondence with the local postmasters, claiming that disclosure would not be compatible with the public interest. The committee expressed full support of the postmaster general's policy. Representative London tried several times to bring up his resolution again but was blocked by Representative Moon.[10]

The Socialist party in the United States had declared its opposition to the war and Socialist papers had in them many articles critical of the war. Several of the papers were denied mailing privileges. Early in July a Socialist leader (Morris Hillquit), a progressive (Amos Pinchot), and a famous criminal lawyer (Clarence S. Darrow) called on Senator La Follette to enlist his support to curb the activities of the postmaster general. They said they had been to the Department of Justice to protest but were told that the Socialist papers should stop criticizing the war "or stay out of the mails."[11]

Pinchot and editor Max Eastman appealed to President Wilson against the barring from the mails of the August issue of the *Masses*, a monthly revolutionary journal. The president discussed the matter with Postmaster General Burleson, stating he thought the editors of that paper were on the whole "well-intentioned." Burleson did not agree and declared that they were discouraging enlistments and were violating the Espionage Act, that if the president did not want the act enforced he would resign. The president backed down.[12]

The publisher of the *Masses* had filed a bill in the southern district court of New York asking for an injunction to restrain execution of the order barring the August issue from the mails. This injunction was granted on July 24; the judge said that cartoons and articles criticizing the president for his inconsistency were merely the "free expression of opinion as to governmental policy" and that as long as this was a free country with freedom of speech no one had the right to prevent a publication from expressing its views on governmental policies.[13]

The Post Office Department appealed and Judge Hough of the Circuit Court of Appeals, Second Circuit, suspended operation of the injunction. He said: "If the Postmaster General has been authorized and directed by Congress not to transmit certain mail matter by mail and is to determine whether a particular publication is non-mailable under the law, his decision must be regarded as conclusive by the courts, unless it is clearly wrong." The department, August 15, issued an order revoking the second-class mailing privileges of the *Masses* on the basis that it had not been issued regularly.[14]

Three other prominent Socialist papers lost their second-class mailing privileges in the summer and fall of 1917: the *American Socialist* in July, Victor Berger's *Milwaukee Leader* in September, and the New York *Call*, the official organ of the Socialist party in New York, in November. In all, about sixty Socialist papers lost their second-class mailing privileges. Some of them, notably the *Call*, continued publication by paying first-class postage.[15]

Many lesser papers ceased publication. Among them was *Freeman's Journal and Catholic Register*, which had had thirteen issues barred from the mail because of articles urging freedom for Ireland. The *Jeffersonian*, published by the well-known Populist Tom Watson, was barred from the mails because of an attack on conscription. His plea to enjoin the postmaster from withdrawing the second-class mailing privileges was denied by Judge Speer of Georgia, who praised the postmaster general for his service to the country in denying the use of the mail to the "dissemination of such poison" as the paper spread. In the last issue, published August 23, Watson wrote: "Without specification of alleged wrongdoing, and without trial by jury and without knowing why it is done, a publisher's business is outlawed and his property scrap heaped, and his presses stopped; still this is not press-censorship. What is it then?"[16]

President Wilson, in most cases, supported Postmaster General Burleson, although sometimes he tried to temper his zeal. The postmaster general wanted to take some action against the Hearst papers, but the president did not think Hearst had "overstepped the bounds of law, outrageous as he has been." Another time he cautioned Burleson to go slow because of the concern of many supporters of the war over freedom of the press. However, the president publicly defended Postmaster General Burleson and declared that he was inclined to be "most conservative in the exercise of these great and dangerous powers."[17]

Even more power was given the postmaster general by the Trading with the Enemy Act of October, 1917. The primary purpose of this act was to regulate exports and imports and trading with German nationals. The act also gave the president the power to create a board to censor communications between the United States and foreign countries and provided punishment for individuals evading this censorship. The bill had passed the House one month after it had been introduced. In the Senate, however, William Henry King of Utah introduced an amendment to give the president the authority to proclaim that it would be unlawful for any comments on the United States government or its foreign policies or the war to be published in the German language unless an English translation was carried in a parallel column. If this were not done the paper could not be carried in the mail. King said his original bill had included all foreign-language publications, but since many foreign-language papers were loyal he had made the requirement applicable only to German papers, many of which were traitorous. This amendment had the approval of the Post Office and Justice departments.[18]

The conference committee replaced this section by what became section 19 of the act. It read as follows:

That ten days after the approval of this Act and until the end of the war, it shall be unlawful for any person, firm, corporation, or association, to print, publish, or circulate, or cause to be printed, published, or circulated in any foreign language, any news item, editorial or other printed matter, respecting the Government of the United States, or of any nation engaged in the present war, its policies, international relations, the state or conduct of the war, or any matter relating thereto: Provided, That this section shall not apply to any print, newspaper, or publication where the publisher or distributor thereof, on or before offering the same for mailing, or in any manner distributing it to the public, has filed with the postmaster at the place of publication, in the form of an affidavit a true and complete translation of the entire article containing such matter proposed to be published in such print, newspaper, or publication, and has caused to be printed, in plain type in the English language, at the head of each such item, editorial, or other matter, on each copy of such print, newspaper, or publication the words "True Translation filed with postmaster . . . ."

Any print, newspaper, or publication in any foreign language which does not conform to the provisions of this section is hereby declared to be nonmailable, and it shall be unlawful for any person, firm, corporation, or association to transport, carry, or otherwise publish or distribute the same . . . .

The president could free a publication from these restrictions by issuing a permit to print, which permit would also be filed with the local postmaster.[19]

This section differed from the King amendment in that: (1) it included all foreign-language papers; (2) it provided for the translation to be filed with the local postmaster, thus giving the Post Office Department more power; (3) it forbade distribution by any means of a paper that did not abide by this act or the Espionage Act. Protests, especially in the Senate, were vociferous. Some declared the conference committee had exceeded its authority since this provision was quite different from the King amendment. Many objected to the additional power given the postmaster general. Senator George W. Norris of Nebraska declared that the postmaster general would now have the power to force any magazine or newspaper he wished to cease publication because any publication declared nonmailable could not be published or distributed by any means. He said he understood the postmaster general had already put out of business thirty-eight or forty newspapers. The conference committee report was adopted by the Senate with only six senators voting against it.[20]

The day the conference report was adopted Postmaster General Burleson announced that he would "enforce strictly those provisions . . . which empower him to bar from mails all foreign language newspapers which contain seditious matter." He said he would "demand absolute obedience of the provision which required literal translations in English of all news items, editorials or other printed matter respecting the Government of the United States." Later he spelled out what papers could not print, that is, they could not say that Wall Street or munition makers controlled the United States government, nor could they criticize conscription, sale of government bonds, or collection of taxes. He declared that Socialist papers would not be barred from the mails unless they contained treasonable matter but then added: "The trouble is that most Socialist papers do contain this matter."

Within a very few days after the passage of the act, foreign-language newspapers began to apply for permits to be exempt from the operation of the act. Some foreign-language papers ceased publication. By the middle of October Burleson told the cabinet that the campaign to suppress seditious newspapers had proceeded so well that he expected that within the month there would be little trouble with newspapers.[21]

The Trading with the Enemy Act had provided for censorship of all communications "by mail, cable, radio or other means of transmission passing between the United States and any foreign country he [the President] may from time to time specify." By executive order censorship of cables and telegrams going outside the country had already been established May 2, 1917. On October 12 a Censorship Board, composed of representatives of the War, Navy, and Post Office departments and the War Trade Board and the chairman of the Committee on Public Information, was created. The chairman of the Censorship Board was Robert L. Maddox, a longtime employee of the Post Office Department and at the outbreak of the war in charge of the foreign mail section. His deputy was Eugene R. White, in service in the department since 1897, and most of the working force were postal employees.[22]

Censorship stations were established in all the important seacoast cities in the United States and also in Honolulu, San Juan, and Shanghai. These were usually in the post offices in the cities. The staff used the sampling method and relied on a list of twenty-one different subjects which if mentioned might cause the deletion or suppression of the letter. The board prepared a list of some 250,000 suspects whose mail was more carefully scrutinized. Most of the mail going from the United States to European neutrals was not censored in the United States, for the Allies had built up a very efficient censorship system. Mail sent to Mexico and Latin America was carefully studied.[23]

## Unamerican Doctrines Nonmailable

In spite of the severity of these laws and the zealousness with which they were enforced by the Post Office and Justice departments, many congressmen favored a stricter law. Several bills amending the Espionage Act of 1917 were introduced in January, 1918. One such bill presented by Edwin Y. Webb passed the House with practically no debate. In the Senate, however, a section providing punishment for wilful criticism of the government, the Constitution, the flag, etc., was added. The debate, however, centered on Title XII of the Espionage Act, which dealt with the power of the postmaster general; Senator Borah of Idaho presented an amendment to repeal that section of the act. Senator Lodge of Massachusetts agreed with Borah that the authority given the postmaster general was "in the highest degree dangerous." Instead of allowing the Post Office Department discretion in regard to foreign newspapers he proposed that no paper printed in the German language should be allowed the use of the mails. Later he modified his proposal so that such a paper could be circulated if an English translation was included. Lodge said he knew many patriotic Germans but most of them read English; he thought language was one of the greatest bonds of unity. King defended the operations of the Post Office Department and said the system established by the Trading with the Enemy Act was working very well. Lodge, however, disliked the secrecy of the proceedings, for only the postmaster passed on the translation. When convinced that his amendment would put an immense burden on the loyal press, which under the system then in force could be exempt, he withdrew it.[24]

Senator King then offered two amendments that were incorporated into the law. The first merely applied Title XII to section 3 of this act as amended, and the other added a section which read as follows:

The Postmaster General may, upon evidence satisfactory to him that any person or concern is using the mails in violation of any of the provisions of this Act, instruct the postmaster at any post office at which mail is received addressed to such person or concern to return to the postmaster at the office at which they were originally mailed all letters or other matter so addressed, with the words "Mail to this address undeliverable under Espionage Act" plainly written or stamped upon the outside thereof, and all such letters or other matter so returned to such postmaster shall be by them returned to the senders thereof under such regulation as the Postmaster General may prescribe.[25]

Because the end of the debate was near, no attention was paid to this amendment with its terrific extension of the power of the postmaster general, and the bill passed the Senate. Some senators were more alert when the conference committee report was presented to the Senate. Senator Thomas Hardwick of Georgia called the Senate's attention to the "arbitrary power" given to the postmaster general by section 4. He said that if a person violated the Espionage Act he had the right of trial by jury, but under this section 4 a person might at the whim of the postmaster general lose forever his right to use the mails. Many senators now spoke on the implications of this amendment, that not only could newspaper publishers be ruined but all a man's business and social relations could be affected. Norris said he would be opposed to giving this power to a saint. "There is no man living in whom this power could be intrusted, however wise or good or great he may be, without, in my judgment, interfering with the very fundamental principles of human liberty and human freedom on which our great Commonwealth is founded," he declared. King defended his amendment, saying it was similar to the lottery and obscenity postal statutes and the language was identical with that used in the fraud statutes. Borah said he believed a great wrong had been done the American citizens during the preceding ten or fifteen years by giving the postmaster general authority to pass on "the question of abusive language, of disloyal language, of contemptuous language, or language calculated to incite opposition to the war." The conference report was accepted by the Senate without a roll call and by an overwhelming vote. When the House heard of the adoption by the Senate it concurred, May 7, 1918, by a vote of 293 to 1 (134 not voting).[26]

This section was not invoked against many American citizens, but the power was there. Two prominent people whose mail was returned under this provision were Arthur C. Townley, organizer of the Non-Partisan League in 1915, and Charles Lindbergh, member of Congress, 1907–1917, and the Non-Partisan League candidate for governor of Minnesota in 1918.[27]

The major test of the postmaster general's power over the press during World War I came in the case of *United States ex rel. Milwaukee Social Democratic Publishing Company* v. *Albert J. Burleson, Postmaster General.* This company published the *Milwaukee Leader*, edited by Victor Berger, a leader in the Socialist movement, the man who claimed credit for converting Eugene V. Debs to that philosophy. Berger had been the first Socialist elected to Congress; he served from 1911–1913. In the summer of 1917 President Wilson had been asked to receive the former congressman but he had refused, saying he had no confidence in Berger, that because of his actions and utterances he could not be trusted as a friend of the government. His speeches and writings did get him into trouble and he was indicted (February 2, 1918) for violation of the Espionage Act. Although under indictment he ran for the United States Senate in the spring of 1918 and polled over one hundred thousand votes.[28]

Shortly before Berger was first indicted a hearing took place on September 22, 1917, before the third assistant postmaster general on the mailability of the *Milwaukee Leader*. The paper had been declared nonmailable under Title XII of the Espionage Act. Then its second-class mailing privileges were revoked on the basis that it had been issued irregularly. The ruling of the Post Office Department was upheld by the lower courts and the case finally reached the Supreme Court. Justice John H. Clarke, delivering the decision for the Court on March 7, 1921, reviewed the history of second-class mailing privileges and pointed out that the postmaster general had been exercising the power for forty years. He stated that the Espionage Act had been passed to prevent disloyalty and disunity and that freedom of the press did not extend "to protection of him who counsels and encourages the violation of the law as it exists. The Constitution was adopted to preserve our government, not to serve as a protecting screen for those who, while claiming its privileges, seek to destroy it." He went on to say that it would not be practical to maintain a reader in every newspaper office in the United States to approve in advance issues to be admitted into the mails and that it was a reasonable assumption that a paper, which had daily for months had in it articles preaching disloyalty, would continue to do so. Therefore it was within the power of the postmaster general to revoke the second-class mailing privileges and the paper could in the future make an application for renewal of the privileges. The power to revoke, he said, was incident to the power to grant and the order had merely withdrawn the second-class mailing privileges but had not prevented the publishing of the paper. He went on to say that administrative decisions made by the head of an executive department within his jurisdiction should not be disturbed by the courts unless clearly wrong.

Justices Holmes and Brandeis dissented. They contended that the statute did not give to the postmaster general power to deny second-class mailing privileges to a paper just because some issues had contained nonmailable matter. Justice Holmes said he was certain the postmaster general could not determine in advance that issues of a newspaper were going to be nonmailable and therefore deny to it the postage rate set by law for newspapers. Justice Brandeis expressed some doubt about the power of Congress to grant the postmaster general so much authority.[29]

The editor of the *New Republic* declared: "The decision reveals a lethal remedy against their [newspapers] misbehavior—or rather the Postmaster General's finding of their misbehavior, for *there* is the rub. The Postmaster General without court or jury, may find the newspapers non-mailable." He stated that more than any other decision this one shook the confidence in the judicial process, for the judges instead of being detached had succumbed to the passions of the times.[30]

Postmaster General Will Hays (1921–1922) restored second-class mailing privileges to the *Milwaukee Leader* on May 31, 1921. The following month he restored them to the New York *Call*, which had been excluded from second-class mailing privileges since November 13, 1917. Postmaster General Burleson had claimed that since the paper had been suspended for violating the Espionage Act it was not a newspaper at all. In January, 1919, after the armistice had been signed, the paper had again applied for the reduced rate. After holding the application for five months, the Post Office Department finally held an oral hearing. After a delay of six more months and after the *Call* had instituted mandamus proceedings, the application had been denied. The editor of the *New Republic* declared this was one of the most arbitrary of Postmaster General Burleson's censorship activities.[31]

Shortly after the armistice Senator Borah proposed an amendment to the Post Office Appropriation Act to repeal the sections in the two espionage acts which referred to mail matter (Title XII, sec. 1,2,3 of the act of June 15, 1917 and sec. 4 of the act of May 16, 1918). He declared these acts had resulted in a complete censorship of the American press. He said they were, of course, war measures and certainly would not even have been proposed if it had not been wartime, so now was the time for their repeal. The Idaho senator received some support from Senator Lodge of Massachusetts, who said he had never liked those laws that led to censorship but that he did not think freedom of speech should be interpreted to mean freedom to advocate resistance to laws. Lee Overman of North Carolina warned the Senate that the Bolshevists were in favor of the repeal of these sections and Knute Nelson of Minnesota said the government needed all the power it had to combat the "Reds" and their propaganda. Borah's attempt to obtain suspension of the rules so his amendment could be acted on was defeated by a vote of 25 to 39.[32]

Some senators favored even stricter laws. Thomas J. Walsh of Montana reported out favorably from the Judiciary Committee a bill to declare unlawful the exhibition of a red flag. It also would broaden the power of the postmaster general so he could ban from the mails anything that advocated violence or strikes to overthrow the government. Robert La Follette wrote his family that he thought the bill would prohibit "carrying (and probably wearing) anything red." Owing to the efforts of La Follette, Borah, and Norris the bill was prevented from coming to a vote.[33]

In the Sixty-sixth Congress (1919–1921) several bills were introduced to increase the power of the postmaster general. The nation seemed to be overwhelmed by fear of a Bolshevik revolution in the United States. The Comintern (third Internationale under Soviet control) and the American Communist party had just been formed. Strikes, bomb scares, and violence were prevalent; several government officials received threats. Most of the states had passed criminal anarchy laws providing penalties for those advocating the overthrow of the government by force and so-called red flag laws. Sedition bills, which would outlaw various political theories and punish severely anyone who sought to overthrow the government by force or impede operation of federal laws or terrorize United States government officials, were introduced in Congress.[34]

This fear was reflected in the bills concerning the mail. Thomas L. Blanton of Texas urged immediate action on his bill, on account of the present emergency. His bill was an elaborate one; it would be unlawful for two or more to combine to hinder railroad movement of the mail or the mining of coal on which movement of the mail depended. It would be unlawful to advocate the overthrow of the government by force, to display any flag or emblem intended to promote its overthrow, or "to transmit or attempt to transmit through the United States mails any of the seditious communications mentioned herein, all of which are declared nonmailable." Another bill, presented by Henry L. Emerson of Ohio, provided punishment for sending through the mail matter tending to stir up racial or religious hatred.[35] Several bills would prohibit admission to the mails of any printed matter or literature printed in a foreign language (some merely specified the German language). Some of these stated that it was the duty of the Post Office officials "to seize any publication sought to be sent through the mails in violation of the provisions of this act." These bills did not get out of committee, but the number of them are evidence of the hysteria prevalent in Congress in 1919.[36]

Bills to exclude foreign-language publications from the mail or at least from second-class mailing privileges continued to be introduced until 1927, by which time the "red scare" had died out. The authors of these bills that year were from Georgia, the home of the reestablished Ku Klux Klan. These bills declared nonmailable any newspaper printed in a foreign language that advocated opposition to organized government or the overthrow of the United States government or the assaulting of officials or destruction of property. However, the papers would not be nonmailable if a "true and complete" English translation was included in the paper. A law of this type was necessary, said the authors, because of the great increase in foreign-language newspapers during the 1920s, their criticism of America, the friction in Europe, and the trouble in Central America, Mexico, and China. America should be for Americans, they proclaimed. The bills were all buried in committee.[37]

This decade, 1917–1927, more than any other period in American history, saw immoderate grants of power to the postmaster general, not only over the press but also over correspondence of individuals. Two of the acts remained on the statute books, but the most extreme (that of May 16, 1918) went out of existence with the end of World War I. The excessive nationalism, as evidenced by the fear of a foreign-language press, was characteristic of the 1920s. During the next decade attention of congressmen was turned to threats of extortion and kidnapping, to scurrilous and libelous attacks on religious groups, and they looked to the Post Office Department for protection against those dangers. Not until the threat of war in Europe in 1939 did congressmen turn their attention again to limiting the dissemination of political doctrines.

# Between Two Wars: Nonmailable Categories Buttress State Laws

During the twentieth century, especially after World War I, there was considerable pressure to develop a federal police power. Since under the Constitution the states have the inherent police power to protect the health and morals of their citizens, regulation by the federal government could be obtained only by indirect means. The commerce clause had been used to regulate railroads, even railroad labor to some extent, to curb trusts, to provide for inspection of meat, food, and drugs, to outlaw interstate traffic in lotteries, and to prevent the transportation of women across state boundaries for immoral purposes. The power to tax had been used less successfully, although laws taxing colored oleomargarine, narcotics, and white phosphorus matches had been upheld by the Supreme Court. It was often found that the use of the postal clause was the most effective method because the Supreme Court had time and time again declared that Congress's power over the postal system was subject to few constitutional restrictions.

It was during the period between World War I and World War II that the use of nonmailable categories to help enforce state laws was used. Before this it had been recognized, as in the case of lotteries, that state laws were ineffective if one state permitted lotteries and their tickets and circulars were not barred from the mails. But before 1914 the laws declaring nonmailable lottery tickets and circulars, obscene matter, and political doctrines did not relate to state laws. Congressmen, then, began to see in the power over the mails a weapon to help states enforce their laws protecting the health and morals of their citizens. Thus the prohibitionists used it to help enforce liquor laws in dry states; law enforcement officers favored its use for gun control, for outlawing of gambling devices, and for the apprehension of kidnappers, and liberals wanted it used to curb fraudulent speculation.

The first time the nonmailable category was used to help enforce state laws was early in 1915 in connection with state plant quarantine laws. An amendment to an agricultural appropriation bill providing for this was passed with no discussion and no recognition of its significance. Officials of the states which provided for terminal inspection of plants were to send to the secretary of agriculture the list of plants and plant products subject to inspection. The secretary would then inform the postmaster general and thereafter all packages containing such plants would be sent by a postmaster to the state official for inspection. If the plant was found free from injurious pests the package would be returned to the postmaster to be forwarded to its destination. If found infected the postmaster would so inform the sender. It would be unlawful for any person to deposit in the United States mails any package subject to inspection without plainly so marking it.[1]

Advocates of prohibition after 1915 worked to prohibit the use of the mails for the advertising of alcoholic beverages (the transmission of liquor itself through the mails had been banned since 1872). By 1915 twenty-seven states had passed laws providing either for statewide prohibition or for local option. These laws had been made more effective by the passage of the Webb-Kenyon Act in 1913, which forbade the shipment of liquor into a state in violation of a law of the state; in other words it divested liquor of its interstate commerce character (no penalty for violation had been included). The law had been upheld in *Clark Distilling Company* v. *Western Maryland Railway Company*.[2]

Representatives from the Southern states, most of which had prohibition laws, took the lead in introducing bills to forbid the use of the mails for the transmission of liquor advertisements. Senator Bankhead of Alabama succeeded in getting his bill reported out and brought up for debate in the Senate early in 1917, two years after he had first introduced it. The first section of the bill said that no letter, circular, or newspaper containing an advertisement of intoxicating liquors should "be deposited or carried in the mails . . . or be delivered by any postmaster" when addressed to someone "in any State or Territory of the United States at which it is by the law in force in the State or Territory at that time unlawful to advertise or solicit orders for such liquors, or any of them, respectively." This last clause is what made this bill different from the other nonmailable statutes. The bill was amended to authorize the postmaster general to designate the states that prohibited such newspapers. There were, at that time, twelve states that did so. This bill was adopted by the Senate on January 11, 1917.[3]

Senator Wesley Jones of Washington, in order to improve its chance of passage, proposed that the Bankhead bill be added as an amendment to the Post Office appropriation bill, which had been passed by the House on January 16. Senator Martine of New Jersey, wishing to defeat the amendment, proposed adding a provision making it unlawful for a person to deposit in the mails any advertisements of cigarettes. He said: "I trust that these splendid specimens of humanity who are advocating prohibition will stand up like men and vote to save the rising generation from the iniquity of tobacco smoking and from the horrors of the poison of nicotine." As was expected, this was defeated. James Reed of Missouri offered an amendment providing punishment for anyone who ordered or purchased liquor to be transported into a dry state or who drank any such liquor. He said he was serious in presenting such an amendment, that most proposals dealt with the liquor manufacturers or newspaper publishers, but his amendment dealt with the consumer. It was charged that the liquor interests supported the Reed amendment, hoping it would lead to a reaction that might bring about the repeal of some of the state laws. The whole amendment was adopted by unanimous vote of the Senate and was accepted by the House with only a little debate on Reed's "bone-dry" amendment.[4]

Section 5 of the Post Office Appropriation Act of March 3, 1917, provided punishment for anyone who caused intoxicating liquors to be transported into any dry state; the part of the Reed amendment providing punishment for a person who drank liquor imported into such a state had been eliminated. The section also made nonmailable into a dry state any newspaper that carried advertisements of liquor and provided punishment for the publisher who deposited in the mail an advertisement that violated this section. The trial could take place either in the district in which a circular was mailed or to which it was carried or where it was delivered.[5]

Congressmen suggested that the sale of firearms also be made subject to state law. Bills were introduced to make it unlawful not only for anyone to deposit in the mails but also for anyone to take from the mails or for any postmaster to accept for transmission or for delivery any package containing a pistol or revolver in violation of any law of a state. The bill reported out by the House Judiciary Committee went on to state: "Any pistol or revolver transported into any State by mail or in interstate commerce shall, upon arrival in such State, be subject to the operation and effect of the laws of such State enacted in the exercise of its police powers and shall not be exempt therefrom by reason of being introduced therein through the mails of the United States or in interstate commerce."[6]

The bill favored by the Committee on the Post Office, however, merely declared nonmailable "pistols, revolvers, and other firearms capable of being concealed on the person." Such articles could be conveyed in the mails to certain personnel under regulations prescribed by the postmaster general. The committee said they had considered a bill making firearms nonmailable if the state or political subdivision had laws prohibiting the sale of firearms but had decided that such a law was unenforceable and would empower every political subdivision to make postal regulations.[7]

Law officials urged passage of some federal law and pointed out that such a law would not harm law-abiding citizens but would help curb crime. They said that because of the mail order business pistols were as plentiful, almost, as pencils. Magazines were full of advertisements stating that the order for a gun need not be accompanied by any money; the customer need only pay the postmaster. Postmaster General New (1923–1929) urged the passage of a law that would make that class of firearms absolutely unmailable with such exceptions as to persons as Congress might think proper.[8] The bill brought about a heated debate in Congress. Advocates of the bill maintained it would help control the lawless element in the large cities, that city ordinances had been made unenforceable because of the mail-order business in firearms. Those opposed declared such a bill would be futile as criminals would acquire firearms anyway, that it infringed on the rights of citizens who wanted to keep arms to protect the family, that it violated the Second Amendment of the Constitution ("the right of people to keep and bear arms shall not be infringed"). Several attacked the growing power of the Post Office Department.[9]

The act, which finally became a law February 8, 1927, made nonmailable firearms capable of being concealed on a person except, under regulations prescribed by the postmaster general, to officers of the army, navy, state enforcement officers who needed them for the performance of their duties, and to manufacturers and bona fide dealers. The maximum penalty for knowingly depositing such articles in the mail was a fine of $1,000 and/or imprisonment for two years.[10] None of the bills barring the use of the mails to newspapers and magazines which advertised firearms for sale passed, so people desiring revolvers and pistols could order them by mail and the guns could be shipped by express. This made the law of 1927 quite ineffective.

The bill (H.R. 9179) in the Sixty-eighth Congress (1923–1925) that would have made pistols and revolvers subject to state regulation also contained sections that would have banned from the mails and interstate commerce gambling and chance slot machines. The committee report on the bill recommended favorable action, declaring that the worst breeders of crime were slot machines accessible to school children, who spent their lunch money on them. Many states and cities had tried to outlaw them but no real relief could come until Congress passed a law.[11]

The House and Senate were unable to agree on bills banning from the mail gambling paraphernalia. The House bill proposed making nonmailable "any article, device, or thing designed or intended for the conduct of such lottery, gift enterprise, or scheme" and any newspaper advertising any such article. It also extended the authority of the postmaster general to issue fraud orders in such cases. Some representatives objected to extending the authority of the Post Office Department to such an extent to "determine the police regulations of the State." Some argued that when the lottery law was enacted it was to correct a national evil, but that this bill would permit the exclusion from the mails of letters sent out by a women's club informing them of a bridge game at a member's home. A supporter of the bill expressed his worry about the effect of gambling; "if this country keeps on with the gambling instinct we will wake up some fine morning and find that we have wiped out the moral law and lost regard for the Ten Commandments and will be next door to the situation that is facing unhappy Russia," he declared. Bills banning lottery paraphernalia passed the House in Sixty-seventh, Sixty-eighth, and Sixty-ninth Congresses (1921–1927).[12]

All the House bills were buried in committee in the Senate. Manufacturers of slot machines convinced the Senate committee that the primary purpose of the machines was the vending of small package merchandise which was wholly legitimate and that they were transformed by unscrupulous purchasers into gambling devices. The Senate bill therefore specified that what should be banned from the mails was an article or device which was "so constructed as to have for its principal and primary use the risk of money or property by lot of chances." This bill was passed by the Senate in both the Seventieth and Seventy-first Congresses (1927–1931). It was supported by Postmaster General Brown (1929–1933). Pringle, the assistant superintendent of the Internal Reform Federation, testified before the Senate committee that the greatest obstacle to enforcement of state antigambling laws was the campaign carried on by the large manufacturers of gambling implements. He said the federal government long ago had closed the mail to lotteries but tons of materials for future lotteries were sent through the mail. If Congress would pass a law it would "greatly diminish the difficulties of enforcing State laws." The bills failed to be passed by the House.[13] It was not until 1961 that an act was passed amending the lottery section of the postal code to include gambling paraphernalia.

An article in *The Nation* described materials that were not censored as gambling devices: marked cards which could be read by means of special glasses, slot machine slugs, dice sold for "magical purposes only, and *not* for gambling." The author stated that the mails were as pure as the Post Office Department wished to make them. He said: "The solicitor at Washington . . . has arbitrary power to bar from the mails anything he may judge to be fraudulent or offensive. His ruling can be reversed only by expensive recourse to the Federal courts."[14]

Up to 1926 the Post Office Department had been relatively successful in using the fraud statute to prosecute cases of blackmail; they had, therefore, not supported efforts of congressmen to make nonmailable written or printed matter "threatening body harm or injury to the person or property of the person addressed." However, in that year the Supreme Court in *Colgero Fasulo* v. *United States* held that "threats to kill or injure unless money is forthcoming do not constitute a scheme to defraud." "Broad as are the words 'to defraud' they do not include threat and coercion through fear or force," Justice Pierce Butler maintained.[15]

The Post Office Department thereupon recommended that Congress pass some legislation that would at least give it the authority it thought it had over use of the mails for blackmailing. Bills to do so were introduced in the Seventieth and Seventy-first Congresses (1927–1931), but they were buried in committee. While similar bills were being discussed in the Seventy-second Congress (1931–1933) the son of aviator Charles A. Lindbergh was kidnapped. The demand for ransom had been sent by mail. The House committee decided this "latest fiendish act" made the chances of passing a bill, preventing the use of the mail for extortion demands, excellent. Such an act would bring "to the assistance of the States and localities the aid of the Federal Government in stamping out this most atrocious form of crime," said the committee report.[16]

The bill (H.R. 96) passed the House on March 9, 1932, with no debate. The Senate substituted its own bill (leaving the enacting clause), which after some discussion was accepted by the House and became a law on July 8, 1932. The act read as follows:

That, whoever, with intent to extort from any person any money or other thing of value, shall knowingly deposit or cause to be deposited in any post office or station thereof, or in any authorized depository for mail matter, to be sent or delivered by the post-office establishment of the United States, any written or printed letter, or other communication with or without a name or designating mark subscribed thereto, addressed to any other person, and containing any threat (1) to injure the person, property, or reputation of the addressee, or of another or the reputation of a deceased person, or (2) to kidnap any person, or (3) to accuse the addressee or any other person of a crime, or containing any demand or request for ransom or reward for the release of any kidnapped person, shall be fined no more than $5,000 or imprisoned no more than twenty years, or both.

Prosecution would be in the district where the matter was deposited unless it was mailed in a foreign country, and then the trial could be either in the district into which the matter was carried or in which it was deposited in the United States mail.[17]

Governmental officials wanted to be able to prosecute a sender of extortion letters in the United States also in the district where the letter was delivered. Attorney General Homer C. Cummings sent a draft of a proposed amendment, suggested by J. Edgar Hoover, chief of the Federal Bureau of Investigation. Cummings pointed out that extortion letters were frequently mailed far from the place of delivery, where the intended victim and necessary witnesses would reside. For illustration he told how extortion notes sent to the glamorous evangelist Mrs. Aimee Semple McPherson Hutton in California had been mailed in North Carolina. Corporation officials in New York City, Walter S. Gifford of American Telephone Company and Cornelius Vanderbilt of the New

York Central Railroad, had received threatening letters mailed in Clinton, Illinois. The proposed amendment passed both houses with little debate and became a law on June 28, 1935.[18]

The following year (May, 1936) Attorney General Cummings suggested two changes. One would make punishable "the transmission of threatening communications of a more serious nature even though it may not be shown that the sender had an intention to extort money or other things of value." He also recommended that the phrase "with intent to extort" be eliminated entirely, as it was so difficult to prove intent. He said that "public policy would seem to demand that the mere preparation and sending through the mails of extortion letters in and of itself should be prohibited and punishable by law," for after all the jurisdiction in these cases rested on the right of Congress to "limit and restrict the use of the United States mails."[19] It was not until May 15, 1939, that these proposals were finally enacted into law. This act, a long and complicated one, divided offenses into three categories: punishment for mailing a communication asking for ransom for release of a kidnapped person or threatening "with intent to extort" was set at a maximum fine of $5,000 and/or imprisonment for twenty years. Letters "containing any threat to kidnap any person or any threat to injure the person" with no intent to extort was punishable with a maximum fine of $1,000 and/or five years' imprisonment. For sending a letter "with intent to extort" containing threat to injure the property or reputation of the addressee the maximum punishment was a fine of $500 and/or imprisonment of two years.[20]

Throughout the twentieth century there had been introduced many bills to extend the lottery and fraud laws to make nonmailable dealings in futures, margin transactions, stock gambling, matter sent out by loan businesses, insurance firms, and stock and produce exchanges not duly chartered and regulated by a state. The campaign received fuel from the Pujo investigation of Wall Street in 1913 and from articles in *Everybody's Magazine* of February, 1913. It was agreed by all that the state laws could not protect the gullible investor from being separated from his savings, for they could not reach beyond the state borders. Some, including Postmaster General New, said the mail fraud statutes were sufficient, and he described how postal inspectors had detected frauds, how fraud orders had put firms out of business, and how indictments had been obtained. He cited the case against ninety-two oil promoters in Texas who had fleeced 70,000 individuals of some $7 million.[21] Many congressmen thought by strengthening the nonmailable laws the state laws regulating speculation could be effective. Others, however, realized that straight federal regulation was necessary; ultimately that viewpoint prevailed. More and more the interstate commerce clause became the constitutional basis for regulation, with the nonmailable category being only incidental.

Federal laws regulating grain exchanges and trading in futures in commodities were put into effect early in the 1920s, but federal regulation of the sale of securities and of the stock exchanges was not realized until after the panic of 1929. It was due to the powerful "farm bloc" established in 1921 under the auspices of the American Farm Bureau Federation that regulation of dealing in grain futures was passed. Here, however, the basis of control was not just the postal clause, although a drastic nonmailable section was included in the act. The first act, the so-called Capper-Tincher Act, was passed August 24, 1921; this provided for a tax of twenty cents a bushel on all transactions except those on boards designated by the secretary of agriculture. This was to be further enforced by making it unlawful to transmit through the mails, by interstate commerce, or by telephone or telegraph any information concerning future contracts in grain other than those dealt with on the legal boards. This act was declared unconstitutional as a misuse of the taxation power (Hill v. Wallace). The Supreme Court hinted that the same ends might be achieved by use of the interstate commerce clause.[22]

A bill giving the secretary of agriculture authority to designate boards of trade as "contract markets" for the conduct of trade in grain was introduced. It contained the same "unlawful" clause but in addition declared that anyone who violated that section or failed to evidence any contract by a memorandum and who delivered "for transmission through the mails or interstate commerce by telegraph, telephone, wireless, or other means of communication false or misleading reports concerning crop or market information or conditions" to affect the price of grain would be guilty of a misdemeanor and subject to maximum fine of $10,000 and/or imprisonment for one year.[23]

Halvor Steenerson of Minnesota attacked the nonmailable provisions. He said: "The use of the taxing power and the power over transportation in interstate commerce to accomplish this illegal purpose of indirectly controlling State matters having failed, it is now proposed to invoke the postal power for the same purpose. Can this be constitutionally done?" He declared that denying mailing privileges to those newspaper publishers who carried in their papers market quotations from markets that had not been approved by the secretary of agriculture was unconstitutional as a denial of due process of law and equal protection of the law. His motion to strike out the postal section failed by a vote of 16 to 57. He then moved that the word "knowingly" be inserted so an innocent person would be protected, but that also was defeated. The bill passed the House on June 27, 1922, by a vote of 211 to 76. It was reported out in the Senate by Arthur Capper of Kansas, August 23, with some minor amendments, substituting "record" for "memorandum" and inserting the word "knowingly"; the bill was adopted with no discussion on September 14, 1922.[24]

During the same session the House of Representatives passed a bill to prevent the use of the mails and other agencies of interstate commerce for transporting securities to any person in a state in which by law it was unlawful to sell such securities. It was also unlawful to send into such state any letter, circular, or newspaper containing advertisements of securities. Maximum penalties would be $2,000 and/or two years for first offense and $5,000 and/or five years for second offense. Edward E. Denison of Illinois said it was apparent that federal legislation was needed to aid in preventing the sale of fraudulent and worthless securities. He stated that this country was far behind other countries in enacting such legislation. England had passed a "blue-sky law" regulating the sale of fraudulent stocks in the middle of the nineteenth century; many other countries had followed her example in the 1890s. Kansas had passed the first such law in the United States in 1910, and by 1922 forty-two states had similar laws. Denison pointed out that these laws were to a large extent nullified by the use of the mails by dishonest promoters. He said his bill simply supplemented state laws and was similar in that respect to several other acts, notably the Webb-Kenyon Act of 1913 and the Reed "bone-dry" amendment of 1917. The bill was supported by the National Association of Securities Commissioners, the American Bankers Association, and acting Postmaster General Hubert Work (1922–1923). The latter had wanted an additional section that would have authorized the postmaster general to deal with such letters with power similar to that of fraud orders, labeling the letters "Illegal Promotion" when they were returned to the senders.[25]

Denison introduced his bill again in the first session of the Sixty-eighth Congress (1923–1924). He urged its passage so that the "strong arm of the Federal Government [could come] to the aid and assistance of these States that are trying to protect their people from this class of fraud by cooperating with the States, if you please, to the extent of forbidding the use of the Federal agencies to violate and nullify the State laws." The bill contained many exceptions so that there would be little or no interference with the transmission through the mails of perfectly valid securities (those of well-established businesses and those listed on certain stock exchanges). Others claimed there were many fraudulent stocks listed on the stock exchanges. Representative La Guardia of New York wanted to make it unlawful to deposit in the mails any communication concerning purchase or sale of stocks on margin. The biggest attack on the bill came from C. William Ramseyer of Iowa. He said: "We have a great postal system in this country. That system is controlled and directed by one central authority, and that one authority is located here in Washington." He argued that if this bill were to pass, then every state in the Union would be empowered to make postal regulations because they could, through their securities commissions, decide what mail could come into a state. The bill is the product of the abnormal postwar psychology, said he.[26] Attempts to get such a bill through were also made in the Sixty-ninth (1925–1927), Seventieth (1927–1929), and Seventy-second (1931–1933) Congresses, but to no avail.[27]

Then came the crash on the stock market in October, 1929, with the consequent loss to individuals of millions of dollars, in many cases owing to the purchase of fraudulent stocks. Subsequent public resentment paved the way for the passage of the Securities Act on May 27, 1933. This was broader than any of the acts introduced in the 1920s; it provided for federal regulation, for the registration with the Federal Trade Commission of all securities publicly offered for sale through the mails or interstate commerce. If there was no registration statement for a security the mails could not be used for buying or selling that security nor could the certificate be carried in the mails.[28] Federal judges declared that this act did not by implication repeal the earlier mail fraud statute, that the two could exist side by side and a person using the mails to defraud in the sale of securities might be liable under both statutes. There could be separate indictments charging a violation of the mail fraud statute and of section 17 of the Securities Act; there could be separate trials or a joint trial.[29]

The Supreme Court in 1938 upheld Congress's denial of the use of the mails as a means of enforcement of the Public Utilities Act (*Electric Bond and Share Co. v. Securities Exchange Commission*). It stated that a public utility holding company engaged in interstate commerce which failed to register could be denied the use of the mails. However, it pointed out that Congress could not use its authority over the mails to enforce a power that was outside its constitutional province.[30]

The postal power was used in 1938 to help enforce the Pure Food and Drug Act. That act, passed in 1906, had been based on the commerce clause of the Constitution and had been upheld on that basis (*Hipolite Egg Co. v. United States*). The court, however, had held that false labeling applied only to ingredients and not to advertised claims for cures (*United States v. Johnson*). In 1910 a bill to deny the use of the mail to persons violating the Pure Food and Drug Act had been introduced but had been pigeonholed. Instead there had been passed (August 23, 1912) the so-

138

called Sherley amendment, which made goods with false labels contraband in interstate commerce.[31]

Several postmasters general had urged Congress to pass an act banning all false advertising of medicines, but nothing had been done. They also had tried to prevent false claims in advertising through the use of fraud orders. One had been issued against a firm selling organo tablets which were held to be good for nervous disorders and sexual decline. When the case ( *Leach* v. *Carlile*, 1922 ) came before the United States Supreme Court the postmaster general's order was upheld, the Court declaring that the claims were so far-fetched that in advertising through the mails the firm was perpetrating a fraud upon the public. The Court refused to review the order. Justices Holmes and Brandeis dissented. Holmes called the circulars letters and therefore protected by the First Amendment guarantee of free speech. He thought the damage done to the buyers of the tablets would be less than damage done to individual freedom by arbitrary orders of the postmaster general.[32] In the Federal Trade Commission Act of 1938 it was specifically stated that it was unlawful for any person to disseminate any false advertising by "United States mails, or in commerce by any means, for the purpose of inducing, or which is likely to induce, directly, or indirectly the purchase of food, drugs, devices, or cosmetics." This was upheld by the United States Court of Appeals, Sixth Circuit; the judge said: "Congressional control of the mails, under the power conferred by the Constitution, includes the power to forbid the use of the mails for deceptive transactions which are detrimental to the financial well being of the nation."[33]

Advertising of foreign divorces was also attacked in Congress. The initiative was taken by Arthur D. Healey of Massachusetts, who first presented his bill in 1935. The bill would make nonmailable any circulars describing how divorce could be obtained in a foreign country. The bill was aimed at the advertisements appearing in papers in the United States stating that legal divorces could be obtained in certain states in Mexico without either spouse even having to appear, that it could all be taken care of by mail. Many states in the United States not only had laws prohibiting

advertisements of foreign divorces in the state but also had refused to recognize these mail-order divorces, and the courts had
upheld the state laws. This had meant great hardship to many
innocent people who had contracted other marriages and thus
were liable to bigamy charges. The Post Office Department had
tried to deal with the problem by the issuance of fraud orders
against operators of these schemes, but they had not been entirely effective. The American Bar Association had urged lawyers to
observe professional ethics and not to appear in such cases of
mail-order divorces, and the United States consular service advised citizens of possible frauds in such divorces. Representative
Healey's bill passed the House in the Seventy-fourth and Seventy-
fifth Congresses (1935–1939).[34]

Postmaster General James Farley (1933–1940) urged passage
of such a bill; in fact Healey's bill had been drafted by the department. Farley's plea was laid before the Senate in the Seventy-sixth
Congress (1939–1941). He had written: "It is a matter of great
importance to the State that the marital status of its citizens be
maintained for the benefit of the community at large and no foreign court should be permitted to dissolve the marriage relation-
ship of persons over whom it has no jurisdiction and in whom it
has no interest." This time the bill passed the Senate with no debate and the House adopted it; it became a law on August 10,
1939.[35] The act declared every letter, card, circular, advertisement giving information how a divorce might be secured in a foreign country to be nonmailable matter and not to be conveyed in
the mails or delivered. Maximum punishment for violating the
law would be a fine of $5,000 and/or imprisonment for five years.
Section 2 said that nothing in the act would preclude criminal
prosecution for using the mails to defraud.[36]

Another evil that the states had tried, unsuccessfully, to regulate was the employment of young children in factories. Most of
the states had passed a law of some kind, but they were not uniform and manufacturers in states where laws were strict were at
a disadvantage in competing with other firms in states with more
lenient laws. As early as 1907 Senator Beveridge of Indiana had
introduced a federal child labor law, but it had received practi-

cally no support because of doubts as to its constitutionality. Finally a law had been passed in 1917 which prohibited the transportation in interstate commerce of goods manufactured in factories that employed children. The Supreme Court, June 3, 1918, had declared the law unconstitutional as too broad a use of the commerce clause.[37]

Senator William S. Kenyon of Iowa then had introduced bills to deny the use of the mails to concerns who employed children to produce goods or commodities. The bills had been buried in committee. Congress had then tried to regulate child labor by taxing the profits of companies employing children, but this also the Supreme Court had declared unconstitutional.[38] A child labor amendment had been passed by Congress in 1924, but by 1935 only twenty states had ratified it. The NIRA (1933) had made the nonemployment of children a condition in the codes of fair competition, but most of the jobs held by children (in agriculture and domestic service) had not been covered by codes. Then the law was declared unconstitutional in 1935.[39]

Representative Henry Ellenbogen of Pennsylvania thereupon decided to try the postal clause again, and in April, 1935, he introduced a bill to make nonmailable articles produced by child labor as well as letters concerning such articles. He said if his bill were adopted child labor would become a thing of the past. "By barring the use of the mails to a firm engaging in child labor I have created an instrument which would be thoroughly effective in abolishing child labor," he said. His bill was pigeonholed in the Committee on the Post Office.[40]

By this time, however, the public attitude had changed and there was little opposition when a ban on employment of children under sixteen was included in the Fair Labor Standards Act in 1938. Also the Supreme Court now accepted the use of the interstate commerce clause to broaden the police power of the federal government over not only child labor but also adult labor conditions in establishments that used the facilities of interstate commerce.[41] The use of the postal clause was no longer necessary.

The abuse of the mails that received the most attention during this period between two wars but that was not corrected was the sending through the mail of unsolicited merchandise. That could not be curbed by state law; it could be dealt with by the Post Office alone. Postmaster General New, in his annual report of 1927, had urged the passage of a bill that would declare unacceptable for mailing unsolicited merchandise, i.e., merchandise a person wished to send for sale to a person who had not ordered it. If the merchandise deposited in the mails was not acceptable to the addressee it would be returned to the sender and he would be charged postage at double the regular rates. The department had received many bitter complaints from individuals who received such merchandise as well as from retail merchants who opposed what they considered unfair competition through the mails. Merchandise would be sent to individuals with a request that they transmit payment for it. If the receiver did not return the article or pay for it he was subject to follow-up letters that were annoying and often abusive and threatening. Sometimes merchandise was sent to people recently deceased, and the family, not being sure it had not been ordered, paid for it. Postmaster General New concluded his plea for a bill to make unmailable unsolicited merchandise with: "The Postal Service is a public service for the legitimate use of the people. It should not be made the instrument of a practice which works an uninvited hardship or inconvenience to recipients of mail matter subjecting them to annoyance and abuse. They have equal rights with the sender."

Postmaster General Walter F. Brown (1929–1933) also supported the declaring of unsolicited merchandise as nonmailable and opposed the suggestion of Senator Goldborough of Maryland that religious, charitable, and eleemosynary institutions be exempt. He said: "While merchandise emanating from such sources is less objectionable than merchandise handled purely for purposes of individual profit, yet to most addressees such shipments constitute an annoyance. Moreover, the administration of the law would be rendered somewhat more difficult by having an excepted class."[42]

In almost every Congress from 1930 to 1943 Senator Carl Hayden of Arizona introduced bills declaring nonmailable unsolicited merchandise. These were passed by the Senate in the Seventy-second, Seventy-third, and Seventy-fourth Congresses (1931–1937). Postmaster General James Farley supported the bills and said that enforcement would not be too difficult, as the Post Office Department knew what firms were in the habit of sending out unsolicited merchandise, they could stop the offense at the source. The senders of such merchandise were vehement in their protests because the passage of such a measure would destroy their businesses. Most vociferous were the senders of greeting cards, for they had been accustomed to sending out their cards to prospects for approval. The mail-order business was a big enterprise, a high-pressure business with many facets; it was estimated that such businesses grossed hundreds of millions of dollars a year. In spite of the protests of hundreds of citizens, who were flooded with unsolicited articles coupled with requests for payment, the support of three postmasters general, and the passage overwhelmingly by the Senate, the bills failed to get out of committee in the House.[13] It was not until 1970 that Congress passed an act dealing with the mailing of unsolicited merchandise.

By the time war broke out again in Europe in 1939 the federal government was exercising substantial police power for the protection of the health and morals of the citizenry. No longer was it necessary to use the subterfuge of the postal power to reinforce state laws. Although many federal laws made provision for denial of the mails, the laws operated directly on individuals and were based on the taxation and interstate commerce clauses of the Constitution. After 1937 the Supreme Court gave a broad interpretation to those two clauses. There were areas in which those two clauses could not operate as effectively as the use of the post office clause. One of these was in the mailing of unsolicited merchandise, which Congress failed to regulate. Obscene matter had long been nonmailable, and the descriptive terms were by then so extensive that no new ones were added, although in practically every Congress bills were introduced to broaden the nonmailable obscenity category and particularly to improve the enforcement of the existing statutes. However, with the outbreak of the war the attention of Congress turned toward keeping subversive political propaganda out of the mails.

143

# Subversive Propaganda Nonmailable

The prospect of war in Europe in 1939 turned the attention of Congress to possible dangers to the American system of government. There were on the statute books two acts dealing with censorship passed during World War I—the Espionage Act of June 15, 1917, and the Trading with the Enemy Act of October 6, 1917. The first act declared nonmailable any matter that violated the provisions of that act or any matter advocating treason or forcible resistance to any law of the United States. The second act provided that no newspaper in a foreign language which discussed the United States government or its policies would be mailable unless an English translation of the articles had been filed with the local postmaster. Early in 1939 a bill was introduced to amend the Espionage Act; it was passed on March 19, 1940. The only change made in Title XII, dealing with the mails, was to make imprisonment mandatory for unlawful use of the mails and the maximum term of imprisonment was increased from five to ten years.[1]

Early in 1941 bills were introduced in both houses of Congress to curb the flood of foreign propaganda coming into the United States. Under the International Postal Convention the United States had agreed to deliver in this country, free of charge, all matter on which postage had been paid in the foreign country of

144

origin. The United States government was therefore distributing huge quantities of Communist, Fascist, and Nazi literature, in reality subsidizing their distribution. The Dies Committee on Un-American Activities proposed drastic legislation that would exclude from the benefits of the International Postal Convention reciprocity all postal matter that might subvert the United States political system. Alfred F. Beiter of New York introduced a bill to prohibit the use of the mails to disseminate certain propaganda. Postmaster General Frank Walker (1940–1945) urged legislative action but wanted regulation and exposure of propaganda sent through the mails rather than exclusion. In accordance with this proposal Senator Wiley of Wisconsin introduced a bill to probihit mailing of propaganda disseminated by agents of foreign ideologies unless the source of such propaganda was identified thereon. He pointed out that under the Foreign Agent Registration Act of 1938 agents were required to register but the propaganda which they disseminated was not regulated. These bills were buried in committee.[2]

The postmaster general, however, on advice of Attorney General Robert Jackson, ruled that propaganda sent to this country by foreign agents abroad who were not registered with the State Department was nonmailable. Over fifteen tons of mail shipped here from Russia, Germany, Italy, and Japan were seized. The Russian government, through her ambassador, filed a protest against the seizure. The editor of the *Washington Evening Star* pointed out that the "Soviet publicists were among the first to discover the advantages that lie in letting the prospective recipient of alien propaganda pay the delivery bill."[3]

Shortly after the United States became involved in World War II, Postmaster General Walker wrote Postmaster Goldman in New York City that a censorship station would be established there under military supervision. Goldman, in his history of the New York City post office, said that for several months before the bombing of Pearl Harbor the problem of censorship of international mails had been studied by officials of the office, several of whom had had experience during World War I. The Post Office was so well prepared that on the morning of December 8 censor-

ship of all mail "destined for Axis countries or countries domi-
nated by the Axis" was begun. Later this censorship was extended
until it included mail to and from almost every foreign country.[4]

The Office of Censorship, established in the First War Powers
Act of December, 1941, supervised the censorship of matter entering or leaving the United States. A force of translators examined all printed matter received from foreign countries; matter
containing propaganda was sent to the solicitor. By 1944 almost
five hundred thousand pieces of mail had been detained; the confiscated mail occupied ten thousand square feet of storage space
and cost of the storage to the government was over seventy-five
hundred dollars annually. At the request of the postmaster general, Senator Kenneth McKellar of Tennessee introduced a bill for
the disposal of certain condemned mail matter. It provided for a
committee composed of the postmaster general and the director
of censorship (or alternates) to dispose of all printed mail matter
mailed to or by persons whose names were on the Proclaimed
List of Certain Blocked Nationals. This matter must have been
censored or condemned by the Office of Censorship "as being inimical to the war effort of the United States or contrary to the
interests of the United States or its Allies." The matter could not
be disposed of until ninety days after it had been condemned.[5]

After the United States entered the war, although publications
from the Axis countries no longer entered the United States,
propaganda from neutral countries and from pro-Nazi groups in
the United States, notably the Silver Shirts, flooded the country.[6]
Representative Dickstein of New York introduced a bill giving the
postmaster general power to bar from the mails matter designed
"to cause racial or religious hatred, bigotry, or intolerance." He
said various groups were taking advantage of the times when
people were emotionally upset to spread intolerance and race
hatred. He hoped the House Committee on the Post-Office and
Post-Roads would find a way to put a stop to having the mails
used by these subversive groups. The New York representative
declaimed: "While our boys are risking their lives to defeat the
forces of fascism and reaction abroad, these people—in a very
subtle way—are trying to break ground for these dark forces in

our own country. The Post Office Department, in permitting this type of propaganda to be distributed through the mails, unwillingly becomes a party to this conspiracy." The bill was buried in committee. The Post Office Department said it had already banned from the mails hundreds of such magazines.[7]

During World War II, as in World War I, although less drastically, the postmaster general by revoking second-class mailing privileges exercised powers of censorship. Father Couglin's *Social Justice*, when the postmaster general announced that its second-class mailing privileges were to be withdrawn, suspended publication rather than fight the decision. Such privileges were revoked in the case of the Trotskyite *Militant* and many other periodicals. In light of the decision after World War I in the case of the *Milwaukee Leader* there was little to be gained by appealing to the courts.[8]

Postmaster General Walker's denial of second-class mailing privileges to some seventy periodicals from May, 1942, through May, 1943, was the subject of a resolution introduced by Senator William Langer of North Dakota asking for an inquiry into the policy of the Post Office Department in excluding matter from the mails. He declared these periodicals had been denied the reduced rates "despite the fact that their contents adhered to the standards previously set by the Post Office" and that the procedures were "undemocratic and arbitrary" and that the hearings "were in fact a mockery of justice." The resolution was buried in the post office committee.[9]

After World War II, in contrast to the post–World War I era, there were few attempts to make nonmailable foreign-language publications. Congressmen were incensed, however, at the transmittal through the mails of threatening letters, defamatory statements, and hate propaganda. The difference is understandable since the American public viewed World War II as a battle against Nazism and Fascism, against an ideology of racism, rather than as a war against Germany and Germans. Jacob Javits of New York, in 1954, introduced several resolutions regarding the transmittal of hate matter. He expressed concern over the great quantity of anti-Catholic, anti-Semitic, and anti-Negro material going through the mails. He asked the postmaster general whether the mails were being used "for the purpose of disseminating false and defamatory statements" about any group of citizens or for the distribution of matter advocating the overthrow of the government. He wanted to know if this matter was coming from outside the United States. Were the laws adequate, he asked, and what measures had the postmaster general taken to prevent the distribution of hate propaganda.

The answer of the postmaster general dealt with the last two questions. He cited the sections of the criminal code that covered mail matter but said that none of them provided expressly for the exclusion of material attacking a particular religious group. He pointed out that in order for matter to be treated as nonmailable it must be proven that it incited to arson, assassination, or murder, or advocated treason, or caused disloyalty or insubordination in the armed forces. He said the courts in interpreting these sections had insisted that "there be a clear and present danger that the things proscribed by the Statute could come about." Because of this interpretation the Post Office Department had seldom been able to declare nonmailable publications of an anti-Semitic, anti-Catholic, or anti-Negro character. Representative Javits, in relating the postmaster general's answer, said the latter had given him a list of ten publications that spread hate propaganda about which he could do nothing. The New York representative declared "The Federal Government should be capable of seeing that its facilities are not abused and exploited for the purposes so contrary to free institutions and the deep convictions of the overwhelming majority of the people of our country."[10]

In 1958 bombings of Jewish synagogues and attacks on Negroes made the public more aware of the dissemination of hate mail. Justice and postal officials met on October 22 to consider the problem but decided there was no statutory basis for action. Much of the mail was sent first class and postal officials could not open such mail without a warrant, which could be obtained only if there was sufficient evidence to believe the mail contained nonmailable matter. Also, most hate literature did not directly suggest arson or murder, and mere defamatory broadsides were not considered illegal. That year the Democratic party's Advisory Council advised passage of a law that would outlaw the use of the mails for the distribution of matter "designed to inflame racial and religious prejudices for the purpose of inciting violence."[11]

In almost every Congress from 1954 to 1967 there were introduced bills to declare nonmailable matter of a defamatory or threatening character as regards an individual or religious or racial group. Not only was this matter not to be conveyed in the mails or delivered but it was to be withdrawn. These bills all died in committee.[12] The only act barring from the mail threatening letters was one (June 1, 1955) that provided punishment for anyone who knowingly and willfully deposited in the mail matter threatening to "take the life of or to inflict bodily harm" upon the president of the United States, the president-elect, or vice-president. The law previously had applied only to the president.[13]

Communist propaganda in the mails received much attention in Congress after 1949. The outbreak of the Cold War, the spread of the Iron Curtain over most of Eastern Europe, the establishment of the Cominform, and especially the report of the Royal Commission on the spy ring in Canada with repercussions in England and the United States led to a second red scare in the United States. A bill, almost identical to that proposed by Senator Wiley in 1941, was introduced in 1949. The purpose of the bill was to identify all mail matter prepared or issued by organizations whose purpose was the overthrow of the government. The bill provided that the attorney general, after a hearing, could designate an organization he considered subversive. Publications issued by that organization would have to have on the wrapper the name and classification of the organization. Matter that was not so identified would be declared nonmailable and be returned to the sender. A district court could set aside the attorney general's order.

Postmaster General Donaldson (1947–1953) thought the act might be difficult to enforce since it applied not only to publications entered as second-class mail matter but also to letters, pamphlets, and books. The American Civil Liberties Union and National Lawyers Guild claimed the bill was unconstitutional. The

House Committee, in its report favoring the bill, pointed out that Congress's power over the postal service was complete and it could declare matter nonmailable and provide criminal punishment for those who violated the law. In this case, however, the congressmen were not declaring matter sent out by certain groups nonmailable, they were merely stating that such mail should be properly identified.[14]

North Korea's attack on South Korea in June, 1950, led to the passage, over President Truman's veto, of the McCarran Internal Security Act on September 23, 1950. Section 2 described the world Communist movement and its revolutionary character and its relation to the Communist movement in the United States. The act made it unlawful for anyone knowingly to conspire with anyone else to help establish a totalitarian dictatorship in the United States. It required the registration of all Communist organizations and all members of such organizations. Any such organization was forbidden to use the mails for transmittal of any publication unless the publication had on it a statement that it was put out by a Communist organization. Control was vested in a Subversive Activities Control Board.[15]

This act did not go far enough to suit many congressmen. Some wanted to exclude from the mails entirely any matter advocating Communism or the overthrow of the government by force. Others wished Communist propaganda designed for use in the public schools to be declared nonmailable. Senator Knowland of California was particularly incensed at the "U.S.S.R. Information Booklet," published by the embassy in Washington and distributed free to public schools. The pamphlet could not be declared nonmailable under the Foreign Agents Registration Act, for it was put out by the diplomatic staff of a foreign country.[16]

Bills receiving the most support were those that would deny second- and third-class mailing rates to Communist propaganda. Those rates were so low they did not cover the cost of mailing; circulation of propaganda by this method was therefore subsidized by American taxpayers. The advocate of this bill in the Eighty-third Congress (1953–1955) was Mrs. Katherine St. George of New York, chairman of the House subcommittee on postal operations. She said she preferred the complete exclusion from the mails of Communist propaganda but such a suggestion had been branded as censorship. Since Communist organizations were listed in the attorney general's "Guide to Subversive Organizations and Publications," then propaganda put out by such organizations could just be declared nonmailable as second- or third-class mail. She pointed out that the preferential rates had been given "to encourage enlightenment and the general intelligence of the people." "It is unconscionable that American taxpayers should be called upon to pay a part of the cost of handling mailings which are intended to undermine our form of government," she declared. In spite of the support of the Post Office Department the bill did not get to the floor of the House.[17] In fact, none of the proposed measures made any headway toward passage.

After the outbreak of the Korean War the Post Office Department had resumed the practice, discontinued in 1946, of confiscating propaganda sent by foreign agents who had not registered under the Foreign Agent Registration Act. Customs and postal officials, with a staff of translators, screened publications coming in from Iron Curtain countries and held from delivery Soviet propaganda. The program of mail-screening operated in secret at first. Subscribers were not told why they had not received Communist publications they had ordered. The government estimated that it seized fifteen million pieces of matter a year. "Uncle Sam's mailman cannot be used to deliver the material designed to destroy the government that employs him," was the explanation.[18]

Gradually the public became aware of the practice and protests grew. As early as 1952 the American Civil Liberties Union, when it learned through the *New Leader* that the Post Office Department had refused to deliver to subscribers Soviet magazines, accused the postal officials of acting as "judges of academic standards."[19] A Quaker organization threatened legal action when peace literature it had ordered from England had been secretly impounded. The officer responsible for the action, the solicitor of the Post Office Department, Abe Goff, replied that universities, libraries, and research groups received the publications they needed for study purposes.[20] Individuals who had subscribed to publications, would, after the department had checked on them, also have the mail delivered to them.[21]

On the first of January, 1959, the Post Office Department began the automatic notification of all persons who had mail of this type awaiting them at the post office. Notice read as follows:

This letter is to advise you that the postal service has received foreign mail addressed to you consisting of certain publications which contain foreign political propaganda.

Such matter ordinarily would be treated as nonmailable. However, such matter may be passed through the mails and delivered to the addressee when it has been ordered, subscribed to or is desired, and is not for dissemination.

The individual was required to sign a card saying that he wished the material and return the card within fifteen days; otherwise the material would be destroyed. In New York City alone it was estimated that less than half of the cards were returned. Some people were afraid they would be branded if they said they wanted to receive Communist publications.[22] The editor of the *Christian Century* not only requested that the material be sent on but wrote an editorial, "Who Censors our Mail?" He stated that the publication he wanted was a release from the Hungarian Church Press and then said: "Censorship of any kind is an insult to the intelligence and patriotism of the American people. But stupid censorship is, to paraphrase a French proverb, 'worse than a sin; it is a mistake.' "[23]

The constitutionality of the practice of intercepting mail from abroad that customs and postal officials considered subversive was questioned. The ruling of the attorney general in 1940 was considered by many a "strained interpretation" of two statutes—the Foreign Agents Registration Act of 1938 and the Espionage Act of 1917. A foreign agent was considered nonregistered and material sent out by him could be considered nonmailable. During the twenty years there had never been a court test of the ruling; a threat of a suit usually resulted in the lifting of the ban.[24]

In 1960 several people filed suits "charging the Government had illegally seized mail addressed to them on the grounds that it was 'foreign propaganda.' " One of the plaintiffs was a social scientist who had attended the United Nations Educational and Scientific Committee Conference in Prague and had subscribed to the *Czechoslovak Woman* and the *Czechoslovak Youth.* The Post Office Department had sent her a card notifying her that if she wished to receive these magazines she should return the card with her signature on it. She had refused and had instituted a suit when she had not received the magazines. She was represented in court by attorneys of the American Civil Liberties Union. The Department of Justice asked for a delay in answering the charges on the basis that it wished to consider the whole policy and also because a new administration was coming into office soon.[25]

On March 17, 1961, President Kennedy announced that on the advice of the secretaries of state and treasury and the attorney general and the postmaster general and following a report of the National Security Council planning board, he had ordered discontinued immediately the program of intercepting Communist propaganda from abroad. He said it had served "no useful intelligence function." The *New York Times*, in an editorial entitled "Of Sealing Wax and Ships," hailed this action, stating: "It took just a little courage to call a halt to this form of censorship; and we are glad to note that the Kennedy Administration has now supplied the same."[26]

This order was opposed by many prominent congressmen, and bills to prevent the distribution of Communist propaganda were introduced. In the House Francis E. Walter of Pennsylvania, chairman of the House Committee on Un-American Activities, said that because of this order "poison will be poured into the veins of our society without restriction and without notice or warning of its nature." He proposed an amendment to section 10 of the Internal Security Act of 1950, which required labeling of Communist propaganda sent out by registered Communist organizations. His amendment required not only the notification of the recipients but also the posting of notices in all post offices warning persons to be alert to Communist propaganda. However, the postmaster general was not authorized by this amendment to open, inspect, or censor any mail. In spite of the opposition of the administration, the bill passed the House on September 18,

1961, by a vote of 369 to 2 (64 not voting). It was reported out of the Judiciary Committee in the Senate on September 26 and a brief discussion followed. Some, including Senator Hubert Humphrey of Minnesota, thought the bill too mild, that we should not subsidize Soviet propaganda unless the Soviets reciprocated.[27] Further action on the bill was postponed pending action on other proposed solutions to the problem of Communist propaganda.

Glenn Cunningham of Nebraska, a member of the House Committee on Post Office and Civil Service, had called Walker's bill "a powder-puff approach" that would not stop the subsidizing of Communist political propaganda. His bill (H.R. 9004), introduced August 31, simply declared that no postal rate would be available to material determined by the attorney general to be Communist propaganda, originating either abroad or in the United States.

Instead of calling for action on his bill he got added to the postal rates bill an amendment that stated that in order "to counteract adverse usage of the mails and to reduce the domestic postal deficit" no international postal agreement would permit the United States Post Office to deliver mail the attorney general had decided was Communist political propaganda. Another section stated that no postal rate in the bill would be available for such Communist political propaganda. This amendment, said the sponsor, would not prevent a person who really wanted to receive Communist material from doing so, as he could receive it by parcel post or by commercial express. During the debate on the floor of the House there was some objection to having such an amendment tacked onto a postal rates bill. On the other hand, Representative John Lindsay of New York criticized the "unlimited powers" granted to the postmaster general and attorney general to "censor" the mails. However, the bill, with the amendment, passed the House on January 24, 1962.[28]

The Senate considered several proposals to restrict the distribution of Communist propaganda. Many senators were worried about the flood of propaganda that had come into the country since President Kennedy issued the order of March 17, 1961. The

## Subversive Propaganda Nonmailable

Customs Bureau noted that about three-quarters of a million pieces of Communist printed matter had arrived in New York port from foreign sources during February, 1962. About half of this pro-Communist propaganda was addressed to the "ordinary American citizen." Senator Goldwater of Arizona, although he did not announce his support of the Cunningham amendment, declared "that a clamp down on Communist propaganda coming into this country is a must."

There was, however, considerable opposition to the Cunningham amendment. Mrs. Neuberger of Oregon pointed out that the International Postal Convention was reciprocal and that the United States had sent out approximately ninety-six million pounds of mail but had received only seventy-six million pounds and to the Iron Curtain countries had sent out sixteen million and received only 2.3 million. The *New York Times* made the same point, that we were anxious to get our propaganda into Communist countries and if we blocked theirs they would retaliate. The editor thought that restriction of the freedom of Americans to read what they pleased did more harm than any propaganda. President Kennedy voiced his disapproval of the Cunningham amendment. The Justice Department issued a memorandum stating that it probably was unconstitutional, a violation of the First Amendment, that it would deprive us of information of value to us and would injure the prestige of the United States.[29]

The Senate Committee on Post Office and Civil Service wrestled with the problem of Communist propaganda. Most of the members thought the Cunningham amendment too strict but feared if they rejected it they would be accused of being "soft" on Communism. They did not want to deprive citizens of the right to receive the reading matter and yet if they did not put in some restriction on Communist propaganda they might jeopardize the passage of the postal rates bill. The Senate committee, finally by a vote of 6 to 3, substituted for the Cunningham amendment the mail-screening program that had been in operation by executive order until March 17, 1961. It would now be a law. The bill directed the Post Office to detain Communist political propaganda, to notify the addressee, and to deliver it "only on his request." If he did not reply within a reasonable length of time the mail would be destroyed. Some exceptions to this ruling were made: subscribers to magazines, mail addressed to government agencies, libraries, and universities, and material mailed under the reciprocal international agreement where the United States government mailed an equal amount of material for delivery in a Communist country.[30]

The amendment was discussed in the Senate from September 25 to 27. Senator Joseph Clark of Pennsylvania led the fight in the Senate against delivery of Communist propaganda. He suggested several amendments, all of which were defeated. Among them was a modified version of the Walker bill: the general public should be alerted to the large quantities of Communist propaganda and obscene matter coming in from abroad by the posting of notices in post offices. Also, a person could file a written request with the local post office to detain propaganda and obscene matter addressed to him and the postmaster general could then dispose of it or return it to the sender. The amendment was voted down, 23 to 51. Another amendment, which would give the president authority to stop delivery of mail from Communist countries when he thought national security required it, was also defeated (48 to 33). The Postal Rates bill with the mail-screening amendment was passed by the Senate and was accepted by the House. Representative Cunningham stated in the House that it merely reinstated the program of President Truman and so he was perfectly satisfied.[31]

The amendment became a law on October 11, 1962, to go into effect on January 7, 1963. It read as follows:

### Communist political propaganda

(a) Mail matter, except sealed letters, which originates or which is printed or otherwise prepared in a foreign country and which is determined by the Secretary of the Treasury pursuant to rules and regulations to be promulgated by him to be "communist political propaganda", shall be detained by the Postmaster General upon its arrival for delivery in the United States, or upon its subsequent deposit in the

## Subversive Propaganda Nonmailable

United States domestic mails, and the addressee shall be notified that such matter has been received and will be delivered only upon the addressee's request, except that such detention shall not be required in the case of any matter which is furnished pursuant to subscription or which is otherwise ascertained by the Postmaster General to be desired by the addressee. If no request for delivery is made by the addressee within a reasonable time, which shall not exceed sixty days, the matter detained shall be disposed of as the Postmaster General directs. . . .

(c) The provisions of this section shall not be applicable with respect to (1) matter addressed to any United States Government agency, or any public library, or to any college, university, graduate school, or scientific or professional institution for advanced studies, or any official thereof, or (2) material whether or not "communist political propaganda" addressed for delivery in the United States pursuant to a reciprocal cultural international agreement under which the United States Government mails an equal amount of material for delivery. . . .[32]

This amendment was immediately challenged in the district court in Los Angeles by a Pasadena truck driver, Charles Amlin. He had received notices from the post office that they were holding for him copies of the *People's Korea*, a pro-Communist weekly printed in English in Tokyo. He was not a Communist, he said, and he had not subscribed to the paper, but he would not tolerate interference with his mail. His suit, sponsored by the American Civil Liberties Union, was to enjoin Postmaster General Day and the postmasters of San Francisco and Los Angeles from detaining such mail. The suit asserted that this interference with mail violated the First Amendment of the Constitution, guaranteeing freedom of speech and press. Also because of the vagueness as to what constituted "Communist political propaganda" it violated judicial rights stated in the Fifth Amendment. A similar suit was instituted in San Francisco on behalf of Leif Heilberg, a toolmaker who wanted a Chinese Communist pamphlet. He feared if he sent in a written request for it that such an action would be used against him when he applied for citizenship. The government lawyers tried to get the suits dismissed on the basis that in each case the plaintiffs would receive their mail regularly if they would state in writing that they wanted it. The American Civil Liberties Union repudiated this solution, as many people were reluctant to have their names on a list stating they wanted Communist propaganda, believing their loyalty then might be questioned. In November, 1964, a three-judge federal court in San Francisco, by unanimous vote, ruled that the amendment to the 1962 Postal Rates Act was unconstitutional "because it inhibited the spread of ideas and was a 'clear and direct invasion of First Amendment territory.' "[33]

In New York another suit had been instituted, this time on behalf of Corliss Lamont's publishing company Basic Pamphlets, whose copy of the *Peking Review* had been held up by the Post Office. After the filing of the suit the Post Office Department informed Lamont that his action was evidence he wanted to receive Communist political propaganda and no more of his mail would be withheld. Lamont then challenged the government for placing his name on a list. The New York district court dismissed Lamont's complaint. He appealed.[34]

It came out at this time that the Post Office Department had kept lists of persons who received such mail, and it was hinted that such lists had from time to time been turned over to the House Un-American Activities Committee. This caused an uproar, and a federal district court expressed concern that the "lists might be used by other agencies for other purposes." This probably influenced the administration's decision to destroy the lists. It was announced early in 1965 that the lists would be ordered burned by March 15 and that no new lists would be compiled. This was considered by many to be a liberal move, but it had the disadvantage that from then on a notice had to be sent and returned for every piece of mail desired; previously there had been a space on the card which could be checked if one wished delivery of any similar publications in the future.[35] This changed procedure presented another issue to the Supreme Court, which was considering the question whether or not the amendment was constitutional.

The Supreme Court handed down its decision on May 24, 1965. Two cases had been joined, that of the postmaster of *San Fran-*

*cisco* v. *Leif Heilberg* on a government appeal and that of *Corliss Lamont* v. *the Postmaster General*. Justice William O. Douglas delivered the opinion. The Court declared the amendment unconstitutional "because it requires an official act (viz., returning the reply card) as a limitation on the unfettered exercise of the addressees' First Amendment rights." Douglas went on to say that the requirement to return the card might have a "deterrent effect" on an individual, especially those whose economic position was a sensitive one, such as a public official or a schoolteacher. Justice Brennan, with whom Justices Goldberg and Harlan concurred, discussed the contention of the government that such propaganda was subsidized by the government and also that it was offensive to many recipients. In regard to the latter he pointed out that the unwilling recipient was protected in that he could file with the Post Office a statement that he did not wish to receive such propaganda and such mail would then be withheld. In regard to the subsidy he said: "If the Government wishes to withdraw a subsidy or a privilege, it must do so by means and on terms which do not endanger First Amendment rights."[36] The decision was unanimous by eight justices, because Justice White took no part in the consideration of the case.[37] The *New York Times* stated that this was "the first time in the 176-year history of the First Amendment that it had been used by the Supreme Court to declare an act of Congress unconstitutional."[38]

Postmaster General Gronouski (1963–1965) hailed the decision. The Johnson as well as the Kennedy administration opposed the screening of Communist political propaganda. Gronouski announced that the department would immediately discontinue enforcement of the act, that it had been unworkable and expensive, costing about a quarter-million dollars a year.[39] Thus was ended a practice which the Post Office Department had engaged in off and on for twenty-five years. It was one of the most controversial of the nonmailable categories of the department. During most of the period the department had withheld the mail on the basis of an executive order; only during the last three years had the Post Office Department been specifically ordered by Congress to carry out such a practice. It may be significant that in this case the Court by a unanimous decision repeated what had been part of a dissenting opinion in 1921: "The United States may give up the post office when it sees fit, but while it carries it on the use of the mails is almost as much a part of free speech as the right to use our tongue."[40]

# Postal Power
# Obstructed

Postmasters general after World War II were hampered by the courts not only in their attempts to prevent the dissemination of Communist propaganda in the United States but also in their efforts to enforce effectively the mail fraud statutes and to prevent the use of the mails for the distribution of obscene matter. Some justices even intimated that Congress's power under the postal clause of the Constitution might have limitations. Usually, however, instead of objections to the postal laws passed by Congress, the courts criticized the manner in which the postmasters general used the power delegated to them by Congress. Justices preferred disagreeing with an administrative official to clashing with Congress.

Before World War II the courts had been reluctant to interfere with the administrative orders of the postmaster general. Judge Hutcheson of the District Court, Southern District of Texas, in *Crane* v. *Nichols* (1924), had said that "the statute authorizing fraud orders was aimed at such a beneficent purpose that only in the extremest cases should courts interfere with their issuances."[1] After World War II the courts did interfere with the attempts of postmasters general to prevent the use of the mails to defraud. A large proportion of the fraud cases never reached court and, of course, an infinitesimal number of them reached the Supreme Court. That court in the 1940s and 1950s handed down some important constitutional decisions dealing with the postmaster general's use of fraud orders and criminal prosecution of those attempting to use the mails to defraud.

The issue of free exercise of religion was brought up in one of the fraud cases, one of the most complicated, long-drawn-out, and fantastic of such cases. In 1931 Guy Ballard, a former promoter of fraudulent stocks, had written a book telling of his experiences on a mountaintop in California where he had been visited by a St. Germain who had proclaimed Ballard to be "The Great I Am." His book, published in 1934, had become an immediate success. The following year, Ballard, his wife, and son had set up headquarters for the "I AM" movement in Los Angeles. This new religion promised to the followers immortality through incarnation and the power of "precipitation," the receiving of material needs without working. A temple was opened and members flocked to attend services and classes. Branches were established throughout the United States with an estimated membership of over a half-million members. Books written by Ballard, and phonograph records of his sermons, "I AM" rings, pictures, charms, charts of "I AM Presence" were sold. Followers donated "love gifts" to St. Germain and a St. Germain Foundation was set up to receive savings of the followers who would no longer need money since the destruction of the world was imminent. Money poured in; Ballard's fortune was estimated at three million dollars. Ballard died in December, 1939, but the enterprise was carried on by his wife and son.[2]

The movement finally came to the attention of the Post Office Department and in 1940 Mrs. Ballard, her son, and top staff members were indicted by a federal grand jury in Los Angeles with conspiracy to violate the mail fraud statutes, in that they had solicited funds "by means of false and fraudulent representations, pretenses and promises." They were convicted in the district court but that conviction was reversed by the circuit court of appeals on the grounds that the jury had been restricted as to issue, that all questions concerning "the truth or falsity of the respondents' religious beliefs or doctrines" had been withheld. The Supreme Court (*United States* v. *Ballard*, 1944) upheld the decision of the district court. It, however, remanded the case to the circuit court to consider other objections made by the respondents. Chief Justice Stone favored merely reinstating the decision of the district court. He said that the constitutional guarantees of freedom of religion should not afford immunity from criminal prosecution "for the fraudulent procurement of money by false statements as to one's religious experiences." The case again reached the Supreme Court (*Ballard* v. *United States*, 1946), this time because the defendants, one of whom was a woman, claimed that the trial in the district court had been in error as women had been systematically excluded from the jury. The Court ruled for the defendants on this issue of procedure. Justices Frankfurter, Vinson, Jackson, and Burton dissented and stated the Court should have squarely met the issue of mail fraud and the constitutional guarantee of freedom of religion. Finally in 1947 the department decided not to bring the case to court a third time. The movement, however, had been practically put out of business by fraud orders first put into effect in 1943 and not removed until 1954.[3]

The Court insisted that when a person was prosecuted for using the mails to defraud that the use of the mails had to be an essential part of the scheme. For that reason the Court threw out several cases where checks, the proceeds of the fraud, were mailed from one bank to another, for the mailing was not for the purpose of executing the fraud.[4] In another case, *United States* v. *Sampson* (1962), concerning the advance fee racket, the Supreme Court sustained the Post Office Department. In this case salesmen, who induced owners to sell their small businesses or real estate, asked for a fee to be paid in advance to show good faith; the salesmen promised, orally, that the fee would be returned when the transaction was completed. Justice Hugo Black said: "We cannot hold that such a deliberate and planned use of the United States mails by defendants engaged in a nationwide fraudulent scheme in pursuance of a previously formulated plan could not, if established by evidence, be found by a jury under proper instructions, to be 'for the purpose of executing' a scheme within the meaning of the mail fraud statute."[5]

Even in the use of the fraud order the postmaster general was sometimes thwarted. In one important case where the constitutionality of the mail fraud statutes was upheld, still the postmaster general had been forced to limit the operation of the fraud order. *Read Magazine* carried puzzle contests which Postmaster General Hannegan (1945–1947) decided were really a scheme to defraud. The puzzles were easy to solve, but since the award was given only after the submission of an essay it was felt to be not a puzzle but an essay contest. The salient points of the advertisement were in very small print, so those who entered the contest found that instead of paying a fee of $3 they might have to pay as much as $42. On October 1, 1945, Hannegan issued an order that the New York City postmaster should refuse to deliver any mail or pay any money orders to the company. This broad fraud order would not only practically put the magazine out of business but also would affect the legitimate functions of the company. The district court enjoined enforcement of the fraud order; this was affirmed by the circuit court of appeals. Hannegan appealed to the Supreme Court.

Jesse Donaldson, who replaced Robert Hannegan in 1947, narrowed the fraud order to apply only to contest mail. The Supreme Court, on March 8, 1948, handed down its decision in *Donaldson, Postmaster General* v. *Read Magazine, Inc.* Justice Hugo Black rendered the decision, which was agreed to by seven justices, with Justices Harold H. Burton and William O. Douglas dissenting. First, he declared that the company could not complain of the modification of the order since it was for their benefit and gave them the "very relief" they had sought "by limiting the number of persons" against whom the order was directed. He went on to say that the purpose of the mail fraud orders was to prevent injury to the public, that they were not a punishment. He felt in this case the advertisements were misleading to contestants as they had been so arranged as to divert the reader's attention from the fine print. He said that no doubt intelligent readers would not have been deceived, but the fraud statutes were to protect ordinary people. He stated that the mail fraud orders were not unconstitutional; they did not violate the First Amendment by authorizing a prior censorship, or the Fourth Amendment as authorizing unreasonable searches and seizures, or the due process clause of the Fifth Amendment. Nor did they deny trial by jury guaranteed by the Sixth Amendment nor inflict unusual punishments in violation of the Eighth Amendment. He pointed out that in 1872 Congress had first authorized the postmaster general to forbid delivery of registered letters and payment of money orders to persons trying to get money under false pretenses; then in 1895 this had been extended to all letters and then further expanded by the Securities and Exchange Act of 1934, which stated that the mails could not be used to sell or offer to buy a security that had not been registered, and the Federal Trade Commission Act of 1938, which made it unlawful for any firm to disseminate false advertising through the mails. In summary he said:

All of the foregoing statutes . . . manifest a purpose of Congress to utilize its powers particularly over the mails and in interstate commerce, to protect people against fraud. This governmental power has always been recognized in this country and is firmly established. The particular statutes here attacked have been regularly enforced by the executive officers and the courts for more than half a century. They are now part and parcel of our governmental fabric.[6]

In the field of medical frauds the postmaster general was greatly hampered by court decisions. Many considered these advertisements of cures for diseases the cruelest of all misleading advertisements, for they raised the hopes of the sick and old who spent needed money for medicine which, if not dangerous, was useless.[7] The Supreme Court had been consistent in overruling the postmaster general in such frauds, insisting on the necessity of proving intent to deceive. The classic case during this period was *Reilly, Postmaster* v. *Pinkus, Trading as American Health Aids Co.* (1949). This company, also known as Energy Food Center, advertised a reducing treatment consisting of one-half teaspoon of Kelp-I-Dine and a diet. The advertisements said a person could eat plenty, would never be hungry, and would yet lose three to five pounds a week. Two doctors testified for the department and stated that Kelp-I-Dine, consisting of granulated kelp, a natural seaweed product containing iodine, was valueless as a weight reducer and the diet could be dangerous.

Justice Black, giving the decision of the Court, admitted that some credulous persons might believe that Kelp-I-Dine would reduce them, but he did not think the fraud order should be enforced. The justice stated that in medical matters experimentation was important for progress. "It would amount to condemnation of new ideas without a trial to give the Postmaster General power to condemn new ideas as fraudulent solely because some cling to traditional opinions with unquestioning tenacity," he said. The Federal Trade Commission could issue cease and desist orders in a case like this without findings of fraud and that action was not nearly so drastic as fraud orders. He concluded, "The strikingly different consequences of the orders issued by the two agencies on the basis of analogous misrepresentations emphasize the importance of limiting Post Office Department orders to instances where actual fraud is clearly proved."[8]

The Court in *United States* v. *Halseth* (1952) limited the definition of lottery schemes, declaring gambling paraphernalia not an existing lottery. The defendant had mailed a punchboard together with a circular, an order blank, and a letter indicating how the addressee might obtain prizes by selling chances on the punchboard. Certain lucky numbers could reward the purchaser with a radio and three Rolpoint pens. The 1948 code, repeating the words of the 1909 code, had made it a criminal offense knowingly to mail matter "concerning any lottery." The Court declared that matter "concerning any lottery" meant an existing lottery and that the "mere mailing of information concerning such schemes and how they may be set up or the mailing of paraphernalia for such schemes does not violate the statute in question." Justice Sherman Minton, handing down the decision for seven justices (Douglas and Burton dissented), said that Congress could have added punchboards to the categories of nonmailable matter if it had wanted to. The fact that since 1915 the department had tried to have the statute amended to include gambling paraphernalia was evidence the postmaster general did not think it included punchboards.[9]

The postmaster general finally succeeded in getting strengthened the laws concerning the use of the mails to carry on gambling activities. An act of September 13, 1961, made it illegal under the lottery statute to use the mails to transmit "any record, paraphernalia, ticket, certificate, bills, slips, token, paper, writing, or other device used, or to be used, or adapted, devised, or designed for use in (a) bookmaking; or (b) wagering pools with respect to a sporting event; or (c) in a numbers, policy, bolita, or similar game." Another act passed on the same date provided punishment for anyone using the mails or interstate or foreign commerce with intent to distribute the proceeds of any unlawful activity or to commit any crime of violence to further any unlawful activity. Unlawful activity was defined as an action concerned with gambling, liquor on which no federal excise tax had been paid, narcotics, and prostitution.[10]

The department received a further setback when the Supreme Court declared the Post Office Department had to comply with the Administrative Procedures Act of June 11, 1946. In light of this ruling the procedure to be followed in postal fraud order cases was prescribed by law. Now, the parties could submit briefs, which meant they had to have access to records; they had the right to receive the initial decision of the trial examiners, and then they were given time to file exceptions. Thus sixty days might elapse before the postmaster general could issue the final order. Postmaster General Donaldson, in a letter of October 16, 1951, pointed out that speed was important if the public was to be protected against fraud and the debasement of morals and that in both cases injury done to the people was irreparable. He said that the statutes "authorizing the Postmaster General to purge such enterprises from the mails are summary and protective rather than remedial." He asked for legislation that would give the postmaster general power to have mail impounded when he was reasonably sure he had grounds for authorizing a fraud or an unlawful order.[11] A bill giving him that power twice passed the

House. In the Senate an amendment suggested by the American Bar Association and approved by the American Newspaper Publishers Association to provide for rapid court action was added, but the bill failed to pass.[12]

The postmaster general received more public support in his fight to prevent the use of the mails for the distribution of pornography. But even in this field the courts blocked many of the efforts of the Post Office Department to "purify" the mails. In dealing with frauds the courts differed with the postmaster general as to intent and procedure. In the case of obscenity the disagreement was over what constituted obscenity. Three methods used by the postmaster general in combating obscenity were challenged by the courts: the withholding of second-class mailing privileges, the barring of obscene matter from the mails, and criminal prosecution for violation of the nonmailable obscenity statute.[13]

The best-known case in which a postmaster general denied second-class mailing privileges to a magazine on grounds of obscenity was that of *Esquire*. Postmaster General Frank C. Walker considered the magazine obscene and issued an order to Esquire, Inc., to show cause why its second-class mailing privileges, granted in 1933, should not be revoked. A three-man board heard thirty-eight witnesses and reviewed 2,500 pages of testimony and handed down a decision, two to one, that second-class mailing privileges should be continued. Postmaster General Walker, however, announced that as of February 28, 1944, they would be revoked. He gave as his reason that the magazine had not met the fourth condition specified in the law of 1879 for receiving second-class rates, i.e., for the "dissemination of information of a public character, or devoted to literature, the sciences, arts, or some special industry." Subscribing to the premise that low rates had been given publishers "because of the special contribution to the public welfare which Congress believes is derived from the newspaper and other periodical press," Walker made it a requirement that a particular periodical, in order to receive the low rates, must deserve them.[14]

Esquire, Inc., brought suit in the federal district court in the

District of Columbia to enjoin the postmaster general from carrying out the order. That court upheld the postmaster general, but the court of appeals reversed the decision. By the time the case reached the Supreme Court Postmaster General Walker had been replaced by Robert Hannegan. Justice William O. Douglas gave the opinion of an unanimous Court in *Hannegan* v. *Esquire* (1946). He said that an examination of the case made it clear that the issue was not whether the magazine published "information of a public character" or was devoted to literature or the arts but whether the contents were "good or bad." He pointed out that to uphold the order of revocation would be to grant the power of censorship to the postmaster general. "Such a power is so abhorrent to our tradition that a purpose to grant it should not be easily inferred," he said. He reviewed the acts that had given special rates to newspapers and decided that Congress had not intended to give the postmaster general the power to decide whether the publication contributed to the public good. He concluded: "The validity of the obscenity laws is recognition that the mails may not be used to satisfy all tastes, no matter how perverted. But Congress has left the Postmaster General with no power to prescribe standards for the literature or the art which a mailable periodical disseminates."[15]

This decision practically destroyed one weapon postmasters general had used to censor publications. Since then it has been very difficult for a publication which kept up regular mailings to lose second-class mailing privileges once they have been granted. The postmaster general still has considerable discretion in the granting of those privileges.

In 1950, however, the postmaster general received another weapon to use in his fight against purveyors of obscene matter. Up to that time he had had the authority to return to senders mail addressed to concerns engaged in selling obscene materials under fictitious names but not to those using their own names. A great deal of this matter was sent first class and therefore could not be opened by a postmaster. The law, passed on August 16, 1950, said that when the postmaster general was convinced that a firm was attempting to obtain money through the mail for obscene matter he could direct the local postmaster to return mail directed to that firm. He was to mark it "unlawful" and return to the sender. Money orders addressed to the firm would not be honored. These unlawful orders or mail blocks were similar to fraud orders issued against lottery dealers or firms using the mail to defraud.[16]

In 1955 the obscenity nonmailable statute was broadened to include phonograph records. A court of appeals had ruled, in *Alpers* v. *United States* (175 F. 2d 137), that records had not been specifically enumerated in the statutes prohibiting transportation of obscene matter. Although the Supreme Court (5 to 3) had overruled the Alpers decision, Postmaster General Donaldson had asked for a clearer statement in the statutes dealing with the mailing of obscene matter. He said that under the existing definition the Post Office Department found it difficult to prevent the shipment through the mails of certain types of matter it thought obscene. He had enclosed with his letter a draft of a bill which became a law on June 28, 1955. The first section declared nonmailable: "Every obscene, lewd, lascivious, indecent, filthy or vile article, matter, thing, device, or substance." This replaced the earlier version which read: "Every letter, packet, or package, or other mail matter containing any filthy, vile, or indecent thing, device, or substance."[17]

In 1956 (July 27) the Post Office Department received authority to impound mail to help enforce the act of August 16, 1950, the one providing for unlawful orders for dealers in smut. This weapon was one of those suggested by the Kefauver subcommittee investigating juvenile delinquency. This committee found that minors were receiving a great deal of pornographic matter. This act provided that when the postmaster general thought action was necessary to enforce the law against mailing obscene matter he could issue an order that mail addressed to a person should be detained by the postmaster for twenty days. Notice of the order, specifying the reasons, was to be sent to the person whose mail was detained. The order would expire in twenty days unless the postmaster general acquired from the United States district court, where the mail was being detained, an order extending the period. The person whose mail was being detained had the right to examine the mail and receive any that was not connected with his unlawful activities. An amendment, added by Senator A. S. "Mike" Monroney of Oklahoma, specified that the provisions of the act should not apply to "mail addressed to publishers or distributors of publications which have entry as second-class matter . . . or to publishers or distributors of copyrighted books." When he presented the amendment he said this was to "safeguard against 'political censorship' by impounding mail matter in which editorial opinion offended the ones with impounding power."[18]

Impounding was an important weapon, directed, as the author of a book dealing with smut peddlers points out, at the hit-and-run operators who hoped to make a fortune out of a "one-shot mailing list." Most of the dealers had several trade names registered, and when the Post Office acted with an unlawful order against a firm under one name, it took its profits, changed its name and address, and sent out another mailing. The power to impound the mail allowed the Post Office to stop the operation immediately while formal proceedings were being carried out.[19]

Dealers in obscene matter, quick to take advantage of any loophole in a law, maintained that the pornographic matter they distributed was copyrighted and therefore exempt from impounding proceedings, for the act had excepted "publishers or distributors of copyrighted books." This was corrected in an act passed August 27, 1958, which deleted those words and left excepted only "mail addressed to publishers of publications which have entry as second-class matter" and to "mail addressed to the agents of such publishers."[20]

The next day a reform long desired by the Post Office Department was written into law; that was one which would make it possible to try violators of the statutes on mailing obscene matter not only at the place from which it was mailed but also at the place it was delivered. Most of the obscene matter was mailed from California or New York and the courts there were swamped with such cases; also, the climate of opinion there seemed to be more lenient toward mailers of obscene matter. Congressmen pointed out that the real crime was committed where the obscene matter was received, for that was where the danger to morals occurred.

This reform was also sponsored by the Kefauver subcommittee. Kefauver's bill, cosponsored by Senator Langer of North Dakota, would permit prosecution where mail was received and also would protect juveniles from receiving pornographic matter. The bill that became law did not include the double penalties for mailers of obscene matter to juveniles, but it permitted prosecution of mailers of obscene mail in a federal district court, in any one of several places: where the mail was deposited, where it was received, or in any district through which it passed.[21]

In 1957 the Post Office Department revised its procedure of dealing with nonmailable matter, chiefly obscene books and magazines. Previously the Post Office Department had held hearings from time to time but on an informal basis. Now, the mailer was to receive written notice of the "alleged reasons for barring his mail." He then would be entitled to a hearing within ten days. In the case of periodicals, the examiner was to make his decision within two days after the hearing. Also, no local postmaster was to decide on his own initiative to exclude material from the mails. A sample had to be sent to the department's assistant general counsel in charge of the fraud and mailability division. If the latter felt there was "probable cause" he was to order a detailed notice served on the mailer. The sender then might answer the allegations in writing and demand a hearing. In every case the mailer might appeal the decision of the examiner to the general counsel. The latter would decide if a fraud or unlawful order should be issued.[22]

The following spring (April, 1958) the Post Office Department established the position of judicial officer to assure a fairer hearing to persons accused of sending obscene or fraudulent material through the mails. The purpose was to separate the prosecuting and judging roles and to reduce the time required to arrive at a final department decision. Complaints would be initiated by the general counsel's office and hearings would be held; then there could be an appeal to the judicial officer. He was to be the postmaster general's "alter ego." Charles D. Ablard was appointed to this new office. The office was legalized by act of Congress in July, 1960.[23]

Arthur E. Summerfield (1953–1961), postmaster general during President Eisenhower's administrations, was zealous in his campaign to rid the mails of obscene matter. His term of service was referred to as the high point of "Comstockery."[24] It was during his administration that the Supreme Court in *Roth* v. *United States* (1957) upheld for the first time the "right of the Federal Government to prosecute, criminally, in obscenity cases." In this case also was handed down the classic definition of obscenity. Samuel Roth had been one of the most notorious purveyors of obscene matter and had been convicted several times in both state and federal courts since 1928. In 1948 orders excluding certain books from the mails had been issued against him by the postmaster general. Only one of the books had been excluded because of obscenity. The others had been held nonmailable on account of fraudulent advertising; they had been misrepresented as salacious. Roth had applied for an injunction to prevent execution of the orders, but this had been denied by both the district court and the Court of Appeals, Second Circuit. The orders had been declared valid. The latter court had declared that the fraud orders were easier to sustain because "standards of fraud are at least somewhat clearer than those of obscenity."[25]

In 1956 Roth was indicted and charged with "mailing books, periodicals, and photographs (and circulars advertising some of them) alleged to be 'obscene, lewd, lascivious, filthy, and of an indecent character.'" He was sentenced to fine and imprisonment. The United States Court of Appeals, Second Circuit, in *United States* v. *Roth* upheld the lower court.[26] Roth applied for release on bail while the case was being appealed to the Supreme Court. This was granted by Justice Harlan because the judges of the circuit court had declared they were foreclosed from giving an opinion on the constitutionality of the obscenity law because of prior decisions of the Supreme Court. Roth's appeal to the Supreme Court was supported by an impressive array of *amicus curiae* briefs, submitted by the American Book Publishers Council, Authors League, *Playboy* magazine, and the American Civil Liberties Union.[27] This case was associated with that of David S. Alberts, accused of violating a California statute.

The defendants' lawyers claimed the obscenity statute violated the First, Fifth, Ninth, and Tenth Amendments. Justice William J. Brennan, Jr., who delivered the majority opinion, summarily dismissed the arguments that the obscenity statute violated the latter amendments and concentrated on the First Amendment. He stated that this was the first time the question of whether or not obscenity was protected by the First Amendment had been squarely presented to the Court. The Court stated positively it was not so protected; obscenity had been rejected as not having social importance. As evidence he pointed out that Congress from 1842 to 1956 had passed twenty laws restraining obscenity and that all forty-eight states had such laws. Sex and obscenity were not the same, he said. He defined obscene matter as "material which deals with sex in a manner appealing to prurient interest." He said the lower courts had applied the tests for obscenity that had been laid down in previous cases, that the trial judge had told the jury to decide if the work as a whole would offend an average person on the basis of present-day community standards. He concluded that the obscenity statute did not "offend constitutional safeguards" and that it was "a proper exercise of the postal power delegated to Congress by Art. I, sec. 8, cl. 7."

Justice Harlan dissented on the ground that the regulation of obscenity was beyond the power of the federal government. Justice Douglas (with whom Justice Black concurred) declared the obscenity statute violated the constitutional guarantees of free speech and press. He said: "The test of obscenity the Court endorsed today gives the censor too free range over a vast domain."[28]

Although the Court upheld the constitutionality of the obscenity statute, still the Roth decision was credited by many with starting a flood of pornography in the mails. The definition of obscenity was a liberal one. The "Roth test" required that a book had to be taken as a whole, it had to be judged in accordance with community standards of morality and the effect on average adults rather than the susceptible. Also the book had to be without any

174

redeeming literary, artistic, scientific, or social significance. This left as obscene only what Justice Potter Stewart later called "hardcore" pornography.

Judges of district and circuit courts, in accordance with the Roth decision, gave a liberal interpretation of the obscenity statute and thus hindered the efforts of Postmaster General Summerfield to purify the mails. Two rulings of the department concerning magazines were not upheld by district court judges. The publishing and distributing companies of *Confidential* magazine were indicted by a federal grand jury on the charge of sending through the mail information on abortions. An article in the magazine entitled "The Pill that Ends Unwanted Pregnancy" told how a pill that had been developed to treat leukemia in children had been used by criminal abortionists without the usual risk of being caught. Federal Judge Joseph Sam Perry in Chicago ruled that the article did not "come within the limits of the law prohibiting the mailing of obscenities."[29]

The Post Office Department tried to bar from the mails the November, 1958, issue of *Playboy*. Action against the magazine had been urged by the Churchmen's Commission for Decent Publications, an organization established in 1957 representing twenty Protestant denominations. The issue contained semi-nude photographs of Brigitte Bardot, clips from her films. District Judge David A. Pine issued a temporary restraining order forbidding the postal officials from acting against the magazine for five days; by that time all copies of the November issue would be mailed. Thurman Arnold, for the magazine, argued that "some kind of hearing must be a prerequisite to Post Office action." The department's appeal to the United States court of appeals for a stay of Judge Pine's order was rejected.[30]

The Justice Department prevented another case, about which there was considerable publicity, from even getting into the courts. It refused to back up the rulings of the Post Office Department in the case of the seizure by the New York City post office of two thousand cards sent out by United Artists. The cards contained a colored photograph of Goya's 155-year-old famous painting of "The Naked Maja." They were being sent out to advertize a motion picture of the same name, which related that Francisco Goya had used the Duchess of Alba as a model for the painting. The action of the New York post office had been upheld by the department examiner and the judicial officer. The inspector had said that the postcard could not be considered a masterpiece— it was "simply a color picture of a nude woman." Since we live in a clothed civilization, he said, a nude woman would strike the average person as indecent. United Artists appealed and the Justice Department declared the cards were "neither obscene, lewd, lascivious, nor filthy." The cards were released.[31]

Postmaster General Summerfield was rebuffed by both the district and circuit court of appeals in the case of *Lady Chatterley's Lover*. This novel by D. H. Lawrence had been circulating openly in England and clandestinely in the United States since 1928. Finally in 1959 Grove Press published an unexpurgated version of it. The post office seized 164 copies of the book and declared nonmailable not only the book but also the advertising circulars of the book put out by the book club, Readers' Subscription, Inc. Postmaster General Summerfield had issued the order over the protest of the judicial officer, Charles D. Ablard. "Any literary merit the book may have," Mr. Summerfield said in his opinion, "is far outweighed by the pornographic and smutty passages and words so that the book taken as a whole, is an obscene and filthy work."[32]

Judge Frederick van Pelt Bryan, on July 21, held the ban "illegal and void." He declared the book was "neither obscene, lewd, indecent nor filthy in content or character." He noted in a thirty-three-page decision that it was the first time since 1933 that a book of "comparable standing" had been alleged to be so obscene as to warrant banning under the federal obscenity statutes.[33] The order of the district court was upheld by unanimous vote of the Court of Appeals, Second Circuit. Justice Clark in his decision in *Grove Press* v. *Christenberry* (1960) rejected the argument of the Post Office Department that "an agency action supported by substantial evidence is beyond judicial review." The lower court, he said, had followed the Roth test when examining *Lady Chatterley's Lover* and added: "We agree with the court below in believing and holding that definitions of obscenity consistent with modern intellectual standards and morals neither require nor permit such a restriction." He also stated that there was little relation between carrying the mails and determining whether or not a work of literature or art was obscene. He concluded: "And courts, not post offices, are the proper places for a determination of what is and is not protected by the Constitution."[34] The case of *Lady Chatterley's Lover* was not reviewed by the Supreme Court.

The power of the postmaster general to issue unlawful orders was taken up by the Supreme Court in connection with nudist magazines. On June 23, 1953, the Post Office Department had ruled that all mail addressed to the publishers of *Sunshine and Health* and *Sun Magazine* be stamped "unlawful" and returned to the sender or to the dead letter office and no payments of money orders to the firm be made. These magazines were published by a Baptist minister as a nonprofit venture to publicize the benefits of nudism. The Post Office banned them because they carried pictures of nude men and women; there was nothing obscene in the text. In this case (*Summerfield* v. *Sunshine Book Co.*, 1954) the court of appeals affirmed the decision of the District Court of the District of Columbia on the basis that the statute did not authorize the banning of future issues of a magazine because an earlier issue had been alleged to be obscene, nor could payment on money orders be refused.[35]

Then the postmaster general directed the postmaster at Mays Landing, New Jersey, to treat as nonmailable issues of *Sunshine and Health* for February, 1955, and the issues of January and February of *Sun Magazine*. The ban was upheld by both the district court and Circuit Court of Appeals, Second Circuit. Judge Danaher, who had dissented in the unlawful-order case in 1954, rendered the decision in this case, *Sunshine Book Co.* v. *Summerfield* (1957). He stated that obscenity was not "within the area of constitutionally protected speech and press" and photographs of nude men and women were obscene "when judged by ordinary community standards" and magazines containing such pictures were nonmailable.[36]

The Supreme Court decided summarily without argument. In a *per curiam* decision it overruled the decision of the lower courts. Copies of the magazine had been filed with the Court and supposedly the justices had seen them. Evidently they did not find them obscene. The decision was interpreted to mean that the Supreme Court was insisting on a narrow definition of obscenity following the rule in the Roth case, that it was not going to permit censorship of anything but "hard-core" pornography.[37]

On the same day the Court also reversed decisions of the lower courts in a case of a magazine dealing with homosexuality, *One, Inc.* v. *Otto K. Oleson* (1958). The postmaster at Los Angeles considered the October issue of *One* obscene and returned copies to the publisher. The publisher sought an injunction against the postmaster, but it was denied by both the district court and the Court of Appeals, Ninth Circuit. Judge Rose for the Court declared that although the magazine purportedly dealt with homosexuality from a scientific point of view, some articles in the magazine "were nothing more than cheap pornography calculated to promote Lesbianism and other forms of homosexuality."[38]

These one-sentence decisions of the Supreme Court nullifying the ban of the Post Office Department on the mailing of three magazines the postmaster general considered obscene aroused the ire of congressmen who feared youth was being corrupted by the circulation of such "filth." The postmaster general reported that the department that year had received 70,000 complaints, that as many as one million children received "pornographic filth" in the family mailbox, and that operators realized one-half a billion dollars annually on mail-order smut.[39] Many bills were introduced in both houses of Congress; most of them provided for stiffer penalties for mailing obscene or crime-inciting matter and several would make mandatory a prison sentence for repeaters. Senator Keating of New York pointed out that most offenders got off with just a fine and that the only way to curb these fly-by-night operators was to put them in jail.[40]

A bill drafted by the Post Office Department was presented in the House by Mrs. Kathryn E. Granahan of Pennsylvania. It was to make more effective the law of 1956. Her bill would permit the holding of the mail for forty-five days and the court, if it were in the public interest, could extend it beyond that time. According to the Granahan bill a person would have to prove that the post-master general had acted "arbitrarily and capriciously" in issuing the original order detaining the mail; the burden of proof, there-fore, would be on the mailer. The bill passed the House with no debate and only one dissenting vote; that was cast by John V. Lindsay, Republican from New York City. He asked "whether it was not a 'rather drastic new concept' to shift the legal burden to the mailer to prove that his material should not be banned."[41]

Opposition in the Senate led to an amendment to the House bill, which really amounted to a new bill. Senator Monroney of Oklahoma was credited with the amendment that made the bill satisfactory to the American Civil Liberties Union, the American Bar Association, and the Justice Department, which had ques-tioned the constitutionality of some features of the House bill. The amendment provided that in preparation for the enforcement of the obscenity mail statutes, the postmaster general could apply to the district court for a temporary restraining order and pre-liminary injunction directing the detention of the defendant's incoming mail. The defendant would be allowed to open his im-pounded mail and remove any matter not related to the offense with which he was charged. This had the advantage of making necessary only one judicial action rather than a multitude of judicial proceedings; there was no time limit on the detention and it gave the court supervision over the power to detain mail. As had been true in the 1956 act publishers enjoying second-class mailing privileges were exempt. The House with no debate concurred in the Senate amendment and it became a law on July 14, 1960.[42]

The Supreme Court in 1961–1962 denied writs of certiorari in three cases involving the use of the mails for advertisements giv-ing information where obscene pictures and smutty books might be obtained. Judges in the circuit courts had pointed out that the obscenity law made it a crime not only to mail obscene matter but also to give information where such could be obtained. The fact that the advertisements exaggerated and the pictures were not as obscene as the advertisements claimed made no difference. Also, it was immaterial whether the pictures portrayed a male rather than a female if they were posed so as to appeal to prurient interest. In the cases the Roth test had been applied in the district courts. In every case the accused was convicted of violating the obscenity statute. The constitutionality of the law of 1958, which permitted trial in the district where obscene matter was received or in transit, was also upheld.[43]

In 1962 the Supreme Court for the first time handed down a plenary review of an order of the Post Office Department holding matter nonmailable when obscene. In the Roth case the Court had specifically declared constitutional the act providing punishment for using the mails for the distribution of smut. The Court had overruled decisions of the lower courts where matter had been banned from the mails as being obscene, but they had done so in brief statements without discussing the constitutionality of the statute. In *Manual Enterprises, Inc.* v. *Day, Postmaster General*, a case similar to *One, Inc.* v. *Oleson*, a long opinion was given. On March 25, 1960, the postmaster at Alexandria, Virginia, withheld delivery of six parcels containing copies of some magazines containing photographs of nude or near nude males, giving names of the models and photographers and addresses of the latter. The postmaster sent copies of *MANual, Trim* and *Grecian Guild Pictorial* to the general counsel and the judicial officer declared these magazines obscene. The district court and the court of appeals for the District of Columbia upheld the ban. These decisions were reversed by the Supreme Court by a six-to-one decision. Justice Harlan, for the majority, first applied the test established in the Roth case to these magazines and decided they could not be "deemed so offensive on their face as to affront current community standards of decency—a quality that we shall hereafter refer to as 'patent offensiveness' or 'indecency.' " He went on to say: "Obscenity under the federal statute thus requires proof of two distinct elements—: (1) patent offensiveness; and (2) 'prurient interest appeal.' Both must conjoin before challenged material can be found 'obscene.' " He then discussed the issue of advertis-

ing and concluded that one could hardly expect magazine publishers to investigate all of their advertisers.

Justice Brennan concurred in the reversal of the decisions of
the lower courts but raised the issue of procedure and procedural
safeguards. To him the main question was whether or not Congress, when it declared matter nonmailable, authorized the postmaster general to censor obscenity. Justice Tom C. Clark, in his
dissent, stated that the Supreme Court, in spite of a clear congressional mandate, in that decision required the United States Post
Office "to be the world's largest disseminator of smut and Grand
Informer of the names and places where obscene material may
be found."[44]

The Supreme Court in March, 1966, revised some of its recent
decisions by upholding (5 to 4) the conviction of Ralph Ginzburg,
New York publisher of *Eros*. Mrs. Granaham said that in 1962
she had called the attention of the Post Office Department to this
fancy, expensive, new quarterly "devoted to the joy of love and
sex" but that the department in light of the decision in the case
of *Lady Chatterley's Lover* had been reluctant to prosecute.[45] The
following year, however, Postmaster General J. Edward Day
(1961–1963) instructed the Justice Department to bring criminal
charges against the owner for mailing copies of an obscene magazine. Ginzburg had been sentenced to five years in prison and to
fines amounting to $28,000 by Judge Ralph C. Body, federal dis-
trict court in Philadelphia. The conviction had been upheld by
the Court of Appeals, Third Circuit, in November, 1964. Ginzburg's appeal to the Supreme Court had been supported by the
American Civil Liberties Union, which had urged the Court to
abandon its test of obscenity laid down in the Roth case and to
declare all published material protected by the First Amendment
unless it created a " 'clear and present danger' of antisocial conduct."[46]

Instead the Supreme Court in *Ralph Ginzburg* v. *United States*
(1966) refused to abandon the obscenity test of the Roth case,
"whether to the average person, applying contemporary community standards, the dominant theme of the material taken as

a whole appeals to the prurient interest." An interesting part in the Ginzburg decision was the role played by advertising, which the Court had entirely eliminated in the Manual Enterprise, Inc., case. Justice Brennan said that in most cases since the Roth decision the Court has "regarded the materials as sufficient in themselves for the determination of the questions." But in this case the question of the setting, that is the method of sale and publicity, was considered as an "aid in determining the question of obscenity." He concluded his decision as follows:

It is important to stress that this analysis simply elaborates the test by which the obscenity vel non of the material must be judged. Where an exploitation of interests in titillation by pornography is shown with respect to material lending itself to such exploitation through pervasive treatment or description of sexual matters, such evidence may support the determination that the material is obscene even though in other contexts the material would escape such condemnation.

Justices Black, Douglas, Harlan, and Stewart wrote dissenting opinions, stating that Ginzburg's conviction violated the First Amendment. Justice Stewart thought the government could constitutionally suppress "hard-core" pornography but only that. To sentence Ginzburg not for mailing the materials but for commercial exploitation of erotica was to deny him due process, he declared.[47] It was the most recently appointed justice, Abe Fortas, who shifted the balance of the Court and brought about the conviction of Ginzburg. This was a surprise, for Justice Fortas, before he was appointed to the Supreme Court, had filed an *amicus curiae* brief on behalf of *Playboy* and had called the federal obscenity law unconstitutional.[48] The Ginzburg decision added to the Roth test another test of obscenity. The Ginzburg rule stated that "a publication advertised in an obscene way could be barred from the mails, and the purveyors could be prosecuted."[49]

Congress since 1962 has attacked the problem of obscene mail matter in a different way, putting the responsibility on the receiver of such mail. In that year the Senate added to the Postal Rates bill, which carried the Communist political propaganda clause, an amendment entitled "Notice with Respect to Obscene Matter Distributed by Mail and Detention Thereof":

In order to alert the recipients of mail and the general public to the fact that large quantities of obscene, lewd, lascivious, and indecent matter are being introduced into this country from abroad and disseminated in the United States by means of the United States mails, the Postmaster General shall publicize such fact (1) by appropriate notices posted in post offices, and (2) by notifying recipients of mail, whenever he deems it appropriate in order to carry out the purposes of this section, that the United States mails may contain such obscene, lewd, lascivious, or indecent matter. Any person may file a written request with his local post office to detain obscene, lewd, lascivious, or indecent matter addressed to him, and the Postmaster General shall detain and dispose of such matter for such period as the request is in effect. The Postmaster General shall permit the return of mail containing obscene, lewd, lascivious, or indecent matter, to local post offices, without cost to the recipient thereof. Nothing in this section shall be deemed to authorize the Postmaster General to open, inspect, or censor any mail except on specific request by the addressee thereof.[50]

In the following Congresses Representative Glenn Cunningham of Nebraska introduced bills carrying this same principle even further. His bills "would permit a person to return unsolicited mail he regards as morally offensive and have future mailings stopped." His bills passed the House but were buried in Senate committee.[51] In February, 1967, the general counsel of the Post Office Department supported this new approach to control obscenity. He said that "hardcore" pornography was no longer much of a problem and the mailing of matter in the "grey area" did not violate the obscenity law. He felt there was little the department could or should do to restrict the reading of a citizen for the department had no desire to be a censor. A person who liked to be titillated by receiving such smut should be allowed to have it sent to him by mail, but the people who did not wish such matter or advertisements of such matter in their homes should have their right of privacy protected.[52]

Representative Cunningham succeeded in getting his bill adopted as an amendment to the Postal Revenue and Federal

Salary Act, which became a law on December 16, 1967. It went into effect on April 15, 1968. The amendment read as follows:

*Prohibition of pandering advertisements in the mails*

(a) Whoever for himself, or by his agents or assigns, mails or causes to be mailed any pandering advertisement which offers for sale matter which the addressee in his sole discretion believes to be erotically arousing or sexually provocative shall be subject to an order of the Postmaster General to refrain from further mailings of such materials to designated addresses thereof.

(b) Upon receipt of notice from an addressee that he had received such mail matter, determined by the addressee in his sole discretion to be of the character described in subsection (a) of this section, the Postmaster General shall issue an order, if requested by the addressee, to the sender thereof, directing the sender and his agents or assigns to refrain from further mailings to the named addressees.

(c) The order of the Postmaster General shall expressly prohibit the sender and his agents or assigns from making any further mailings to the designated addressees, effective on the thirtieth calendar day after receipt of the order. The order of the Postmaster General shall also direct the sender and his agents or assigns to delete immediately the names of the designated addressees from all mailing lists owned or controlled by the sender or his agents or assigns and, further, shall prohibit the sender and his agents or assigns from the sale, rental, exchange, or other transaction involving mailing lists bearing the names of the designated addressees.

(d) Whenever the Postmaster General believes that the sender or anyone acting on his behalf has violated or is violating the order given under this section, he shall serve upon the sender, by registered or certified mail, a complaint stating the reasons for his belief and request that any response thereto be filed in writing with the Postmaster General within fifteen days after the date of such service. If the Postmaster General, after appropriate hearing, if requested by the sender, and without a hearing if such a hearing is not requested, thereafter determines that the order given has been or is being violated, he is authorized to request the Attorney General to make application, and the Attorney General is authorized to make application, to a district court of the United States for an order directing compliance with such notice . . . .

The order could be issued by the court either in the district where the matter was mailed or where received.[53]

According to postal regulations following this law advertisements of pornography must be contained in an envelope on the outside of which is printed some sort of warning, such as:

ADULTS ONLY

NOTICE TO ADDRESSEE

This envelope contains an UNSOLICITED offer for Adult Merchandise. If you do not wish this mail DO NOT OPEN! Simply mark this envelope "REFUSED," sign your initials and return to your Mailman. Upon the return of this envelope, we will endeavor to remove your name from our files. Thank you![54]

Some publishers and mail-order concerns instituted a suit to overturn the law of 1967. They claimed they had been deluged by the orders from individuals to stop sending out their advertisements and that some citizens had taken advantage of the law to attack the reception of advertising matter which was in no way obscene. To remove a name from their mailing list cost five dollars, they declared. They maintained the law violated the constitutional guarantees of freedom of speech and press.[55]

The Supreme Court, in a unanimous decision (*Rowan* v. *United States Post Office*) handed down May 4, 1970, upheld the constitutionality of the law. Chief Justice Warren E. Burger declared that "the asserted right of a mailer stops at the outer boundary of every person's domain" and that the "right of every person 'to be let alone' must be placed in the scales with the right of others to communicate."[56]

The so-called Goldwater amendment to the Post Office Reorganization Act took this individual responsibility one step farther. Now, an individual, on his own behalf and on behalf of any children in his household under nineteen, may file with the Postal Service a card indicating that he does not wish to receive any "sexually oriented advertisements." This will give him blanket protection and he need not wait until he receives smut before he files his statement that he does not wish to receive any. The Post Office will compile a list of such names which mailers of such matter may purchase. Any person who mails such matter to a person on the list and also anyone who manufactures such "sexually related mail matter" knowing it would be deposited in the mail in violation of the act would be subject to punishment (maximum fine of $5,000 and/or imprisonment up to five years for the first offense). Also a mailer of a "sexual oriented advertisement" is required to indicate on the outside wrapper his name and address and the character of the matter.

Civil action may also be taken by the Postal Service against any person it believes is violating the act. The court may (1) direct the defendant "to refrain from mailing any sexually oriented advertisement to a specific addressee," or (2) direct the postmaster of the office where the matter is mailed to refuse to accept such advertisements for mailing; or (3) direct the postmaster of the office where such mail is received to return the letters to the senders.[57]

This may well be the solution to the nonmailability of obscene matter. It is difficult to know what the Court may decide is obscenity. Also there is a growing sentiment that an adult should be allowed to read what he pleases. This opinion was expressed by the Federal Commission on Obscenity and Pornography, created in 1967, which in its recent report declared: "We believe there is no warrant for continued governmental interference of the full freedom of adults to read, obtain or view what materials they wish."[58]

186

# The United States
# Postal Service

The American postal system celebrated its bicentennial on July 26, 1975. In some respects the new United States Postal Service resembles the one established by the Continental Congress rather than the United States Post Office Department. The postmaster general from 1775 to 1782 had more power, e.g., the designation of post roads and post riders, than did the ones from 1782 to 1970. He also was not involved in politics or policy determination. The Continental Congress did investigate and did meddle with the postal system, but it did not make regulations tying the hands of the postmaster general. The postmaster general in 1970 had no control over postage rates, over salaries or working conditions of employees, over transportation facilities, or over post offices and post roads; these were determined by Congress. Congressmen, also, had much to say about the appointment of postmasters and rural mail carriers, although they were technically in the civil service system. The postmaster general, as a member of the president's cabinet, was a political appointee and there was little continuity in that office.

Postmaster General Lawrence O'Brien (1965–1968) startled politicians when he suggested on April 3, 1967, that the Post Office should be a nonprofit government corporation managed by a professional executive and that the postmaster general should cease to be a member of the president's cabinet and should be a businessman, not a politician. He pointed out that the Founding Fathers realized that aside from defense few functions of the government were as important as the postal service and that the Constitution had given Congress a mandate to establish post offices and post roads. He stated that the big difficulty with the Post Office was that the postmaster general had too little control over the postal service—that Congress had kept almost complete control in its own hands. It operated, said O'Brien, within a "restrictive jungle of legislation and custom" and unless drastic changes were made a catastrophe would result.[1]

President Johnson took his postmaster general's suggestion seriously and appointed a commission headed by Frederick R. Kappel, chairman of the board of directors of the American Telephone and Telegraph Company, to study the question. The report, made public on July 16, 1968, followed the suggestions made by Postmaster General O'Brien. It recommended a government-owned corporation similar to the Tennessee Valley Authority which could raise its own capital, set postal rates, make contracts for transporting the mail, and set wages and working conditions for postal employees, who would be removed from the civil service.[2] Congressmen who had hailed Postmaster General O'Brien's speech now tended to look askance at Congress's potential loss of power. Congressional attitude was well expressed by Senator McGee, chairman of the Senate Committee on Post Office and Civil Service, when he said: "It is not the Post Office Department which establishes policies of postal service; it is Congress. It is we who answer to the people, not the Postmaster General."[3]

Postal reform bills were introduced in both houses early in the Ninety-first Congress. The major bill considered by the Senate committee followed the recommendation of the president's commission and provided for the creation of a corporation with full power. The committee blamed the catastrophe toward which the postal system was racing on its poor management and on its backwardness, for it operated in the same manner as it had one hundred years before. They recognized that one major cause was the unproductive labor-management relations due to the highly unionized postal service, which exerted its influence not at the bargaining table but with Congress.[4]

In the House, however, the Committee on Post Office and Civil Service was unwilling to turn the postal service into a corporation. The chairman, Thaddeus Dulski of New York, said the public had become "bewitched" by the word "corporation." He favored reform but not replacement. His bill, introduced on January 3, 1969, would keep the postmaster general in the cabinet, prohibit political recommendations, and give the Post Office some fiscal independence, but Congress would still determine salaries of postal employees and have a veto over postal rates set by a commission.[5]

President Nixon, on May 27, 1969, sent a special message to the House asking for a "total reform of the Nation's postal system." He had made the first move toward eliminating politics from the Post Office by announcing shortly after his inauguration that he was not going to ask congressmen for their recommendations in postmaster or rural carrier appointments. Now he urged that the postmaster general be eliminated from the president's cabinet and that the Post Office become a government-owned corporation. With the message he sent in a bill "carefully drawn to permit the Post Office to be run in an efficient, responsible, businesslike manner in the public interest." The bill, introduced by Morris Udall of Arizona, was cosponsored by Gerald R. Ford of Michigan and Ken Hechler of West Virginia; it was referred to committee.[6]

Thus the lines were drawn—not on the basis of party affiliation, for a government postal corporation had been endorsed by both President Johnson (Democrat) and Nixon (Republican) and their postmasters general. It was opposed by those in Congress, especially in the House, who saw it as a revolutionary measure, removing the governmental body that was closest to the people from public control through their representatives. Rural America feared service in the country would be cut under the new plan. It was also opposed by the third-class mailers who, through their lobby, had received favorable rates from Congress.[7]

The most vehement opposition came from the postal workers, whose unions had been able to exert political pressure on Congress when asking for salary adjustments. They objected to being removed from the civil service and felt that without the right to strike they would be at the mercy of the postal corporation. George Meany, president of the AFL-CIO, appeared before the House committee in opposition to the government bill; he said labor wanted the government to continue to carry the mail. "Stripping Congress of its continuous right of review of postal operations," he stated, "would work an injustice on American mail users and taxpayers because they would lose a highly important opportunity to contribute their views through elected officials."[8]

The House committee held public hearings for four months and then went into executive session on the postal bill. The two major proposals being considered were Representative Dulski's bill (H.R. 4) and the one sponsored by Postmaster General Blount (H.R. 11750). President Nixon in September again appealed for passage of the postal corporation measure. He was supported by the Citizens' Committee for Postal Reform headed by Lawrence O'Brien and Thruston B. Morton, former chairmen of the Democratic and Republican national committees. On April 8 Representative Dulski's bill was reported to the House, evidently by a very close vote of the committee.[9]

Meanwhile a crisis developed that drastically changed the situation. Led by postal workers in New York City, wildcat strikes took place in many parts of the United States. There were bitter denunciations on both sides. The postmaster general blamed Congress for being so slow in passing a postal reform bill; Representative Dulski said Blount was stubborn and had insisted on his own program with no changes. Finally an agreement was reached between the government and the seven craft unions. All federal employees would receive a 6 percent raise, retroactive to December 27, 1969, and the postal employees would receive an additional 8 percent raise as part of the postal reorganization act. This "little bribery," as Representative William Scott of Virginia called the agreement, won the support of the craft unions, although the members of the two industrial unions were disgruntled.[10]

In the House the Committee on Post Office and Civil Service immediately (April 16) began work on a new postal bill presented by the administration. Progress was rapid and the bill was reported out by a vote of 13 to 10. Debate began in the House in committee of the whole on June 16, 1970. The bill avoided the word "corporation" and proposed the United States Postal Service, an independent establishment within the Executive branch. There was comparatively little debate on the measure and so little interest that there had to be several calls for quorum. Congressmen seemed to have become weary of the issue and wanted to get rid of it so the blame for postal inefficiency could be put on someone else. All attempts to eliminate the part of the bill dealing with reform, leaving only the pay raises for postal employees, were defeated. Only one important amendment was adopted and that stated that every employee in the Postal Service had the right to form, join, or refrain from joining a union. Many feared that the bill would make possible a union shop. After three days of debate the bill passed the House, on June 18, by vote of 360 to 24, with 45 not voting.[11]

The Senate had its own bill, which had been introduced on May 14; it was the result of a conference with Gale W. McGee of Wyoming, Hiram Fong of Hawaii, and the postmaster general. However, on June 30, the House bill was substituted for the Senate bill. Senator Javits of New York immediately attacked the "right to work" amendment passed by the House; he thought postal unions should have the right of collective bargaining to obtain a union shop if they wished. His motion to eliminate the provision in the House bill was adopted by a vote of 52 to 38. He also substituted the section in the Senate bill on rate-making for the House bill, which had provided that rates should be subject to congressional veto; he said it was like the old log-rolling on the tariff. An amendment providing for a uniform rate for the whole country on books, prints, and records was adopted. There were also added two new categories of nonmailable matter. The bill was adopted that same day by a vote of 77 to 9, with 14 not voting.[12]

Before the bill went to conference committee the House instructed its conferees to insist on the House amendment dealing with the right to work. After three weeks in conference the bill was adopted by the Senate on August 3 by a vote of 57 to 7, with 35 not voting and in the House on August 6, by a vote of 338 to 29, with 62 not voting.[13] In both houses there were a few irreconcilables; the most prominent were members of the conference committee. In the House H. R. Gross of Iowa deplored the fact that the Post Office would be removed from any possible control by the people. He declared that "the public service concept of the postal service which has been carefully developed by Congress over a period of many, many years, will be completely subverted by the enactment of this new legislation." Senator Ralph W. Yarborough of Texas said: "This Postal Corporation bill is the Tonkin Gulf Resolution of Domestic Legislation. I know of no precedent for this bill. The Constitution provides that Congress shall establish the Post Office and post roads. We abdicate this constitutional responsibility when we turn the function over to a corporation."[14] The president in the presence of Postmaster General Blount and six past postmasters general signed the bill on August 12, 1970, in the ornate reception room of the Post Office Department building.[15]

The Postal Reorganization Act began: "The United States Postal Service shall be operated as a basic and fundamental service provided to the people by the Government of the United States, authorized by the Constitution, created by Act of Congress, and supported by the people." The Postal Service is directed by a Board of Governors, nine of whom are appointed by the president with the advice and consent of the Senate for a term of nine years and removable only for cause. The governors appoint and have the power to remove the postmaster general and deputy postmaster general. The term and compensation of these officers are fixed by the board. The officers are also members of the Board of Governors. The Postal Service as "an independent establishment of the executive branch of the Government of the United States," can sue, be sued, enter into contracts and buy, sell, and hold property.

The employees, no longer in the United States civil service, are members of the new postal career service. They have the right to make collective bargaining agreements but not the right to strike. Disputes are subject to compulsory arbitration. Rates of pay are to be "comparable to rates and types of compensation paid in the private sector of the economy of the United States." Political recommendations are prohibited but inquiries "in order to determine whether such person meets the loyalty, suitability and character requirement for employment with the government" are permitted.

Postage rates are set by a special commission of five professionals appointed by the president for a term of six years. The proposed rates can be rejected by the Board of Governors but only by unanimous vote of the nine members appointed by the president. They are also subject to judicial review. There is in the Treasury the Postal Service Fund and revenue from the Postal Service is put in that fund; if there were a surplus it could be invested for the benefit of the Postal Service. During the first eight years appropriations equal to 10 percent of the total cost of running the postal establishment in 1971 are to be made by Congress. That amount will be decreased by 1 percent each year for the next five years. Then the Postal Service is supposed to be self-supporting. By this act Congress has given up practically all control over the postal system. As long as Congress is making appropriations for the service they may try to interfere in internal matters. The act does state, however, that Congress "reserves the power to alter, amend, or repeal any or all the sections of this title."[16]

Congress still has the power to decide what matter is nonmailable; most of the nonmailable statutes are also part of the criminal code. The Postal Reorganization Act of 1970 (chapter 30) retains the phrase, "Matter the deposit of which in the mails is punishable under section 1302 [lotteries], 1341, 1342 [frauds], 1461, 1463 [obscenity], 1714 [foreign divorces], 1715 [firearms],

1716 [injurious articles], 1717 [treasonable] is nonmailable." This section then continues:

Matter otherwise legally acceptable in the mails which
    (1) is in the form of, and reasonably could be interpreted or construed as, a bill, invoice, or statement of account due; but
    (2) constitutes, in fact, a solicitation for the order by the addressee of goods or services, or both;
is nonmailable matter, shall not be carried or delivered by mail, and shall be disposed of as the Postal Service directs, unless such matter bears on its face, in conspicuous and legible type in contrast by typography, layout, or color with other printing on its face, in accordance with regulations which the Postal Service shall prescribe
    (A) the following notice: "This is a solicitation for the order of goods or services, or both, and not a bill, invoice, or statement of account due. You are under no obligation to make any payments on account of this offer unless you accept this offer." or
    (B) in lieu thereof, a notice to the same effect in words which the Postal Service shall prescribe.

This section entitled: "Solicitations in Guise of Bills or Statements of Account" had been included in the Postal Rate and Federal Salary Act in 1967 because of the practice of some shady promoters who sent out bills and invoices to mislead the addressees into believing they were actually bills for goods previously delivered or services rendered. In the same act was the section, "Prohibition of pandering advertisements."[17]

Another act passed the following year (1968) was included in chapter 30 of the Postal Reorganization Act. This declared nonmailable "any motor vehicle master key, any pattern, impression, or mold from which a motor vehicle master key may be made, or any advertisement for the sale of any such key, pattern, impression, or mold." Anyone knowingly depositing such could be fined up to $1,000 and/or be imprisoned up to one year. This was another attempt to use the postal power to curb crime. The sponsor, Representative Nix of Pennsylvania, pointed out that 63 percent of the car thefts were by youths under the age of eighteen. For ten dollars one could get a set of master keys that would open almost any automobile made in the United States.

There were advertisements of them in most of the girlie magazines. Many bills to restrict mailing of master automobile keys had been introduced in the two previous Congresses. The bill was supported by the American Automobile Association and the Justice and Post Office departments. There was little opposition in either house to this nonmailable category.[18]

There was a good deal of discussion in the 1960s of broadening the section making unmailable concealed weapons (1927) and switchblade knives (1958) to include other firearms. The campaign was intensified after President Kennedy was assassinated, ostensibly by means of a rifle obtained through the mail. The assassinations of Dr. Martin Luther King, Jr., and Senator Robert Kennedy in the spring of 1968 aroused the public to demand some gun control law. Postmaster General W. Marvin Watson (1968–1969) announced on June 12 that as an interim measure he would classify sawed-off shotguns and short-barrel rifles as concealable weapons, "thus barring them from the mails unless sent to authorized recipients such as law enforcement officers." The packages had to be labeled with the word "firearms" and the postmaster was instructed not to make delivery until he had notified the law enforcement officer of the community. Watson was not optimistic about the effectiveness of his ruling, as he pointed out most firearms were not sent through the mail but through private express companies. He urged stronger legislation. A gun control law was passed October 22, 1968, but the emphasis was on the restriction of the transportation of arms through interstate commerce to licensed manufacturers, dealers, and collectors. The nonmailable section (1715) was not broadened.[19]

Other sections in the "Nonmailable Matter" chapter taken from earlier acts are the ones dealing with "Mail bearing a fictitious name or address" and "False Representations: lotteries." The latter title in 1968 replaced "Fraudulent and Lottery Matter." The major change was the elimination of the necessity for establishing the intent to deceive. Under the existing law the postmaster general had to prove: (1) that advertising through the mail had been used, (2) advertising contained false representations of fact of a material nature, and (3) that such representations were intended to deceive. In *Reilly* v. *Pincus* (1949) it had been stated that the postmaster general must prove the person intended to deceive. This bill was aimed particularly at medical, insurance, and land frauds. The latter had grown to tremendous proportions and many people had bought real estate in Florida and Arizona only to find it practically worthless. The bill substituted "false representations" for "false and fraudulent pretenses, representations or promises" in number 4005.[20]

Two new nonmailable categories were added in the Postal Reorganization Act: "Mailing of sexually oriented advertisements" and "Mailing of unordered merchandise." Throughout the 1920s and 1930s congressmen had tried to remedy the abuse by businesses that would mail unsolicited merchandise to a person who would then be dunned for payment. The lobbies, especially the greeting card mail-order houses, were too strong, so it was not until 1970 that an act defined what merchandise could be sent through the mail and the legal obligations of the receiver of the goods. The new section read as follows:

(a) Except for (1) free samples clearly and conspicuously marked as such, and (2) merchandise mailed by a charitable organization soliciting contributions, the mailing of unordered merchandise or of communications prohibited by subsection (c) of this section shall constitute an unfair method of competition and an unfair trade practice . . . .

(b) Any merchandise mailed in violation of subsection (a) of this section, or within the exceptions contained therein, may be treated as a gift by the recipient, who shall have the right to retain, use, discard, or dispose of it in any manner he sees fit without any obligation whatever to the sender. All such merchandise shall have attached to it a clear and conspicuous statement informing the recipient that he may treat the merchandise as a gift to him and has the right to retain, use, discard, or dispose of it in any manner he sees fit without any obligation whatsoever to the sender.

(c) No mailer of any merchandise mailed in violation of subsection (a) of this section, or within the exceptions contained therein, shall mail to any recipient of such merchandise a bill for such merchandise or any dunning communications.[21]

Violations of two of the earliest congressional fiats were discussed during the debates on the Postal Reorganization Act: the

# The Postal Service

inviolability of sealed letters and the Post Office monopoly of the transportation of letters. Congressmen were worried about a new postal order by the postmaster general and the secretary of the treasury to permit the Bureau of Customs to open first-class foreign mail believed to contain prohibited or dutiable material. Before, when a letter was believed to contain prohibited matter, the addressee was informed and requested to allow it to be opened in his presence. If he refused, the letter was returned to the foreign mailer. A district court had held that nondelivery of the mail was unconstitutional, so the Post Office washed its hands of the whole practice by turning the letters over to the Customs Bureau. Their right to open sealed mail of foreign origin had been upheld by the courts in several instances. Domestic letters may be opened if a special search warrant has been obtained. In 1975 the Rockefeller investigation revealed that the CIA and FBI had, from 1952–1973, opened mail of Americans going to the Soviet Union. The organizations claimed this was done in order to protect national security and to prevent sabotage. This program was clearly a violation of the sanctity of the mails and Post Office officials asserted they had had nothing to do with it.[22]

In the first Post Office Ordinance in 1782 the Post Office was given the monopoly of carrying letters. This was its only specific function, but the postmaster general could license post riders to carry newspapers. Congress gradually gave to the Post Office other functions, the carrying of magazines, books, and small packages. The parcel post was set up in 1912. It also undertook some banking functions, such as the issuance of postal money orders (1864) and acceptance of savings in the Postal Savings Banks (1910). Some of these have been discontinued or have declined in importance. The Postal Savings Banks were discontinued in 1966 and the parcel post system has been outdistanced by the United Parcel System. Even the carrying of letters has competition, although that is illegal. During the debates on the Postal Reorganization Act an amendment was introduced in the House to permit private enterprise to undertake delivery of first-class mail. The amendment was defeated, but the act made provision for a commission to study private mail delivery. Postmaster General Blount opposed it. He favored a continuation of the monopoly by the Postal Service, saying that private operators would take over delivery of letters in high population density areas, the more profitable, and not provide mail service to other sections in the United States.[23]

The Postal Service Act was to go into effect on July 1, 1971, but President Nixon announced interim appointments for the Board of Governors in January and they selected as their chief Postmaster General Blount, who had held that office throughout President Nixon's administration. Before then he had been president of the United States Chamber of Commerce. In an interview he said his purpose was to "insulate the new postal service from the Congress, from the White House—from all of the external pressures that operated on it all these years—and let it run with the proper checks and balances, as any nation-wide utility would run."[24]

Is this the end of an era in congressional control of the postal service? If the United States Postal Service remains an independent organization in the Executive department, Congress will have as little authority over it as it has over the Federal Reserve Board. Many congressmen have not yet accepted it. The committees on the Post Office in both houses still scrutinize the operations of the Postal Service. There were many speeches in the Ninety-second, Ninety-third, and Ninety-fourth Congresses enumerating the defects of the system: the delay in delivery of mail, the decline in service, the increase in rates, the large deficits, and the turnover in top management.[25] There were many bills in each session proposing the abolition of the United States Postal Service and the restoration of the old Post Office Department. Other bills were designed "to recapture some measure of congressional jurisdiction over the U.S. Postal Service." They suggested the abolition of the Board of Governors and the appointment of the postmaster general and the deputy by the president subject to confirmation by the Senate and their annual appearance before Congress to present their request for appropriations. The greatest criticism concerned the Rate Commission. Representatives wanted Congress to have the veto over rates set by the commission and if necessary were willing to vote annual subsidies to make up postal deficits, they said.[26]

One power that Congress still has in regard to the semi-independent Postal Service is to decide what may or may not be carried in the mails. Since the passage of the act in 1970 more things have been removed from the nonmailable list than added to it. The government found itself in a somewhat embarrassing position because of the Comstock Law of 1873, which declared nonmailable contraceptive devices or information about them. This did not accord with the government's program of encouraging birth control, not only in overpopulated countries but also for certain groups in the United States. In 1962 the general counsel of the Post Office Department overruled the Chicago postmaster, who had refused to accept copies of Dr. Alan F. Guttmacher's *Complete Book of Birth Control*, which was being sent to paperback distributors. The counsel approved mailing to distributors or retail book outlets and "to individuals with a legitimate professional interest in the subject, such as physicians, clergymen, and psychologists."[27]

The Post Office Department and other government officials urged changes in the law. Representative James Scheuer of New York took the initiative in getting the law changed and finally succeeded (January 8, 1971) in getting removed the prohibition on mailing contraceptive articles and advertisements of such articles. The act did declare nonmailable unsolicited samples except to specified persons. The Court in 1973 in *Associated Students for University of California at Riverside* v. *Attorney General of the United States* declared that "mailing of handbook presenting straightforward, critical manner information concerning abortion and birth control could not be proscribed on the ground that the same might constitute trafficking in obscene materials, nor, since the lifting of prohibition on the sale and use of contraceptives and since the Supreme Court decision on abortions, on the ground that such material might be 'crime-inciting.' "[28]

Other laws defining nonmailable matter that caused embarrassment were the law of 1868 which forbade the mailing of lottery tickets and the law of 1890 which made it a crime to send through the mail any advertisement of a lottery. The latter restricted newspapers from printing the full list of winners in state lotteries, although they could print stories about the lucky people. These laws had been directed against the Louisiana State Lottery and had driven it out of business. In 1964, led by New Hampshire, states again began to set up state lotteries, usually with the aim of raising money for some laudable purpose. Congressmen from those states, as early as 1963, introduced bills to allow the transmission through the mail of lottery tickets and other materials relating to a lottery operated by a state or a political subdivision. They were all buried in committee.

The matter came to a head in 1974 when Attorney General Saxbe announced he would seek an injunction to halt lotteries unless Congress clarified the law within three months. State officials claimed that the federal laws did not apply to state-run lotteries. Congressmen protested that they could not hope to get any action from Congress in so short a time. Congress got busy and by January 2, 1975, had passed a law stating that nothing in the section headed "False Representations: Lotteries" would prohibit the mailing of "(1) a newspaper of general circulation published in a State containing advertisements, lists of prizes, or information concerning a lottery conducted by that State acting under the authority of State law, or (2) tickets or other materials concerning such a lottery within that State to addresses within that State."[29]

Congressmen still introduced bills to make various things nonmailable. The major categories deal with unsolicited advertisements, unsolicited credit cards, drug and cigarette samples, and especially mailing lists, either from girlie magazines, businesses, or government agencies. None of these got out of committee. The emphasis in them is on invasion of privacy and the enforcement is more on the householder than on the Post Office. The fraud statutes still put the responsibility on the Postal Service and the main activity of P-men is to prevent the use of the mail for fraudulent schemes. The Postal Inspection Service is the "nation's oldest federal law-enforcement agency." The great increase in the mail-order business has brought many consumer complaints on undelivered merchandise.[30]

Obscenity is still the category that most interests congressmen and many bills dealing with this topic were introduced in recent Congresses. The bills were to remedy defects in the Postal Reorganization Act. They added to the list of nonmailable matter "salacious advertising" and prohibited sending offensive sex material to youths under eighteen. They defined obscenity, taking the definition recommended by the minority of President Johnson's Commission on Obscenity and Pornography, that material found to appeal to prurient interest automatically be deemed without social value. Several bills proposed to limit judicial review in cases of obscenity because the Supreme Court had overturned so many state and federal obscenity decisions. Congressmen admitted that there were many laws concerning obscenity but they thought it well to have more in case the Supreme Court declared some unconstitutional. Also, in one decision two of the justices expressed doubts that parents should have the right to speak for all minors in refusing pornographic matter.[31]

All of the recent bills emphasize the responsibility of the householder and the Supreme Court seems willing to allow him wide authority. In a recent decision, *Rowan* v. *Post Office Department* (1970), Chief Justice Burger ignored the brief filed by the Direct Mail Advertising Association and made the law "Prohibition of pandering advertisements in the mail" apply to "junk mail" also. He said:

today's merchandising methods, the plethora of mass mailings subsidized by low postal rates, and the growth of the sale of large mailing lists . . . have changed the mailman from a carrier of primarily private communications and has made him an adjunct of the mass mailer who sends unsolicited and often unwanted mail into every home. Everyman's mail today is made up overwhelmingly of material he did not seek from persons he does not know.

Then he added:

in effect, Congress has erected a wall or more accurately permits a citizen to erect a wall—that no advertiser may penetrate without his acquiescence. The continuing operative effect of a mailing ban once imposed presents no constitutional obstacles. The citizen cannot be put to the burden of determining on repeated occasions whether the offending mailer has altered his material so as to make it acceptable.

The contrast between the first nonmailable law, March 3, 1865, which also dealt with obscene matter, and the latest ones is striking. The first law put the burden on the Post Office while the later ones "allow the parent to police his own mail box."[32]

# Notes

## Chapter 1

1. Clyde Melville Kelly, *The United States Postal Policy*, pp. 20–21. See also Wayne E. Fuller, *The American Mail*.

2. William Smith, "The Colonial Post Office," *American Historical Review* 21 (Jan., 1916): 260–68. Regular delivery of mail throughout England and Wales by "post boys" was established by Charles I in 1635 and the "Post Office Charter" setting up the British Post Office was passed in 1660. See *New York Times*, Sept. 18, 1960.

3. Smith, "Colonial Post Office," pp. 270–71; John Bach McMaster, *Benjamin Franklin as a Man of Letters*, pp. 158–59; James Parton, *Life and Times of Benjamin Franklin*, I:76, 330–33. Andrew Hamilton and then his son, John, had been deputy postmasters general for the colonies from 1692 to 1730. John was then replaced by Alexander Spottswood, who in 1737 made Franklin his deputy. From 1753 to 1761 he shared the office of postmaster general for the colonies with William Hunter. See *New York Times*, Aug. 30, 1970.

4. Jared Sparks, ed., *The Works of Benjamin Franklin*, VIII: 113–14 (Feb. 15, 1774).

5. Peter Force, ed., *American Archives*, 4th series, I: 500–501 (Feb. 5, 1774). He also wrote: "It was that gentleman [Franklin] that brought the Post Office in *America* to be of some consequence, and to yield something of a revenue to the mother country. The people there never liked the Institution, and only acquiesced in it out of their unbounded affection for the person that held the office."

6. Ibid., 1: 500–504; II: 481–82, 536, 802–803, 900, 981–83, 1160.

7. Harry Alonzo Cushing, ed., *The Writings of Samuel Adams*, III: 80–82. See also p. 93 (Adams to J. Warren, March 31, 1774).

8. Edmund Cody Burnett, *The Continental Congress*, pp. 63–70.

# Notes for Chapter One

9. Worthington C. Ford and Gaillard Hunt, eds., *Journals of the Continental Congress*, II: 71. The committee consisted of Benjamin Franklin, Thomas Lynch of South Carolina, R. H. Lee of Virginia, Thomas Willing of Pennsylvania, Sam Adams of Massachusetts, and Philip Livingston of New York.

10. Ibid., II: 203, 208–209. The postmaster general's salary was $1,000 a year; the secretary and comptroller each received $340 and deputy postmasters received 20 percent of sums collected. The operation of the British postal act had been suspended September, 1774, although the royal mail limped along until the end of 1775.

11. Ibid., II: 209. Franklin wrote Thomson in 1788, "It was indeed an office I had some kind of right to, as having previously greatly enlarged the revenue of the post by the régulations I had contributed and established while I possessed it under the crown." (See Parton, *Franklin*, II: 595). Richard Bache became postmaster general, November 7, 1776, "in the room" of Franklin when the latter left on a mission to France. (See *Journals of the Continental Congress*, V: 827; VI: 931.)

12. Force, ed., *American Archives*, 5th series, I: 442; John N. Makris, *The Silent Investigators*, pp. 62–63. The office of surveyor had been created in the British postal system in 1772.

13. *Journals of the Continental Congress*, III: 358, 360–61, 467; IV: 288; V: 574–75.

14. Force, ed., *American Archives*, 4th series, III: 956; John C. Fitzpatrick, ed., *The Writings of George Washington*, VI: 305–306 (to Major General Lee, Nov. 24, 1776); XXI: 489–91 (to Marquis La Fayette, April 22, 1781); XXII: 131 (to John Sullivan, May 29, 1781), 167–68 (to President of Congress, June 6, 1781).

15. *Journals of the Continental Congress*, VI: 926; VII: 29–30.

16. Ibid., V: 719–20.

17. Julian P. Boyd, ed., *The Papers of Thomas Jefferson*, II: 18–19.

18. Edmund Cody Burnett, ed., *Letters of Members of the Continental Congress*, II: 375 (May 26, 1777).

19. *Journals of the Continental Congress*, V: 718; VII: 30, 127, 153; IX: 898; XI: 550.

20. Ibid., IX: 817.

21. Ibid., XIII: 26. The members of the committee were Sam Adams, Richard Henry Lee, William Paca of Maryland, William Ellery of Rhode Island, and Henry Laurens of South Carolina. (See Burnett, *Continental Congress*, pp. 721–22.)

22. *Journals of the Continental Congress*, XIX: 219.

23. Jennings B. Sanders, *Evolution of Executive Departments of the Continental Congress*, p. 162; Leonard D. White, *The Federalists*, p. 399.

24. *Journals of the Continental Congress*, XXII:60. Franklin wrote Thomson in 1788: "When I was sent to France, I left it [the Post Office] in the hands of my son-in-law, who was to act as my deputy. But soon after my departure it was taken from me and given to Mr. Hazard." (See Parton, *Franklin*, II:595.)

25. *Journals of the Continental Congress*, XXII: 121–26, 402; XXIII:670–79; Burnett, ed., *Letters of the Continental Congress*, VI: 220 (Roger Sherman to Jonathan Trumbull, Sept. 15, 1781); VI:387 (Charles Thomson's notes, July 23, 1782), VI:394 (Connecticut delegates to Governor of Connecticut, July 29, 1782). The ordinance provided pay of $1,500 for the postmaster general, $1,000 for his assistant, and 20 percent of the revenue of the office for deputy postmasters. Punishment for opening letters was set at $300 and one convicted would be incapable of ever holding an office of the government.

26. *Journals of the Continental Congress*, XXIX:680 (Sept. 5), 685 (Sept. 7, 1785); XXXI: 909 (Oct. 23, 1786 repassed by unanimous vote).

27. Fitzpatrick, ed., *Writings of George Washington*, XXVIII:467–68 (to G. W. Fairfax, June 26, 1786); XXIX:409 (to La Fayette, Feb. 7, 1788); Albert J. Beveridge, *The Life of John Marshall*, I:266n.

28. *Journals of the Continental Congress*, XXXIV:232 (June 13), 239 (June 18, 1788).

29. Burnett, *Continental Congress*, pp. 721–22; Burnett, ed., *Letters of the Continental Congress*, VIII:48 (John Sitgreaves to J. G. Blount, Feb. 28), 73 (J. Wadsworth to W. S. Johnson, March 13), 180 (R. H. Lee to J. Madison, Aug. 11), 225 (W. Grayson to Washington, Oct. 3), 243 (R. H. Lee to Jefferson, Oct. 29, 1785), 334 (W. Grayson to R. H. Lee, March 22, 1786).

30. *Journals of the Continental Congress*, XXXII:45–46 (Feb. 14); XXXIII:672 (Oct. 11, 1787); XXXIV:144 (May 7, 1788). See XXXIV:462–65 for a comprehensive report on the Post Office made August 27, 1788. It stated there were 69 deputy postmasters, that the Post Office had receipts of $29,243 and had paid into the treasury $1,839 in 1787.

31. Max Farrand, ed., *Records of the Federal Convention* I:243; II:135, 159, 168, 182, 304, 308, 328, 569.

32. Jonathan Elliot, ed., *The Debates in the Several State Conventions on the Adoption of the Federal Constitution*, II:406.

# Notes for Chapter One

33. *The Federalist,* ed. Jacob E. Cooke, p. 287.

34. *New York Journal,* Jan. 10, 14, 21, 23, Feb. 11, 12, 15, 25, 26, March 11, 21, 1788.

35. Ibid., March 21, 25, April 10, 1788.

36. Burnett, ed., *Letters of the Continental Congress,* VIII: 716–17 (to George Thatcher, April 13, 1788). See 793n (J. Belknap to Hazard, Sept. 23, 1788).

37. U.S. Congress, *Annals of Congress,* 1st Cong., 1st sess., pp. 80, 82, 684, 927–28.

38. Edmund C. Burnett, "Samuel Osgood," in *Dictionary of American Biography,* ed. Allen Johnson and Dumas Malone, 20 vols. (New York: Charles Scribner's Sons, 1928–1936), XIV: 81–82. Osgood had at first been opposed to the Constitution but had become reconciled to it. (See White, *Federalists,* p. 193.)

39. James D. Richardson, comp., *A Compilation of the Messages and Papers of the Presidents,* I: 66.

40. John C. Fitzpatrick, ed., *The Diaries of George Washington,* IV: 71; Fitzpatrick, ed., *Writings of George Washington,* XXXI: 349.

41. *American State Papers: Documents, Legislative and Executive of the Congress of the United States,* Class III, *Finance,* I: 24.

42. *Annals of Congress,* 1st Cong., Appendix, 2107–14 (Jan. 20, 1790).

43. Ibid., 1st Cong., 2d sess., pp. 1114, 1308, 1327, 1528–29, 1640–43, 1644.

44. Ibid., pp. 1027, 1041, 1061, 1713; William Maclay, *The Journal of William Maclay,* pp. 294, 299–300, 306–309. In 1790 there was the postmaster general who received a salary of $1,500 (half that received by the secretary of war), one assistant postmaster general and one clerk, and 75 deputy postmasters. There were 1,875 miles of post roads; the receipts were $37,937 and the expenses, $32,140. See Wesley Everett Rich, *The History of the United States Post Office to the Year 1829,* pp. 68, 116.

45. John C. Hamilton, *History of the Republic of the United States of America as Traced in the Writings of Alexander Hamilton,* IV: 515. "Should he [Paine] be intrusted with the patronage of the Post Office Department, pervading the whole country, this channel for the dissemination of insurrectionary opinions would be entirely under Jefferson's command; for, both as to politics and religion, Paine and Jefferson have similar views."

46. White, *Federalists,* p. 194.

47. Charles W. Upham, *Life of Timothy Pickering,* II: 496; III: 3, 39.

48. Richardson, comp., *Messages and Papers,* I: 107–108.

206

# Notes for Chapter One

49. *Annals of Congress*, 2nd Cong., 1st sess., pp. 79, 147, 229–42.

50. Ibid., 303–11; Upham, *Pickering*, III: 5–6.

51. *Annals of Congress*, 2nd Cong., Appendix, pp. 133–41. The salary of the postmaster general was set at $2,000, his assistant at $1,000. Postage on letters up to 30 miles was 6¢, 30–60 miles was 8¢, etc. May 8, 1794, the act was renewed without a time limit (see 3rd Cong., Appendix, pp. 1431–33). Salaries were raised to $2,400 and $1,200 and four clerks were added to the staff. This act imposed a fine for enclosing letters in newspapers. Deputy postmasters were given the franking privilege.

52. Richardson, comp., *Messages and Papers*, I:128 (Nov. 6, 1792).

53. *Annals of Congress*, 4th Cong., 1st sess., pp. 1386, 1392, 2061–62, 2352, Appendix, pp. 2957–62; *American State Papers*, Class VII, *Post Office*, p. 16.

54. John C. Miller, *Crisis in Freedom*, p. 31; Philadelphia *Aurora*, July 12, 1800.

55. Paul Leicester Ford, ed., *The Writings of Thomas Jefferson*, VIII:480; IX:83–85 (to James T. Callender, Oct. 6, 1799). See also IX:40 (to A. Stuart, Feb. 13, 1799), 57–58 (to R. Livingston, Feb. 23, 1799), 89 (to J. Madison, Nov. 22, 1799), 244 (to G. Granger, March 29, 1801); Worthington Chauncey Ford, *Some Letters of Elbridge Gerry of Massachusetts*, pp. 22, 24.

56. Robert Preston Brooks, "Joseph Habersham, 1751–1815," *Dictionary of American Biography*, VIII:70. He was born in Georgia, educated in New Jersey and England, and in 1771 he returned to Savannah and entered business. He was one of the advanced group of revolutionists and rose to be a colonel in the revolutionary army. He served as speaker of the assembly of Georgia, delegate to the Continental Congress, 1785–1796, and as a member of the Georgia convention ratifying the Constitution. White, *Federalists*, p. 193, said Habersham "was a person of little color although a competent man of affairs who managed the post office business with energy and integrity."

57. *American State Papers*, Class VII, *Post Office*, pp. 17–21; *Annals of Congress*, 5th Cong., Appendix, pp. 3942–43. See White, *Federalists*, pp. 177–78.

58. *Massachusetts Mercury*, Aug. 22, 1800, quoting the *Courant*.

59. William A. Robinson, "Gideon Granger," *Dictionary of American Biography*, VII:483–84. In 1800 there were 903 post offices and 20,817 miles of post roads.

60. *American State Papers*, Class VII, *Post Office*, p. 22 (to James

Jackson, chairman, committee of the Senate on the post office establishment, March 23, 1802).

61. *Annals of Congress*, 7th Cong., 1st sess., Appendix, pp. 1369–72. In 1801 special agents replaced surveyors (see Makris, *Silent Investigators*, p. 65).

62. Everett Somerville Brown, ed., *William Plumer's Memorandum of Proceedings in the United States Senate*, pp. 73–74, 95–96, 130. One senator said: "The duties of that officer are greatly increased— He is frequently obliged to write all night till one o'clock in the morning. He is a great man, his duties & patronage are great." In January, 1803, Granger reported there were 1,283 post offices and 24,458 miles of post roads.

63. *Annals of Congress*, 11th Cong., 2nd sess., p. 1792, Appendix p. 1335; 2 *Stat.* 592–604. In 1813 an act was passed authorizing the postmaster general to contract for carrying mail by steamboats but not at a rate greater proportionately than that paid for carriage by stages on post roads adjacent.

64. Lindsay Rogers, *The Postal Power of Congress*, p. 47.

65. Brown, ed., *Plumer's Memorandum*, pp. 485–86; *American State Papers*, Class VII, *Post Office*, p. 40. In 1808 a standing committee on post offices and post roads, consisting of one member from each state, was established in the House of Representatives. There were at that time eight other standing committees in the House. (See *Annals of Congress*, 10th Cong., 2nd sess., p. 472.)

66. William B. Utter, "Return Jonathan Meigs," *Dictionary of American Biography*, XII:509–10; Leonard D. White, *The Jeffersonians*, pp. 301–302.

67. *Annals of Congress*, 14th Cong., 1st sess., Appendix, pp. 1809–11; *American State Papers*, Class VII, *Post Office*, p. 112 (Meigs to Montfort Stokes, chairman, committee on Post Office and Post Roads in the Senate, Feb. 21, 1823). He criticized Secretary of State Adams for sending through the mail several cartloads of books; the result was "many newspapers have been rubbed to pieces and lost and letters damaged."

68. White, *Jeffersonians*, p. 314: see Francis P. Weisenburger, *The Life of John McLean*, chs. 1, 2, 3.

69. Richardson, comp., *Messages and Papers*, II:215. President Monroe introduced the practice of having the postmaster general make his annual reports directly to the president. For a description of postal system at that time see *Niles' Weekly Register* 30 (June 3, 1826): 243–44.

70. Ibid., II:311. An act approved March 3, 1825, codified various acts regulating the Post Office but made no substantive change. This

act forbade the writing of any memorandum on a newspaper or printed paper transmitted by mail. It used the term "Post Office Department." See 4 *Stat.* 102–15.

71. 4 *Stat.* 238–39; Rich, *United States Post Office*, p. 126.

72. *Register of Debates*, 19th Cong., 1st sess., p. 2663; 2nd sess., p. 59; *American State Papers*, Class VII, *Post Office*, pp. 145–46; Rich, *United States Post Office*, p. 112.

## Chapter 2

1. Dorothy Ganfield Fowler, *The Cabinet Politician*, pp. 2–6. It is interesting to note that in Great Britain the postmaster general became a member of the cabinet in 1830.

2. Richardson, comp., *Messages and Papers*, II:460–61.

3. *Register of Debates*, 22nd Cong., 1st sess., pp. 875–83. In 1845 newspapers were carried free to subscribers within thirty miles (see 5 *Stat.* 733) and in 1851 free circulation within a county was provided for (see 9 *Stat.* 588).

4. W. T. Barry to Daniel Worley, July 14, 1829, in Postmaster General Letterbooks (National Archives).

5. *Register of Debates*, 22nd Cong., 1st sess., p. 191. See also Joseph Howard Parks, *Felix Grundy*, pp. 252–54.

6. *American State Papers*, Class VII, *Post Office*, pp. 313–15 (report of the Postmaster General, Jan. 5, 1830), pp. 253–56 (report of March 19, 1830, describing the organization of the department); Makris, *Silent Investigators*, p. 66; Leonard D. White, *The Jacksonians*, pp. 279–80.

7. White, *Jacksonians*, p. 251. Barry had served in the Kentucky house of representatives, 1807–1808, 1814 (speaker), in the House of Representatives, 1810–1812, Senate, 1815–1816, as lieutenant governor of Kentucky, 1821–1824, chief justice, Kentucky Supreme Court, 1824–1826. See also Claude Bowers, *The Party Battles of the Jacksonian Period*, pp. 372–73.

8. *Register of Debates*, 21st Cong., 2nd sess., pp. 4–5 (Dec. 15, 1830).

9. U.S. Congress, *Congressional Globe*, 23rd Cong., 1st sess., pp. 42, 439, 474; Parks, *Grundy*, pp. 244–61. The committee was set up on resolution of Senator Clayton, who became the chairman. There were also reports of letters being opened, e.g., Henry Clay wrote Daniel Webster to send his letters under cover of another to "guard against the treachery of the post office." See Fletcher Webster, ed., *The Writings and Speeches of Daniel Webster*, XVII:505. Senate Document 422, 23rd Cong., 1st sess., esp. pp. 25, 31.

10. House Report 103, 23rd Cong., 2nd sess. The majority members were Henry W. Connor, North Carolina; James K. Polk, Tennessee; Samuel Beardsley, New York; Albert G. Hawes, Kentucky. Minority members were Elisha Whittlesley, Ohio; Horace Everett, Vermont; John G. Watmough, Pennsylvania.

11. *William and Mary Historical Magazine* 14(1905–06): 239–40; Jackson to Barry, April 11, 1835, in Jackson Papers (Library of Congress); F. P. Blair to Martin Van Buren, Aug. 26, 1835, in Van Buren Papers (Library of Congress). Barry died in Oct., 1835, in England; he never reached Spain.

12. White, *Jacksonians*, pp. 270–74; Fowler, *The Cabinet Politician*, pp. 22–24.

13. 5 *Stat.* 80–90; *Congressional Globe*, 24th Cong., 1st sess., p. 288. During the debate on the act Senator Calhoun of South Carolina declared, "Unless the power of the Postmaster General should be most vigilantly guarded, it would become enormously increased." See White, *Jacksonians*, pp. 277–78; Lloyd Milton Short, *The Development of National Administrative Organization in the United States*, pp. 177–84. The power of appointing assistant postmasters general was transferred from the postmaster general to the president, March 3, 1853. Postmaster General Kendall reported on the organization in 1836: the first assistant postmaster general was in charge of the contract office, the second assistant headed the appointment office, the third assistant was in charge of the inspection service, and the auditor supervised departmental accounts.

14. Richardson, comp., *Messages and Papers*, III: 174–75, 257; *Congressional Globe*, 27th Cong., 3rd sess., Appendix, p. 7.

15. Richardson, comp., *Messages and Papers*, III, 257, 393; *Congressional Globe*, 27th Cong., 2nd sess., pp. 25–27. His recommendation that the law of 1825 concerning the carrying of mail by private contractors be tightened was done by act of March 3, 1845. Section 15 of the act (5 *Stat.* 736–37) described mailable matter as follows: "That 'mailable matter' and 'matter properly transmittable by mail' shall be deemed and taken to mean, all letters and newspapers, and all magazines and pamphlets periodically published, or which may be published in regular series or in successive numbers, under the same title, though at irregular intervals, and all other written or printed matter whereof each copy or number shall not exceed eight ounces in weight, except bank notes, sent in packages or bundles without written letters accompanying them; but bound books, of any size shall not be held to be included within the meaning of these terms." When the telegraph was invented Postmaster General Cave Johnson proposed that exclusive control over it should be given to

the Post Office since it had been created by the Constitution "to exercise exclusive power for the transmission of intelligence." See *Congressional Globe*, 29th Cong., 2nd sess., Appendix, pp. 19–22.

16. Russel B. Nye, *Fettered Freedom*, p. 55.

17. Charles M. Wiltse, *John C. Calhoun: Nullifier*, pp. 270–71; *William Allen Butler: A Retrospect of Forty Years*, ed. Harriet Allen Butler, pp. 78–79.

18. Dennis Tilden Lynch, *An Epoch and a Man*, p. 385, maintains that this postmaster in Calhoun's own state raised the issue mainly to hurt Van Buren in the South. The New Yorker had just been nominated for the presidency on May 20, 1835. See Bowers, *Party Battles*, p. 435; it was known that Van Buren was opposed to the extension of slavery, so Southerners thought raising the issue of abolitionist literature might embarrass him.

19. Huger to Gouverneur, Aug. 1, 1835, in Samuel Gouverneur Papers (New York Public Library). Gouverneur had been private secretary to President Monroe and his son had married one of Monroe's daughters.

20. *Congressional Globe*, 27th Cong., 2nd sess., Appendix, p. 981, quoting the Charleston *Courier*; Wiltse, *Calhoun: Nullifier*, p. 272; Theodore Jervey, *Robert Y. Hayne and His Times*, pp. 379–81.

21. Huger to Gouverneur, Aug. 1, 8, Gouverneur to the American Anti-Slavery Society, Aug. 6, resolution of the society, Aug. 8, 1835, in Gouverneur Papers. Bowers intimated that Gouverneur's action was prompted by Van Buren; see Bowers, *Party Battles*, p. 435.

22. *Niles' Weekly Register* 48 (Aug. 22, 1835): 448.

23. John Spencer Bassett, ed., *Correspondence of Andrew Jackson*, V:360–61 (Jackson to Kendall, Aug. 7, 1835).

24. *Niles' Weekly Register*, 49 (Sept. 19, 1835):45; Nye, *Fettered Freedom*, pp. 58–59.

25. Dwight L. Dumond, ed., *Letters of James Gillespie Birney*, I:244 (to Gerrit Smith, Sept. 13), 250 (to Joseph Healy, Oct. 2), 256 (S. Wright to Birney, Nov. 5, 1835).

26. *Congressional Globe*, 24th Cong., 1st sess., Appendix, p. 9.

27. Richardson, comp., *Messages and Papers*, III:175–76.

28. *Congressional Globe*, 24th Cong., 1st sess., pp. 36–37.

29. Senate Document 118, 24th Cong., 1st sess. See letter of Calhoun to Christopher Van Deventer, Feb. 7, 1836, in American Historical Association, *Report, 1899*, II: 357–58. "I made a few days since a report on the part of the President's Message, which relates to incendiary publications, in which I have discussed some very important points. The report, I think, was well received on all sides."

30. *Congressional Globe*, 24th Cong., 1st sess., pp. 150–51, 284–

85. Fines were set at a minimum of $100 and maximum of $1,000.

31. Ibid., pp. 288–89, 298–99, Appendix, pp. 282–87.

32. Ibid., pp. 301–302 (April 13); William M. Meigs, *Life of Thomas Hart Benton*, pp. 336–37. Years later Benton wrote that the bill was based on the same nullification theories Calhoun had advocated for some time and that he was "tired of the eternal cry of dissolving the Union." Benton was a faithful follower of President Jackson.

33. *Congressional Globe*, 24th Cong., 1st sess., Appendix, p. 439; Glyndon G. Van Deusen, *The Life of Henry Clay*, p. 314. See *Life*, Sept. 12, 1960, for picture of Clay addressing the Senate on this issue (Old Crow advertisement).

34. *Congressional Globe*, 24th Cong., 1st sess., Appendix, pp. 437–40; Claude Moore Fuess, *Daniel Webster*, II:46.

35. *Congressional Globe*, 24th Cong., 1st sess., Appendix, pp. 437–38; George Tichnor Curtis, *Life of James Buchanan*, I:338–58.

36. *Congressional Globe*, 24th Cong., 1st sess., p. 338. Grundy was a Southerner, a slaveowner, and opposed to the abolitionists. He was defeated for reelection in 1837 and was appointed attorney general by President Van Buren, Sept., 1838.

37. Ibid., pp. 416, 430; Wiltse, *Calhoun: Nullifier*, pp. 273–77 says that the tie forcing Van Buren to cast a vote to pass the bill to a third reading was "a bit of strategy engineered, in all probability, by Calhoun to get the Democratic candidate on the record." Carl Schurz, *Life of Henry Clay*, I:81–85, says Van Buren was a "Northern man with Southern principles."

38. *Congressional Globe*, 24th Cong., 1st sess., pp. 26, 258, 391. See W. Sherman Savage, *The Controversy over the Distribution of Abolition Literature, 1830–1860*, pp. 64–65.

39. 5 *Stat.* 87 (July 2, 1836); White, *Jacksonians*, p. 520.

40. South Carolina, *Acts and Joint Resolutions of the General Assembly, 1835*, pp. 26–28.

41. North Carolina, *Journal of the House of Representatives, 1835*, pp. 101–102, 179, 183; *Journal of the Senate, 1835*, pp. 7, 53, 80; *Session Laws, 1835*, pp. 119–21. See also Georgia, *Acts and Resolutions of the General Assembly of the State of Georgia, 1835*, pp. 297–300; Alabama, *Acts of the General Assembly, 1836*, pp. 174–75; Mississippi, *Laws, 1836*, pp. 101–102; Kentucky, *Acts Passed at the First Session of the Forty-Fourth General Assembly of the Commonwealth of Kentucky, 1836*, pp. 683–86.

42. New York, *Laws of the State of New York, 1836*, p. 811; Massachusetts, *Resolves of the General Court of the Commonwealth*

*of Massachusetts, 1836*, pp. 297–98; Ohio, *Acts of a General Nature, 1835*, p. 957; *Congressional Globe*, 24th Cong., 1st sess., p. 291.

43. Vermont, *Acts and Resolves Passed by the Legislature, 1833–1836*, p. 44; see Savage, *Distribution of Abolition Literature*, pp. 55–60.

44. Maryland, *Laws Made and Passed by General Assembly of the State of Maryland, 1835*, ch. 325 to supplement act of Dec., 1831. In 1842 (1841, ch. 272) an act provided ten to twenty years' imprisonment for any free Negro or mulatto knowingly receiving any abolition matter from any post office. It also provided that grand juries were to summon before them at every term of court postmasters of their county and examine them whether they had received inflammatory pamphlets. Similar laws were passed in Tennessee, Feb. 13, 1836 (*Public Acts, 1835–1836*), Missouri, Feb. 1, 1837 (*Laws, 1836*). See Clement Eaton, "Censorship of Southern Mails," *American Historical Review* 48 (Jan., 1943): 266–81.

45. Virginia, *Acts of the General Assembly of Virginia, 1835–1836*, ch. 66. A similar law was passed in South Carolina in 1859.

46. *Congressional Globe*, 27th Cong., 2nd sess., pp. 977–78 (Jan. 24, 1842).

47. J. Collamer to J. B. Netton, postmaster at Pendleton, S.C., Oct. 9, 1849, in Postmaster General Letterbooks. Collamer had spent most of his life in Vermont, was graduated from the university, spent four terms in the legislature, was assistant judge of the superior court, 1833–1842, member of the House of Representatives from the state, 1842–1849. He was defeated when he ran for the Senate and so recommended himself to President Taylor for a position in the cabinet.

48. Dunbar Rowland, *Jefferson Davis, Constitutionalist, His Letters, Papers, and Speeches* II:103–105 (Robert Bowman and others to Davis, Dec. 21, 1856), III:107–108 (M. D. Hayes to Davis, Sept. 28, 1856).

49. Fowler, *Cabinet Politician*, pp. 78–81. James Campbell, having organized the Irish Catholic vote, was an important local politician in Philadelphia. He had been a supporter of James Buchanan in the Democratic convention of 1852; Buchanan recommended that President Pierce include him in his cabinet.

50. U.S. Department of Justice, *Official Opinions of the Attorneys General of the United States Advising the President and Heads of Departments in Relation to their Official Duties*, VIII (compiled by Caleb Cushing), 489–502. Cushing had begun his political career as a Whig, representing Massachusetts in Congress, 1835–1842; he had

then become the United States' first envoy to China. From 1852–1853 he had been judge of the Massachusetts Supreme Court. His hatred of abolitionists may have influenced his decision. See Claude M. Fuess, *Life of Caleb Cushing*, II:185.

51. Fowler, *Cabinet Politician*, pp. 100–101.

52. *New York Tribune*, Dec. 18, 1859; Nye, *Fettered Freedom*, p. 69.

53. Howard K. Beale, ed., "The Diary of Edward Bates," American Historical Association, *Annual Report, 1930*, IV:95–96.

54. *New York Tribune*, Feb. 8, 1860; Beale, ed., "Diary of Edward Bates," p. 96; *National Intelligencer*, Feb. 6, 1860.

55. *Congressional Globe*, 36th Cong., 1st sess., pp. 795, 3055.

56. J. Holt to A. Huger, Dec. 29, 1860, in Postmaster General Letterbooks.

57. *Congressional Globe*, 36th Cong., 2nd sess., pp. 498, 775–76, 1044–45, 1077–82, 1164. Another act, Feb. 27, 1861, defined mailable matter as: maps, engravings, lithographs, books not exceeding four pounds, and seeds, cuttings not more than eight ounces (see Appendix, p. 325).

## Chapter 3

1. Richardson, comp., *Messages and Papers*, VI:8.

2. William Ernest Smith, *The Blair Family*, I:96–97. The department staff at that time consisted of three assistant postmasters general, a chief clerk, and four messengers. The first assistant postmaster general was John A. Kasson of Iowa. See Edward Younger, *John A. Kasson*, p. 130n.

3. M. Blair to S. Colfax, July 12, 1861, in Postmaster General Letterbooks (National Archives).

4. *Congressional Globe*, 37th Cong., 1st sess., p. 115. See Beale, ed., "Diary of Edward Bates," pp. 182, 185–86. Memorandum of cabinet meeting, April 15, 1861. Attorney General Bates gave his opinion that the mails ought to be stopped in the revolting states immediately. He repeated his recommendation, April 23, and complained that they had cut off our mails but we continued to "furnish theirs gratis."

5. Department of War, *War of Rebellion Records*, series 2, II:12–13 (John A. Kasson to Simon Cameron, Secretary of War, June 28, 1861); *New York Times*, Aug. 22, 26, 1861.

6. *New York Times*, Sept. 13, 1861.

7. *War of Rebellion Records*, series 2, II:59 (3rd asst. postmaster general to secretary of war, Sept. 11, 1861); p. 162 (F. W. Seward

to J. P. Trott, Nov. 30, 1861); p. 179 (Seward to Blair, Dec. 19, 1861); p. 191 (Trott to Seward, Jan. 17, 1862).

8. *New York Times*, July 13, 1861; New York *World*, Aug. 11, 1861.

9. Robert S. Harper, *Lincoln and the Press*, p. 129.

10. William Howard Russell, *Diary North and South*, p. 136.

11. House Misc. Document 16, 37th Cong., 3rd sess., p. 9.

12. *The American Annual Cyclopaedia and Register of Important Events of the Year*, 1861, p. 329.

13. *Journal of Commerce*, Aug. 17, 23, 26, 1861; *National Intelligencer*, Aug. 27, 1861.

14. *Journal of Commerce*, Aug. 29, 31, Sept. 22, 1861. The *World* (Sept. 2) agreed that denying treasonable newspapers the use of the mails would bring papers to an end effectually, although not as speedily as an order from the War Department forbidding their publication. The editor approved of the action; he emphasized his devotion to freedom of the press but felt this was one of the necessities of war. *New York Times* (Aug. 22) considered the *Journal of Commerce* "one of the most mischievous, irritatious and influential organs of Southern treason."

15. *World*, Sept. 2, 6, 16, 1861; *War of Rebellion Records*, series 2, II:496 (John A. Kennedy, supt. of Metropolitan Police, New York City, to Seward, Sept. 14, 1861).

16. *World*, Aug. 26, 1861; Harper, *Lincoln and the Press*, p. 159; Morgan Dix, comp., *Memoirs of John Adams Dix*, II:30–31.

17. *War of Rebellion Records*, series 2, II:70 (Seward to Blair, Sept., 17, 1861); *New York Times*, Sept. 19, 1861. The editor was arrested and the paper suspended the same night.

18. *War of Rebellion Records*, series 2, II:82 (*Plymouth Democrat*, Indiana), pp. 493–501 (New York *National Zeitung* and *Staats Zeitung*), pp. 940, 943, 951, 953–956 (*Franklin Gazette*); Ray H. Abrams, "The Jeffersonian Copperhead Newspaper," *Pennsylvania Magazine of History and Biography* 57 (July, 1933): 260–88. Postmaster General Blair explained to the son of a friend of his father that he did not really think great harm would come from these papers but he did not think they should be aided by the machinery of the government in their traitorous purposes. See *New York Times*, Sept. 9, 1861, for copy of letter to James W. Wall, who had protested the barring from the mails of the *True American* of Trenton, N.J.

19. *National Intelligencer*, Dec. 6, 1861. See Beale, ed., "Diary of Edward Bates," p. 209.

20. Senate Executive Document 4, 37th Cong., 2nd sess., pp. 582–84; *New York Times*, Dec. 3, 1861.

# Notes for Chapter Three

21. *Congressional Globe*, 37th Cong., 2nd sess., Appendix, p. 334. In this Congress (Jan. 13, 1863) Congressman Vallandigham (later exiled from the United States as a Copperhead) introduced a bill to abolish the Post Office (see ibid., p. 399); *New York Times*, Jan. 24, 1862. In November, 1861, the postmaster general had decided that the act of 1825 empowered him to declare the streets of cities post routes and he did so and ordered private postal service discontinued (see *New York Times*, Nov. 19, 1861).

22. *New York Times*, Feb. 26, 28, 1862.

23. *World*, March 25, 1862; Benjamin P. Thomas and Harold M. Hyman, *Stanton, The Life and Times of Lincoln's Secretary of War*, p. 176. Some said that then Stanton had taken over the Post Office Department.

24. Harper, *Lincoln and the Press*, p. 153. He relates how the postmaster at Leavenworth, Kan., gathered up a stack of *World*s and rushed into the street and burnt them; the local paper commented, "Thus *The World* passed away with a great noise and fervent heat."

25. *Annual Cyclopaedia*, 1863, pp. 423–24, lists the papers suppressed by military order.

26. *War of Rebellion Records*, series 1, L, part 1, pp. 896–97 (Feb. 24, 26, 1862). Many papers in California and Oregon were barred from the mails in 1862 (see Harper, *Lincoln and the Press*, p. 232).

27. House Misc. Doc. 16, 37th Cong., 3rd sess.

28. *Congressional Globe*, 37th Cong., 3rd sess., pp. 321, 349–50, 390. The postmaster general had proposed in April, 1862, restoring mail facilities to newspapers that had been excluded, but the War Department had asked that this be postponed "believing it would be premature, pernicious in its tendency and prejudicial to the public safety, if made at this time." See *War of Rebellion Records*, series 2, II:283 (P. Watson to Kasson, April 9, 1862).

29. Senate Executive Document 19, 37th Cong., 3rd sess. (2 pages).

30. *New York Times*, March 25, April 23, 1862, June 12, 1863, describes a mass meeting of Democratic clubs held in the Brooklyn Academy of Music denouncing "the suspension of several newspapers and the denial of mail transportation to others."

31. *Annual Cyclopaedia*, 1863, p. 424. See Donald Bridgman Sanger, "The Chicago Times and the Civil War," *Mississippi Valley Historical Review* 17 (March, 1931): 557–81; Theodore Pease and James G. Randall, *The Diary of Orville Hickman Browning*, I: 632–33.

32. *World*, May 23, June 18, 23, 1864; Fletcher Pratt, *Stanton, Lincoln's Secretary of War*, pp. 363–64, says Seward insisted on the

suppression of the *World* and the *Journal of Commerce*, "two scur-rilous sheets." Stanton sent off the order to arrest the editors without presidential approval.

33. *New York Times*, May 19, 21, 23; *New York Tribune*, May 18, 19, 1864.

34. *World*, May 24, 1864.

35. Ibid., July 8, 9, 19, 1864.

36. Ibid., Aug. 5, 6, 8, 1864. The editor of the *Tribune* (Aug. 6) declared that he was not disposed to "impeach the moral integrity of the Post Office Department" and stated that he did not believe "that the mails are interfered with from any malicious design, though it is quite possible that *The World* or its friends may have lost letters which they knew had been addressed to them. Such incidents are by no means uncommon."

37. Fowler, *Cabinet Politician*, pp. 123–25.

38. Beale, ed., "Diary of Edward Bates," p. 419n.

# Chapter 4

1. *Congressional Globe*, 37th Cong., 3rd sess., pp. 837–39, Appendix, p. 201.

2. Heywood Broun and Margaret Leech, *Anthony Comstock*, pp. 75–76.

3. House Misc. Document 16, 37th Cong., 3rd sess., pp. 8–9, 16.

4. *Congressional Globe*, 38th Cong., 2nd sess. (S. 390), pp. 654–56, 660–62; *New York Times*, Feb. 9, 1865.

5. The bill did provide that a postmaster, in order to ascertain the author, could open letters in case postage had not been prepaid and there was no way of learning who the writer was from the outside. The Senate and House disagreed on this; finally the act provided that all such letters be sent unopened to the dead letter office.

6. *Congressional Globe*, 38th Cong., 2nd sess., pp. 661–62, 965–66, 1256–57, 1311, 1391. It was pointed out that this was really a criminal statute.

7. 13 *Stat.* 507. The importation of obscene articles had been forbidden in acts of 1842 and 1857.

8. *Congressional Globe*, 39th Cong., 1st sess., p. 874; 2nd sess., p. 1994.

9. *New York Times*, March 1, 1866.

10. *Congressional Globe*, 40th Cong., 2nd sess., pp. 1230, 1681, 2973, 2995, 3504, 4175, 4412; Marshall Cushing, *Story of Our Post Office*, p. 505.

11. 15 *Stat.* 196. The postmaster general's annual report of 1866

gave the number of pieces in the dead letter office as 4.5 million; 60 percent were business circulars, advertisements of lottery and gift enterprises (see *Congressional Globe*, 39th Cong., 2nd sess., Appendix, p. 55). The Internal Revenue Law of July 13, 1866, had levied a tax of $100 on lottery ticket dealers and provided a penalty for selling tickets that had not been duly stamped in accordance with the law of 1863 (see ibid., 39th Cong., 1st sess., Appendix, p. 346).

12. Department of Justice, *Official Opinions of the Attorneys-General* XII: 399–401, 538–40. Evarts said the postmaster might be liable to indictment and to suit by aggrieved party if he refused to deliver letters that were not clearly nonmailable.

13. *New York Times*, Feb. 2, 1870, Dec. 6, 1871; *Congressional Globe*, 41st Cong., 2nd sess. (H.R. 2295), pp. 2962, 4799; 3rd sess., pp. 30, 35, 86, 509, 957–59; 42nd Cong., 1st sess. (H.R. 1), 2nd sess., pp. 15, 31, 42, 71, 171, 232, 380, 978, 2640–52, 3893, 3949, 4092, 4105, 4459.

14. 17 *Stat.* 322–23. The act retained the provision that no newspaper should be received in the mail unless sufficiently dried and enclosed in a wrapper. Note that this act specifies illegal lotteries, which the act of 1868 did not. In June, 1870, an act had been passed providing that some officer of the Department of Justice should be designated to care for prosecution of penal offenses against postal laws (see *Congressional Globe*, 41st Cong., 2nd sess., Appendix, p. 669).

15. Cushing, *Our Post Office*, pp. 614–17; Broun and Leech, *Comstock*, pp. 102–28.

16. *Congressional Globe*, 42nd Cong., 3rd sess., Appendix, pp. 168–69. See James C. N. Paul and Murray L. Schwartz, *Federal Censorship*, pp. 19–24.

17. *Congressional Globe*, 42nd Cong., 3rd sess., pp. 1436–37, 1524–25, 1571, 2004, 2210. See Charles Gallaudet Trumbull, *Anthony Comstock, Fighter*, pp. 83–99.

18. 17 *Stat.* 599 (sec. 2). This act omitted the word "vulgar" and left only "indecent character" and also eliminated the phrase "disloyal devices" from items not to be printed on the outside of envelopes and postal cards. Punishment was not only for depositing in the mails but also for taking the article out of the mail.

19. *New York Times*, March 12, 1873; Broun and Leech, *Comstock*, p. 145.

20. Trumbull, *Comstock*, p. 100; Broun and Leech, *Comstock*, pp. 149, 152, 219. Comstock lost his commission in 1906 but was reappointed the next year at a salary of $1,500. He died in 1915. Up to 1893 he had made 1,792 arrests, seized 45 tons of obscene matter

and 17 tons of lottery material (see Cushing, *Our Post Office*, pp. 614–17). The committee of the YMCA on the suppression of vice was formally incorporated as a separate body. Similar organizations were formed in other parts of the country. In the west R. W. McAfee was Comstock's counterpart.

21. James Jackson Kilpatrick, *The Smut Peddlers*, p. 38; *United States* v. *Bott*, 11 Blatchford 346 (1874).

22. *Congressional Record*, 44th Cong., 1st sess. (H.R. 1239), pp. 474, 695–96; see Paul and Schwartz, *Federal Censorship*, pp. 27–28.

23. *Congressional Record*, 44th Cong., 1st sess. (H.R. 2575), pp. 3656, 4261–64. During the debate it was suggested that the use of the mails be prohibited for everything that was for an immoral use. Senator Conkling of New York said that whiskey was kept out of the mails as it was included in the phrase "adapted to an immoral purpose." Senator Sherman of Ohio corrected him, saying that one could send whiskey through the mails in a can but not in a glass bottle as the bottle might break. 19 *Stat.* 90.

24. 20 *Stat.* 359 (sec. 15). Rogers, *Postal Power*, p. 40, says in case of the copyright "the postal power is used to make more effectual legislation which it was competent for Congress to enact."

25. House Executive Document 7, 45th Cong., 2nd sess., pp. 242–51.

26. House Executive Document 8, 45th Cong., 3rd sess., pp. 51–53.

27. *Congressional Record*, 45th Cong., 3rd sess., p. 697.

28. 20 *Stat.* 359 (sec. 13, 14).

29. *In the Matter of A. Orlando Jackson*, 96 U.S. 727 (1879).

30. House Executive Document 22, 46th Cong., 2nd sess., letter of Postmaster General Key (1877–1880) in response to resolution of the House of Representatives, Dec. 16, 1879.

31. House Executive Document 8, 46th Cong., 2nd sess., pp. 340–43 (*In Re Commonwealth Distribution Co.* v. *Postmaster, Louisville, Kentucky*); House Executive Document 8, 46th Cong., 3rd sess., p. 39.

32. In 1879 the legislature of Louisiana abrogated the charter of the Louisiana State Lottery, but a United States judge declared that was a violation of the contract given in 1868 for 35 years. The Louisiana Constitutional Convention in 1879 stated that gambling was a vice and that after Jan. 1, 1895, all lotteries in the state would be illegal (see Cushing, *Our Post Office*, p. 505).

33. House Executive Document 8, 46th Cong., 3rd sess., pp. 529–42 (*Maximilian A. Dauphin* v. *David M. Key*, postmaster general).

34. House Executive Document 9, 48th Cong., 1st sess., p. 31; Matilda Gresham, *Life of Walter Quintin Gresham, 1832–1895*, II:

491–93; *New Orleans National Bank* v. *Merchant,* 18 Fed. 841 (1884).

35. Rogers, *Postal Power,* p. 264.

36. C. H. Cramer, *Royal Bob,* pp. 172–73.

37. T. Harry Williams, ed., *Hayes, The Diary of a President, 1875–1881,* pp. 183–84, 188.

38. *United States* v. *Bennett,* 16 Blatchford 338 (1879). The court stated in more explicit terms the fact that sending obscene matter to a fictitious person was no defense in *Bates* v. *United States,* 10 Fed. 92 (1881) Robert Ingersoll tried to persuade President Hayes to pardon Bennett but, as Hayes said in his diary, he decided to mind his own business and not interfere with the province of the judiciary (see Williams, ed., *Hayes,* pp. 233–34, 237–38, 240; Cramer, *Royal Bob,* pp. 171–75).

39. *United States* v. *Williams,* 3 Fed. 484 (1880).

40. *United States* v. *Loftis,* 12 Fed. 671 (1882). In Congress that year a bill adding the word "letter" passed the House but was buried in the Senate committee (see *Congressional Record,* 47th Cong., 1st sess., H.R. 4963).

41. *United States* v. *Gaylord,* 17 Fed. 438 (1883).

42. *United States* v. *Morris,* 18 Fed. 900 (1884); see also *United States* v. *Hanover,* 17 Fed. 444 (1883).

43. *United States* v. *Leslie G. Chase,* 135 U.S. 255 (1890).

# Chapter 5

1. *Congressional Record,* 48th Cong., 1st sess., H.R. 1807, H.R. 2744; House Report 523; 49th Cong., 1st sess., H.R. 1058; 50th Cong., 1st sess., H.R. 1518. Many of these bills were to prevent the use of the mails for advertisement of medicines, cordials, and bitters unless they were certified by the Patent Office as not being detrimental to health. These foreshadow the Pure Food and Drug Act of 1906.

2. *Congressional Record,* 49th Cong., 1st sess., S. 1961, H.R. 7544; House Report 2676; 25 *Stat.* 188. The word "scurrilous" was in the acts of 1872 and 1873 but was omitted in act of 1876.

3. *Congressional Record,* 50th Cong., 1st sess., S. 3303. In 1895 a federal district judge gave a broad definition of the word "delineation." A proprietor of a small collection agency sent to delinquent debtors a dunning letter enclosed in a pink envelope. If the debtor did not pay, the next demand was sent in a black envelope addressed in white letters. Postal officials knew that such a letter meant the third demand for payment. The judge declared that the use of such en-

# Notes for Chapter Five

velopes was a violation of the statute prohibiting the mailing of postal cards or envelopes on which there is any delineation or other matter intended to reflect "injuriously upon the character or conduct of another." The department then ruled that all envelopes of any color when it was evident the sender intended to reflect injuriously upon the conduct of the addressee should be banned from the mails. See *United States* v. *Dodge*, 70 Fed. 235 (1895); House Document 11, 54th Cong., 2nd sess., p. 3487.

4. *Congressional Record*, 50th Cong., 1st sess., pp. 6041, 6104, 7661; 25 *Stat.* 496. See Paul and Schwartz, *Federal Censorship*, p. 259.

5. *Congressional Record*, 50th Cong., 1st sess., pp. 6499, 7660–62.

6. 25 *Stat.* 496. The Supreme Court shortly after the passage of this act declared "writing" in the act of 1876 did not include a private letter enclosed in an envelope. The Court refused to consider the 1888 amendment. See Rogers, *Postal Power*, p. 49.

7. Department of Justice, *Official Opinions of the Attorneys-General*, XIX: 667–68; see Herbert Adams Gibbons, *John Wanamaker*.

8. Cushing, *Our Post Office*, pp. 609–13; House Executive Document 13, 52nd Cong., 1st sess.

9. Senate Report 747, 52nd Cong., 1st sess. The report was on a bill to ban any publication devoted principally to crime news or stories of lust and immoral deeds.

10. *William Grimm* v. *United States*, 156 U.S. 604 (1894).

11. *Dan K. Swearingen* v. *United States*, 161 U.S. 446 (1896).

12. House Document 256, 55th Cong., 3rd sess., p. 3.

13. *Lew Rosen* v. *United States*, 161 U.S. 29 (1896).

14. *Joseph R. Dunlop* v. *United States*, 165 U.S. 486 (1897).

15. *Warren E. Price* v. *United States*, 165 U.S. 311 (1897).

16. *Arthur D. Andrews* v. *United States*, 162 U.S. 420 (1896).

17. House Document 4, 54th Cong., 2nd sess.

18. Cushing, *Our Post Office*, pp. 566–85. The office of chief inspector had been established in 1880 and in 1891 was made responsible to a fourth assistant postmaster general. See Makris, *The Silent Investigators*, pp. 67–68, 99–100.

19. Senate Report 2566, 50th Cong., 2nd sess.; House Report 1501, 50th Cong., 2nd sess.

20. *Congressional Record*, 50th Cong., 1st sess., H.R. 9268 was substituted for H.R. 4373.

21. 25 *Stat.* 873.

22. House Executive Document 9, 48th Cong., 1st sess., pp. 32–33.

23. *Congressional Record*, 48th Cong., 1st sess., S. 1017, introduced by Philetus Sawyer of Wisconsin. Senate Report 233. Charles

H. Van Wyck of Nebraska tried to add an amendment that would also prevent newspapers from advertising sale of stocks on margin. H.R. 1910 was introduced by Thomas M. Browne of Indiana. He had wanted his bill referred to the Judiciary Committee, but this was defeated by a vote of 60 to 68 and it went to the Committee on the Post Office and Post-Roads. See House Report 826. Bills to delete the word "fraudulent" were introduced in both houses and received favorable reports but were pigeonholed. See S. 1018 and Senate Report 288, and H.R. 1911 and House Report 472.

24. Senate Report 11, 49th Cong., 1st sess., pp. 12–13.

25. *Congressional Record*, 49th Cong., 1st sess., S. 260, S. 1072, H.R. 2030, H.R. 2290, H.R. 2296, H.R. 3337, H.R. 6522, H.R. 9121, House Report 2678. Postmaster General Vilas (1885–1888) suggested that the cheaper pound rate be denied to all newspapers which contained lottery advertisements and that there be published in an official guide the names and descriptions of fraudulent schemes. See House Executive Document 10, 49th Cong., 1st sess. See also *Congressional Record*, 50th Cong., 1st sess., S. 1868, H.R. 1315, H.R. 1842, H.R. 3320, H.R. 3324; House Report 787 on the latter two bills was adverse.

26. Cushing, *Our Post Office*, p. 520.

27. Richardson, comp., *Messages and Papers*, IX:80.

28. House Executive Document 10, 51st Cong., 1st sess., pp. 39–40; Senate Executive Document 196.

29. *Congressional Record*, 51st Cong., 1st sess., S. 568, S. 2768, S. 4323, H.R. 177, H.R. 241, H.R. 242, H.R. 3321, H.R. 8981, H.R. 11569, H.R. 12150.

30. Ibid., pp. 8439, 8698–8721, 9510, 10085; House Report 2844, Senate Report 1579 (on S. 4323).

31. 26 *Stat.* 465. Anthony Comstock's biographer claims this act incorporated his bill which had been introduced in 1885 and which he had kept before Congress for five years; see Trumbull, *Comstock*, p. 114. Cushing, *Our Post Office*, p. 524, says the bill was written by Assistant Attorney General Tyner. The Supreme Court declared that a man could be tried in the district where the letters were delivered even if he were not present (see *Salinger* v. *United States*, 265 U.S. 224 (1924), 272 U.S. 542 (1926). Proof that a letter properly directed was placed in a post office creates presumption it reached its destination and trial could be held in court where letter was delivered, declared the Court. Defendants claimed offense was committed where letter was mailed; see *Hagner* v. *United States*, 285 U.S. 427 (1932).

# Notes for Chapter Five

32. Hannis Taylor, "A Blow at the Freedom of the Press," *North American Review* 155 (1892): 700.

33. *Official Opinions of the Attorneys-General*, XIX: 679–82; House Executive Document 10, 51st Cong., 2nd sess., pp. 14–15.

34. Cushing, *Our Post Office*, pp. 525–36, 533.

35. *Ex parte John L. Rapier*, 143 U.S. 110 (1892).

36. Hannis Taylor, *Origin and Growth of the American Constitution*, p. 230.

37. House Executive Document 11, 52nd Cong., 2nd sess., pp. 8–9.

38. Cushing, *Our Post Office*, p. 562; *Edward H. Horner* v. *United States*, 143 U.S. 207 (1892). Justice Blatchford used as the definition of a lottery "a game of hazard in which small sums are ventured with the chance of obtaining a larger value, either in money or in other articles."

39. *Congressional Record*, 53rd Cong., 2nd sess. (S. 1620), pp. 2211, 3766, 3808–3809, 4312–14, 4986, 5089, 7941, 8667; 3rd sess., pp. 3013, 3038–39, 3130.

40. 28 *Stat.* 963. Sealed letters containing lottery circulars came under custom laws. In accordance with the Universal Postal Treaty the customs officers treated these letters as "forfeited goods," for they were marked unlawfully. When they reached their destination the postmaster required the addressee to open the package in the presence of a customs officer and if it contained lottery tickets or circulars they were confiscated. See House Executive Document 13, 52nd Cong., 1st sess., p. 21.

41. Reports on fraud orders issued are given in: House Executive Document 12, 53rd Cong., 2nd sess.; House Executive Document 13, 53rd Cong., 3rd sess.; House Executive Document 13, 54th Cong., 1st sess.; House Executive Document 11, 54th Cong., 2nd sess., House Executive Document 13, 55th Cong., 3rd sess.; House Executive Document 16, 56th Cong., 1st sess.; House Executive Document 4, 56th Cong., 2nd sess.

|  | Fraud Orders Issued | Revoked |
|---|---|---|
| 1893–94 | 223 | 21 |
| 1894–95 | 218 | 70 |
| 1895–96 | 193 | 44 |
| 1896–97 | 244 | 64 |
| 1897–98 | 62 | 4 |
| 1898–99 | 99 | 4 |
| 1899–1900 | 84 | 1 |

42. *Jay T. Stokes* v. *United States*, 157 U.S. 187 (1895).

# Notes for Chapter Six

43. *Louis F. Streep* v. *United States*, 160 U.S. 128 (1895).

44. *John H. Durland* v. *United States*, 161 U.S. 305 (1896). For similar cases in the lower courts see *MacDonald et al.* v. *United States*, 59 Fed. 563 (1893), 63 Fed. 426 (1894). Judge Grossup of the district court of Illinois said: "The mails of the United States are intended for legitimate business or friendly communication, and are defiled by the dissemination and promotion of such a scheme as the evidence in this case admittedly discloses."

45. *American School of Magnetic Healing and J. H. Kelly* v. *J. M. McAnnulty*, 187 U.S. 94 (1902).

46. *Public Clearing House* v. *Frederick E. Coyne*, 194 U.S. 497 (1904). Justice Peckham dissented. For similar case see *Fitzsimmons* v. *United States*, 156 Fed. 477 (1907). In that case Judge Gilbert cited the Supreme Court decision of 1904.

47. House Executive Document 11, 54th Cong., 2nd sess., pp. 59–69; House Executive Document 16, 56th Cong., 1st sess., p. 33; House Executive Document 4, 57th Cong., 1st sess., pp. 36–37.

48. House Executive Document 4, 54th Cong., 1st sess., p. 35; House Executive Document 11, 54th Cong., 2nd sess., pp. 47–49; House Executive Document 4, 57th Cong., 1st sess., pp. 35–36, 44–45.

# Chapter 6

1. *Congressional Record*, 56th Cong., 1st sess. (S. 2494, S. 2495, H.R. 6957, H.R. 8923), pp. 893, 1021, 2688, 5476; 2nd sess. (H.R. 13423), pp. 803, 825, 1222, 1586.

2. Senate Document 394, 59th Cong., 2nd sess., pp. 17, 42–51; Makris, *Silent Investigators*, pp. 68–69. The office of chief inspector became an independent office in 1905.

3. Senate Document 394, 59th Cong., 2nd sess., p. 226. Postmasters general had had power to exclude from the mails certain injurious and dangerous matter, but there had been no penalty for depositing such matter in the mail. Many postmasters general had recommended penalties, especially severe ones if postal employees were hurt or killed. See House Executive Document 4, 47th Cong., 1st sess., p. 52 (1881); House Executive Document 4, 54th Cong., 1st sess., p. 38 (1895); House Executive Document 4, 58th Cong., 2nd sess., p. 9 (1903).

4. Senate Document 394, 59th Cong., 2nd sess., pp. 231–33, 280–99.

5. Ibid., pp. 269, 342–43. Anthony Comstock complained about the "demoralizing French pictures" coming in from France, so the State Department requested the aid of the French government "to

prevent the mailing of objectionable photographs or pictures." See *Evening Post* (New York), Feb. 6, 1905.

6. House Executive Document 4, 57th Cong., 2nd sess., pp. 32–42. Tyner reported that during the year ending June 30, 1902, there had been 785 official written opinions, 567 dealing with mailability of matter under act of Sept. 19, 1890, 163 calls to persons to appear and 92 hearings. See *Congressional Record*, 57th Cong., 2nd sess., S. 6888, H.R. 16654 (bills to review rulings of the Post Office Department). In the next Congress Senator Hoar of Massachusetts presented a resolution that the Committee on Post-Offices and Post-Roads consider whether or not legislation was necessary to provide for prompt judicial hearing of a person complaining about the action of the Post Office Department. He recited protests he had received from individuals whose correspondence, containing medical advice and preparations, had been excluded from the mail (see *Congressional Record*, 58th Cong., 2nd sess., p. 3029).

7. *Congressional Record*, 59th Cong., 1st sess. (H.R. 16548), p. 3710; 2nd sess., pp. 460–61, 703–12.

8. House Report 4919, 59th Cong., 1st sess.

9. George B. Cortelyou, "Frauds in the Mail," *North American Review*, 184 (April 19, 1907): 808–17. See also House Document 17, 59th Cong., 1st sess.

10. *Bates and Guild Co.* v. *Henry C. Payne, Postmaster General*, 194 U.S. 106 (1904). Chief Justice Fuller and Justice Harlan dissented. For similar decision see *Smith* v. *Hitchcock*, 266 U.S. 53 (1912). In this case some magazines were denied second-class mailing privileges as the postmaster general said each issue contained a single story complete in itself. They were really books and should therefore go third class. The Court refused to review the facts and upheld the postmaster general.

11. *Congressional Record*, 58th Cong., 2nd sess., S. 3380; Senate Report 827.

12. *Congressional Record*, 59th Cong., 1st sess., pp. 3223–25; House Document 650.

13. *Congressional Record*, 59th Cong., 1st sess., H.R. 24823, H.R. 24935; 60th Cong., 2nd sess., H.R. 22325. All the bills were introduced by Oliver C. Wiley of Alabama.

14. Elting E. Morison, et al., eds., *Letters of Theodore Roosevelt*, V: 186 (March 19, 1906).

15. Ibid., VI:977–78 (March 20, 1908).

16. Department of Justice, *Official Opinions of the Attorneys-General*, XXVI: 555–72.

17. *Congressional Record*, 60th Cong., 1st sess., pp. 4526, 6132,

# Notes for Chapter Six

6756; Senate Report 622; 35 *Stat.* 416. By an oversight this section was omitted when the postal laws were codified in 1909, so it was inserted in another Post Office Appropriation Act in 1911 (36 *Stat.* 1339).

18. Morison, ed., *Letters of Theodore Roosevelt*, VI: 1080–81 (to Lyman Abbott, June 17, 1908).

19. Robert Baral, *Turn West on 23rd Street*, pp. 17–19; *New York Times*, Feb. 5, 1907.

20. *New York Times*, Feb. 1, 2, 3, 5, 6, 8, 9, 1907.

21. Ibid., Feb. 10, 12, 13, 1907. The trial ended with no verdict, March 27, 1907.

22. Ibid., Feb. 12, 15, 16, 1907.

23. *Congressional Record*, 60th Cong., 1st sess., pp. 496, 979; House Report 2; Senate Report 10.

24. *United States* v. *Moore*, 104 Fed. 78 (1900).

25. *Hanson* v. *United States*, 157 Fed. 749 (1907). See also *United States* v. *O'Donnell*, 165 Fed. 218 (1908) in which a judge said that a sealed envelope in which a third party was called scurrilous names did not violate the obscenity statute as it was not likely to incite immorality.

26. *Congressional Record*, 60th Cong., 1st sess., pp. 995–98, 2391-- 92; 2nd sess., pp. 283–84.

27. 35 *Stat.* 1129. A Chicago postmaster in 1911 barred from the mails, because it discussed with frankness things usually not mentioned in polite society, the report of the Chicago Vice Commission. The commission had been appointed by the mayor and had on it prominent lawyers, teachers, and clergymen and the report had been sent out by John D. Rockefeller to sociologists and social workers. See "The Vice Report and the Mails" *Outlook* 99 (Oct., 1911): 353– 54; "Discussing the Social Evil," *Nation* 93 (Oct. 5, 1911): 308–309. It was not until 1932 that the Supreme Court handed down a decision concerning the adding of "filthy" in the statute; it declared that Congress had in 1909 "added a new class of unmailable matter—the filthy." See *United States* v. *O. B. Limehouse*, 285 U.S. 424 (1932).

28. The section read: "Every article or thing designed, adapted, or intended for preventing conception." The courts held that there should be required "an intent on the part of the sender that the article mailed or shipped by common carrier be used for illegal contraception or abortion or for indecent or immoral purposes." See *Youngs Rubber Corp.* v. *C. I. Lee and Co.*, 45 F. 2d 103 (1930). The courts also held that the "intent of a person mailing a circular conveying information for preventing conception" must be considered in the conviction of a person, that the section should be given a reasonable construction.

# Notes for Chapter Six

See *Davis* v. *United States*, 62 F. 2d 473 (1933). See also House Report 304, 80th Cong., 1st sess.

29. The court did, however, declare that the wrapper did not include the outside sheet of a newspaper; see *United States* v. *Higgins*, 194 Fed. 539 (1912). One postmaster under this clause banned from the mails postcards sent out by ex-President Theodore Roosevelt asking citizens of Pennsylvania to vote for Gifford Pinchot instead of Boies Penrose, as the latter stood "for all those forms of evil against which every clean and decent citizen should unflinchingly stand." (See New York *Sun*, Oct. 3, 1914.)

30. *Congressional Record*, 60th Cong., 1st sess., p. 987; 2nd sess., pp. 285–95, 322–40. Similar bills were introduced in every subsequent Congress until the United States entered the war in 1917.

31. House Document 17, 59th Cong., 1st sess.

32. 35 *Stat.* 1130. The Supreme Court declared that the phrase "concerning schemes devised for the purpose of obtaining money or property under false pretences" in the lottery section was limited to schemes similar to a lottery. George Stever had advertised high-grade cattle for sale and had entered in correspondence with interested buyers. When the buyers came to his place he offered for sale only inferior cattle. Although he was not found guilty under the lottery section, he was for using the "mails to carry on any scheme or artifice to defraud." See *United States* v. *George F. Stever*, 222 U.S. 167 (1911).

33. 35 *Stat.* 1131. Punishment had been a maximum of $500 and/or 18 months' imprisonment. Another fraud had been declared nonmailable in 1906, i.e., stamping gold or silver merchandise as being of finer metal than it was (see 34 *Stat.* 260).

34. 35 *Stat.* 1131. In 1905 an act had been passed declaring nonmailable matter containing various kinds of moth and boll weevil in a live state as injurious to crops (see 33 *Stat.* 1269). The postmaster general in 1910 provided that medicine containing poison could be admitted to the mails when sent from manufacturer to physician, if the package label bore the name of the manufacturer. A court, however, declared that the postmaster general's powers concerned only regulation as to packing. At the request of Postmaster General Burleson, Congress passed an act on May 25, 1920 (41 *Stat.* 620) permitting the transmission in the mails from manufacturer to dealer, to licensed physicians, dentists, pharmacists, of medicine containing poison. This was extended June 10, 1934, to cosmetologists and barbers (49 *Stat.* 1063).

35. *Congressional Record*, 60th Cong., 1st sess., pp. 479, 701; 2nd sess., p. 342.

36. Ibid., 62nd Cong., 2nd sess. (S. 7027, H.R. 24962), pp. 7501, 7890, 8234–36, 8551, 9304–9309, 9447, 9988; House Report 858; 37 *Stat.* 240.

37. *Congressional Record*, 62nd Cong., 2nd sess., pp. 5122, 5463, 5512, 5753, 10667; 37 *Stat.* 553.

38. House Document 641, 59th Cong., 1st sess.; *Congressional Record*, 62nd Cong., 1st sess., pp. 927, 1561–1564, 1584–1585, 1591; Senate Document 26. Senator Jeff Davis of Arkansas made a bitter attack on Postmaster General Hitchcock for what he termed the persecution of Lewis.

39. *Lewis Publishing Co.* v. *Edward M. Morgan, Postmaster, New York City*, 229 U.S. 288 (1913).

40. "Mr. Hitchcock's War On Swindlers," *Independent* 69, no. 3235 (Dec. 1, 1910): 1221–22; Andre Tridon, "The Post Office, Guardian Angel to the 'Easy,'" *Harper's Weekly* 55 (June 10, 1911): 12; *Congressional Record*, 62nd Cong., 2nd sess., pp. 5471–72.

41. *United States* v. *Young*, 232 U.S. 155 (1914). Young was president of a hardware company and sent falsified statements about his company through the mail to his broker to get him to sell notes of his company.

42. *United States* v. *Kenofsky*, 243 U.S. 440 (1917).

43. *United States* v. *New South Farm and Home Co.*, 248 U.S. 349 (1916).

44. *United States* v. *Comyns*, 248 U.S. 349 (1919). In this case the defendants, representing themselves as lawyers practicing before the United States land office, induced people to give them money to purchase land under the Timber and Stone Act of June 3, 1878. They claimed they could buy land for their clients more cheaply than it could be bought directly from the government. A fee was to be paid in advance which would not be returnable even if the land was not obtained. They were convicted of using the mails to defraud.

45. *Badders* v. *United States*, 240 U.S. 391 (1916).

46. *Degg* v. *Hitchcock*, 229 U.S. 162 (1913).

## Chapter 7

1. *Congressional Record*, 64th Cong., 2nd sess. (S. 8148), pp. 3408, 3490.

2. Ibid., 65th Cong., 1st sess., S.2 by Senator Charles A. Culberson of Texas; H.R. 291 by Edwin Y. Webb of North Carolina.

3. Ibid., pp. 1167, 1816–19. The Gard amendment (censorship provision) passed by a vote of 191 to 185. *New York Times*, April 26,

# Notes for Chapter Seven

May 1, 3, 4, 5, 1917. See also Frederic L. Paxson, *America at War*, pp. 61–62.

4. *Congressional Record*, 65th Cong., 1st sess., pp. 1594–95, 1600–1601, 1820–23, 1841; House Report 30, p. 9. There was no discussion in the House of section 1101, which had been patterned after the lottery law.

5. *Congressional Record*, 65th Cong., 1st sess., pp. 1845–49.

6. Ibid., pp. 1867–73, 2056–72. In 1912 La Follette had claimed that his mail had been subjected "to espionage almost Russian in character." He had sent out 15,000 letters to postal employees asking about conditions in the service, especially in regard to union membership. Some newspapers made fun of him but others thought his charge was probably valid. See "The Postal 'Espionage' Charges," *Literary Digest* 45, no. 9 (Aug. 31, 1912): 326.

7. La Follette voted against the bill when it was sent to conference by a vote of 77 to 6. He thought the measure was the "worst legislative crime of the war because it menaced freedom of the press, freedom of speech, freedom of assembly, freedom from unwarranted search and seizure, and other rights which had been won by generations of struggle and sacrifice." See Belle and Fola La Follette, *Robert M. La Follette*, II: 732–33.

8. *Congressional Record*, 65th Cong., 1st sess., pp. 3124, 3138, 3144, 3439–40, 3492; House Report 65; Senate Document 37. See *New York Times*, May 23, 24, 1917 for description of administration pressure for censorship clause. See 40 Stat. 230 for text.

9. James R. Mock, *Censorship, 1917*, pp. 132–33; Paxson, *America at War*, p. 64.

10. *Congressional Record*, 65th Cong., 1st sess. (H. Res. 115, S. Res. 119), pp. 4931, 5407, 5569, 5634, 6109 (postmaster general's answer to resolution of Senator Hardwick of Georgia Aug. 17), pp. 6257–62 (postmaster general's answer to House Resolution, Aug. 22); House Report 109.

11. La Follette, *La Follette*, II: 739–40.

12. Ray Stannard Baker, *Woodrow Wilson*, VII: 165 (to Amos Pinchot, July 13, 1917).

13. *Masses Publishing Co. v. Patten*, 244 Fed. 535 (1917).

14. *Masses Publishing Co. v. Patten*, 245 Fed. 102–106 (1917); William Hard, "Mr. Burleson, Section 481 1-2B," *New Republic* 19 (May 17, 1919): 76–78.

15. H. C. Peterson and Gilbert C. Fite, *Opponents of War, 1917–1918*, pp. 47, 95, 97, 99.

16. William Hard, "Mr. Burleson, Espionagent," *New Republic* 19 (May 10, 1919): 42–45; *Jeffersonian Publishing Co. v. West, Post-*

*master*, 245 Fed. 585 (1917); C. Vann Woodward, *Tom Watson*, pp. 457–58.

17. Baker, *Wilson*, VII:291, 301, 318. See in *Congressional Record*, 65th Cong., 2nd sess., pp. 7062–63 for Burleson's defense for not acting against the Hearst papers. For the case of the *Nation* see "The Nation and the Post Office," *Nation* CVII (Sept 28, 1918): 336–37. The editor stated that it was due to President Wilson's interference that the ban on the issue of Sept. 14 was raised Sept. 18. The issue had been banned because of its article criticizing Samuel Gompers and the administration's labor policies.

18. *Congressional Record*, 65th Cong., 1st sess. (H.R. 4960), pp. 3484, 4989, 6298, 7019–21.

19. 40 *Stat.* 425. A fine of $500 and/or one year imprisonment was to be imposed for a person making a false affidavit.

20. *Congressional Record*, 65th Cong., 1st sess., pp. 7322, 7340–52. Vote in the Senate was 48 to 6 (Albert Cummins of Iowa, Hiram Johnson of California, Joseph France of Maryland, William Kirby of Arkansas, George Norris of Nebraska, and James E. Watson of Indiana were the six opposing).

21. *New York Times*, Sept. 25, 26, Oct. 10, 13, 1917; Mock, *Censorship, 1917*, pp. 140–41 cites 1,600 applications. See also Baker, *Wilson*, VII:324.

22. Mock, *Censorship, 1917*, pp. 15, 55–58; Senate Document 186, 65th Cong., 2nd sess.

23. House Report 1473, 65th Cong., 3rd sess.; Mock, *Censorship, 1917*, pp. 62, 64–65, 110; *New York Times*, Sept. 26, Oct. 17, 1917. In a note dated May 3, 1917, President Wilson had stated that Secretary Lansing urged censorship of the mails but that Burleson thought it unnecessary as it would be a "duplication of work that is being better performed by our allies." Lansing urged that there be at least censorship of mail going to Latin American countries (see Baker, *Wilson*, VII:47).

24. *Congressional Record*, 65th Cong., 2nd sess. (H.R. 8753, S.2522), pp. 908, 1169, 1497, 3002–3004, 3467, 3816, 4426, 4565–66, 4628, 4775, 4889–93. See *New York Times*, April 3, 10, May 4, 1918, in favor of a stronger law.

25. *Congressional Record*, 65th Cong., 2nd sess., pp. 4897–98; 40 *Stat.* 554. House conferees added "when the United States is at war."

26. *Congressional Record*, 65th Cong., 2nd sess., pp. 5937–38, 5943–50, 5978–84, 6053–57, 6174–75, 6185. The negative vote was cast by Representative London of New York, who had introduced several resolutions asking the postmaster general to furnish information on suspended newspapers.

27. Mock, *Censorship, 1917*, pp. 126, 130; Peterson and Fite, *Opponents of War*, p. 189.

28. Baker, *Wilson*, VII:170 (to William Kent, July 17, 1917); Peterson and Fite, *Opponents of War*, pp. 162–66. Berger was sentenced to twenty years in the penitentiary, but the Supreme Court overruled the sentence because Judge Landis had refused a change of venue. In 1919 and 1920 he was elected to the House of Representatives but was denied a seat because of his conviction by the Court.

29. *United States ex Rel. Milwaukee Social Democratic Publishing Co. v. Albert J. Burleson, Postmaster General*, 255 U.S. 407 (1921): for Wilson's attitude toward the preliminary hearing see Baker, *Wilson*, VII: 312–13 (Wilson to Burleson, Oct. 18, 1917). See also Zechariah Chafee, *Government and Mass Communications*, p. 296. He states that no act gave the postmaster general power to punish a paper with loss of "low postal rates for future issues" because of some bad issues. See also Giles J. Patterson, *Free Speech and a Free Press*, p. 212.

30. "Press Censorship by Judicial Construction," *New Republic* 26, no. 330 (March 30, 1921): 123–25.

31. "Burleson and the Call," ibid. 21 (Jan. 7, 1920): 157–58.

32. *Congressional Record*, 65th Cong., 3rd sess., pp. 2936–43, 2968. La Follette after Borah's failure wrote his children, "Men are making records these days that ought to make the framers of the Constitution open their eyes in their coffins." (See La Follette, *La Follette*, II: 939.)

33. *Congressional Record*, 65th Cong., 3rd sess. (S. 5207), p. 4561; La Follette, *La Follette*, II: 939.

34. Robert K. Murray, *Red Scare*, ch. 14.

35. *Congressional Record*, 66th Cong., 1st sess., H.R. 10235; 3rd sess., H.R. 14658. See also 2nd sess., H.R. 11277, H.R. 11281.

36. *Congressional Record*, 66th Cong., 1st sess., S. 2097, S. 2099, S. 2524, S. 2604; 67th Cong., 1st sess., S. 555; 69th Cong., 1st sess., S. 759, H.R. 5386; 2nd sess., H.R. 16768.

37. Ibid., 70th Cong., 1st sess., S. 1436, H.R. 7912.

# Chapter 8

1. *Congressional Record*, 63rd Cong., 2nd sess., p. 4518; 38 *Stat.* 1113.

2. Alfred H. Kelly and Winfred A. Harbison, *The American Constitution*, p. 676; Carl Brent Swisher, *American Constitutional Development*, pp. 550–54.

# Notes for Chapter Eight

3. *Congressional Record,* 63rd Cong., 3rd sess., S. 7739; 64th Cong., 2nd sess. (S. 4429), pp. 634, 949, 1166–72. In 1913 a bill had been introduced to deny second-class mailing privileges to publications containing pictorial advertisements relative to cigarettes, tobacco, and intoxicating liquors (see ibid., 63rd Cong., 2nd sess., H.R. 10155).

4. Ibid., 64th Cong., 2nd sess., pp. 2107, 2825, 3324, 3328, 3330, 3343, 3792, 3957.

5. 39 *Stat.* 1069. Maximum punishment was set at a fine of $1,000 and/or imprisonment for six months.

6. House Report 910, 68th Cong., 1st sess. (H.R. 9179).

7. *Congressional Record,* 68th Cong., 1st sess., H.R. 9093; 69th Cong., 1st sess., p. 9692. Bills to prohibit the use of the mails for transporting newspapers or other mail matter containing advertisements for the sale of pistols or revolvers were introduced also (see 68th Cong., 1st sess., H.R. 9161; 2nd sess., H.R. 10895; 69th Cong., 1st sess., H.R. 8586).

8. House Report 610, 69th Cong., 1st sess.; Senate Report 1107.

9. *Congressional Record,* 68th Cong., 2nd sess., pp. 725–37; 69th Cong., 1st sess. (H.R. 4502), pp. 6050, 9692–96; 2nd sess., pp. 236, 641, 2805, 2983; Senate Report 865, 68th Cong., 2nd sess.

10. 44 *Stat.* 1059. An act of May 15, 1939, added members of the coast guard to the officers to whom firearms might be mailed (53 *Stat.* 744) and an act of March 7, 1942, added "officers and employees of enforcement agencies of the United States" (56 *Stat.* 141).

11. House Report 910, 68th Cong., 1st sess.

12. *Congressional Record,* 67th Cong., 1st sess. (H.R. 6508), pp. 6286–97; House Report 137, 68th Cong., 1st sess., H.R. 9179; 69th Cong., 1st sess. (H.R. 6982), pp. 10114–19, 10150; House Report 560.

13. *Congressional Record,* 70th Cong., 1st sess. (S.2751), pp. 1842, 7791, 8291, 9574, 9786; Senate Report 994; *Congressional Record,* 71st Cong., 2nd sess. (S. 1446), pp. 10973, 11565–67, 11745.

14. Paul Jelco, "How Pure are the Mails?", *Nation* 131 (Aug. 6, 1930): 144–45. The courts did declare a game called "keno," similar to bingo, under the lottery law (see *Boasberg* v. *United States,* 60 F. 2d 185 (1932). The Supreme Court denied petition for writ of certiorari (see 287 U.S. 664).

15. *Congressional Record,* 67th Cong., 2nd sess., S. 3962. This bill was introduced by Harry S. New of Indiana, who became postmaster general the next year (1923). A similar bill was introduced in the 68th Cong., 1st sess., H.R. 6870; *Fasulo* v. *United States,* 272 U.S. 620.

16. *Congressional Record,* 70th Cong., 2nd sess., H.R. 14147; 71st Cong., 1st sess., H.R. 1205; 2nd sess., H.R. 12660; House Report 692, 72d Cong., 1st sess.

17. *Congressional Record,* 72d Cong., 1st sess., pp. 5581, 7250–51, 8362–63, 8851–53, 13828, 14599–600; Senate Reports 498 and 727; 47 *Stat.* 649.

18. *Congressional Record,* 74th Cong., 1st sess., H.R. 6717; House Report 823; Senate Report 873; 49 *Stat.* 427.

19. *Congressional Record,* 74th Cong., 2nd sess. (S. 4656), p. 8447; Senate Report 2095. Bill passed the Senate, June 1, 1936, but was pigeonholed in Judiciary Committee of the House; 75th Cong., 1st sess., S. 1138, H.R. 3909 were merely reported out, Senate Report, 1190; *Congressional Record,* 76th Cong., 1st sess. (S. 200, H.R. 3230), pp. 20, 68, 804, 1968, 3729, 3763, 4909, 5112, 5160, 6357; House Report 102, Senate Report 349.

20. 53 *Stat.* 742. This law changed the jurisdiction back to the district court where the matter was mailed.

21. Harry S. New, "Closing the Mail Box to Frauds," *World's Work* 46, no. 3 (July, 1923): 255–64. He said that one-half of the time of postal inspectors was spent on detecting frauds.

22. Swisher, *American Constitutional Development,* pp. 830–31.

23. *Congressional Record,* 67th Cong., 2nd sess. (H.R. 11843), pp. 9175–77, 9411; House Report 1095. J. N. Tincher of Kansas had spent the last thirty years urging legislation regulating grain exchanges.

24. *Congressional Record,* 67th Cong., 2nd sess., 9424–25, 9440–47, 9462, 9508, 11665, 12567–68; Senate Report 871; 42 *Stat.* 999.

25. *Congressional Record,* 67th Cong., 2nd sess. (H.R. 10598), pp. 5963–82, 6067–90; House Report 760.

26. *Congressional Record,* 68th Cong., 1st sess. (H.R. 4), pp. 25, 4503–30. Two more states passed "blue sky" laws (Pennsylvania and Washington) in 1922–1923.

27. Ibid., 69th Cong., 2nd sess. S. 5769; 70th Cong., 1st sess., H.R. 20, H.R. 11462; 72nd Cong., 1st sess, S. 127, H.R. 8932, H.R. 9447.

28. 48 *Stat.* 77.

29. 85 Law 539–40.

30. 49 *Stat.* 812; *Electric Bond and Share Co.* v. *Securities and Exchange Commission,* 303 U.S. 419 (1938).

31. *Hipolite Egg Co.* v. *United States,* 220 U.S. 45 (1911); *United States* v. *Johnson,* 221 U.S. 488 (1911); *Congressional Record,* 61st Cong., 3rd sess., S. 9193. See Merlo Pusey, *Charles Evans Hughes,* I:292.

32. *Leach* v. *Carlile*, 258 U.S. 138 (1922); Kilpatrick, *Smut Peddlers*, p. 90. Bills to amend the obscenity statute to prevent transmission through the mails of advertisements relating to venereal diseases, sexual debility, etc., were introduced in 66th Cong., 1st sess., S. 1189, H.R. 5123, and 69th Cong., 1st sess., S. 3834, H.R. 10989.

33. 52 *Stat.* 114; *Kenneth W. Shafe* v. *Federal Trade Commission*, 256 F. 2d 661 (1958).

34. *Congressional Record*, 74th Cong., 1st sess., H.R. 8180; 2nd sess., p. 727; House Report 1643; 75th Cong., 1st sess. (H.R. 6961), p. 8023; House Report 1289.

35. *Congressional Record*, 76th Cong., 1st sess. (S. 2245, H.R. 6051), pp. 4426, 4820, 7934, 8654, 8795, 10257, 10549, 11171; Senate Report 683.

36. 53 *Stat.* 1341. Another act, passed the same month, prohibited the dissemination by mail of false advertisements concerning seeds (see 53 *Stat.* 1282).

37. *Hammer* v. *Dagenhart*, 247 U.S. 251 (1918); Claude Bowers, *Beveridge and the Progressive Era*, pp. 245–47, 250–55, 265–66.

38. *Congressional Record*, 65th Cong., 2nd sess., S. 4732, 4760; *Bailey* v. *Drexel Furniture Co.*, 259 U.S. 20 (1922).

39. Kelly and Harbison, *American Constitution*, pp. 730–31.

40. *Congressional Record*, 74th Cong., 1st sess. (H.R. 7017), pp. 4490, 4882–83.

41. 52 *Stat.* 1060; *United States* v. *Darby Lumber Co.*, 312 U.S. 100 (1941).

42. *Congressional Record*, 72nd Cong., 1st sess., pp. 2609–11, 5736.

43. Ibid., 71st Cong., 1st sess., S. 610; 72nd Cong., 2nd sess., S. 1663; 73rd Cong., 1st sess., S. 2101; 74th Cong., 1st sess., S. 1226; Senate Report 9878. In the House bills were sponsored by Henry W. Watson of Pennsylvania and Hampton P. Fulmer of South Carolina.

## Chapter 9

1. *Congressional Record*, 76th Cong., 1st sess. (S. 1398), pp. 1461, 7205, 8371–73; 3rd sess., pp. 3010–11; Senate Report 598, 76th Cong., 1st sess.; House Report 1716, 76th Cong., 3rd sess.

2. *Congressional Record*, 77th Cong., 1st sess. (S.313, H.R. 4051), pp. 144–45, 2348.

3. Ibid., p. 1865, Appendix, p. 831. The attorney general ruled that foreign agents living abroad who distributed propaganda should be registered. If they were not registered they committed a felony and mail sent by them could be confiscated under postal laws.

4. Albert Goldman, *The New York, N.Y. Post Office during the War Years, 1941–1945*, pp. 19, 351.

5. Ibid., pp. 54–55; *Congressional Record*, 78th Cong., 2nd sess. (S. 1971), pp. 5273, 8482, 9431, 9547, 9780; Senate Report 1227; 58 *Stat*. 913. For description of censorship see Byron Price, "Governmental Censorship in War Time," *American Political Science Review* 36, no. 5 (Oct., 1942): 837–49.

6. Goldman, *New York Post Office*, p. 55; *Congressional Record*, 77th Cong., 2nd sess., p. 2566. William Pelley, leader of the Silver Shirts, was finally convicted of sedition as the propaganda distributed by his group followed too closely the Nazi party line.

7. *Congressional Record*, 78th Cong., 1st sess., pp. 1819–20. See Chafee, *Government and Mass Communications*, p. 125, for criticism of the bill.

8. Osmund Kessler Fraenkel, *Our Civil Liberties*, pp. 37–38, 86.

9. *Congressional Record*, 78th Cong., 1st sess. (S. Res. 145), pp. 3820–24.

10. Ibid., 83rd Cong., 2nd sess. (H. Res. 602, H. Res. 603, H. Res. 632), pp. 9076, 9120, 10542, 12760, Appendix, p. 5590. Senator Joseph McCarthy of Wisconsin got the Post Office Department to bring charges against a Herman Greenspun, publisher of the Las Vegas *Sun*, that he had mailed matter tending to incite murder or assassination; in his papers Greenspun had predicted that McCarthy would come to a more violent end than had Senator Huey Long. Greenspun, however, was acquitted. See Richard H. Rovere, *Senator Joe McCarthy*, p. 69n.

11. *New York Times*, Oct. 21, 23, 26, Dec. 9, 1958.

12. *Congressional Record*, 83rd Cong., 2nd sess., H.R. 10286; 84th Cong., 1st sess., S. 446, H.R. 5418, H.R. 7427; 2nd sess., H.R. 10294; 86th Cong., 1st sess., S. 122, H.R. 1817, H.R. 1818, H.R. 1838, H.R. 1849, H.R. 1934, H.R. 3128; 87th Cong., 1st sess., H.R. 289, H.R. 521, H.R. 610; 89th Cong., 1st sess., S. 2548, H.R. 837; 2nd sess., H.R. 16011.

13. 69 *Stat*. 80.

14. *Congressional Record*, 81st Cong., 1st sess. (H.R. 5265) p. 8084; House Report 1374.

15. 64 *Stat*. 987. Minor changes were made in this act in Jan., 1968 (see 81 *Stat*. 766).

16. *Congressional Record*, 82nd Cong., 1st sess. (H.R. 3634), p. 3606; 2nd sess. (S. 2990), pp. 1585, 5140; 83nd Cong., 1st sess., S. 1409, S. 1824, H.R. 4365, H.R. 5426; 84th Cong., 1st sess., S. 1508.

17. Ibid., 82nd Cong., 2nd sess., (S. 3174); 83rd Cong., 2nd sess. (H.R. 9317), pp. 7093, 7119; *New York Times*, May 8, 1954. The

postmaster general revealed that the United States government by giving second-class mailing privileges to the *Daily Worker*, the Communist paper, subsidized it to the amount of $40,000 annually. He said he was investigating to see if such a publication could be declared nonmailable on the basis of the Communist Control Act, passed Aug. 24, 1954 (see *Congressional Record*, 84th Cong., 1st sess., p. 3324).

18. Murray L. Schwartz and James C. N. Paul, "Foreign Communist Propaganda in the Mails: A Report on Some Problems of Federal Censorship," *University of Pennsylvania Law Review* 107 (March, 1959): 621–66; "Propaganda in the Mails: A Postscript," ibid. (April, 1959): 796–801; Paul Howard, "Ban on Foreign Propaganda," *Wilson Library Bulletin* 30 (Oct., 1955): 120, 123.

19. *Publishers' Weekly* 162, no. 24 (Dec. 13, 1952): 2322.

20. Dorothy Kahn, "Abe Goff, Our Chief Censor," *Reporter*, 12, no. 10 (May 19, 1955): 27; *New York Times*, July 10, 1956.

21. George Sokolsky, "Open Letter to the Post Office," *Saturday Review* 38 (April 23, 1955): 9–10. This prominent anti-Communist protested that he was entitled to receive Soviet publications not as a special privilege but because he had subscribed to them. "They can do me no greater harm than some American publications I buy. If I am to be saved from my reading habits I do not want it to be done by the Post Office, the business of which is to deliver the mails," he wrote.

22. Postmaster General, *Annual Report, 1959*, p. 94; *New York Times*, Aug. 2, 1959, May 23, 1960; *New Republic*, 140, no. 19 (May 11, 1959): 3–4; see also *Commonweal* 72, no. 10 (June 3, 1960): 245–46.

23. *Christian Century* 76 (March 11, 1959): 285.

24. George Du Shane, "Neither Snow Nor Rain Nor . . .," *Science* 133 (Feb. 24, 1961): 549.

25. *New York Times*, May 23, 1960, Sept. 14, 1960, Feb. 13, 14, 1961.

26. Department of State, *Bulletin*, XLIV, no. 1136 (April 3, 1961), pp. 479–80; *New York Times*, March 23, 1961.

27. *Congressional Record*, 87th Cong., 1st sess. (H.R. 5751), pp. 8907–8908, 12269, 12953, 13201, 19195, 20052–58, 20618, 21295. There were a number of bills to deny the use of the mails for Communist propaganda (see H.R. 9004, H.R. 9023, H.R. 9025, H.R. 9039, H.R. 9064, H.R. 9095, H.R. 9099, H.R. 9279, H.R. 9281, H.R. 9411, H.R. 9455, H.R. 9465; 2nd sess., S. 2738, S. 2740, H.R. 9620, H.R. 9644, H.R. 9721, H.R. 9755).

28. Ibid., 87th Cong., 1st sess., pp. 17814–19, 17881, 18578, 20052;

2nd sess., pp. 328, 744–48, 769–70, 826; Glenn Cunningham, "The Cunningham Amendment," *Science* 135 (June 8, 1962): 908–909.

29. *Congressional Record*, 87th Cong., 1st sess., pp. 20198, 21295–98; 2nd sess., pp. 2099, 3838–39, 8498–99; *New York Times*, April 18, May 28, July 22, 24, 1962.

30. *New York Times*, Sept. 19, 21, 25, Oct. 6, 1962; *Library Journal* 87, no. 20 (Nov. 15, 1962); *American Library Association Bulletin* 56 (Dec., 1962): 990. The latter association was opposed to the Cunningham amendment and many librarians and educators appeared before the Senate committee. The American Association of University Professors was also opposed to the amendment.

31. *Congressional Record*, 87th Cong., 2nd sess., pp. 20636–45, 20854, 20920, 20979–87; *American Library Association Bulletin* 57 (Jan., 1963): 17–19.

32. 76 *Stat.* 840.

33. *New York Times*, June 1, Oct. 24, 1963, Nov. 20, 24, 1964.

34. Ibid., Oct. 24, 1963, April 12, 1964.

35. Ibid., Feb. 25, April 14, 17, 1965.

36. 381 U.S. 301 (1965).

37. Justice White had been deputy attorney general in the Kennedy administration and at that time had prepared a memorandum attacking restrictions on the mail from Communist countries. There had been objection in the Senate at the time of his appointment to the Court. One senator said: "Is the Senate of the United States going to approve the appointment as Associate Justice of the Supreme Court one who will permit a 'Trojan Horse' to be wheeled into every library and home in the Nation?" (see *Congressional Record*, 87th Cong., 2nd sess., p. 6268).

38. *New York Times*, May 31, 1965.

39. Ibid., May 25, 1965.

40. Justice Holmes in *ex rel. Milwaukee Social Democratic Pub. Co.* v. *Burleson*, 255 U.S. 407 (1921).

## Chapter 10

1. *Crane* v. *Nichols*, 1 F. 2d 33 (1924).

2. Makris, *Silent Investigators*, ch. 12, has a detailed description of the "I AM" movement.

3. *United States* v. *Ballard et al.*, 322 U.S. 7 (1944); *Ballard* v. *United States*, 329 U.S. 173 (1946).

4. *Gustav H. Kann* v. *United States*, 323 U.S. 88 (1944); *Parr* v. *United States*, 363 U.S. 370 (1960). See *Pereira* v. *United States*, 347 U.S. 1 (1954) for a decision in which the mailing of a check was

declared to be use of the mails to defraud. The defendant married a woman, got her to draw a check on an out-of-state bank, and then left her. The Court declared it was not necessary to prove that the scheme contemplated the use of the mails in the fraud. A person causes the mails to be used where he does an act with the knowledge that mails are usually used.

5. *United States* v. *Sampson et al.*, 370 U.S. 73 (1962).

6. *Donaldson, Postmaster General* v. *Read Magazine, Inc.*, 333 U.S. 178 (1948). The dissenting judges said the advertisements "fully disclosed the real character of the promotion project, and that the Postmaster General's act, in issuing the order constituted an abuse of his discretion."

7. William J. Slocum, "No Frauds are Crueler than These: The Postal Inspectors," *Colliers* 125 (Feb. 4, 1950): 34–35, 66.

8. *Reilly, Postmaster* v. *Pinkus*, 338 U.S. 269 (1949); see also *Owen Laboratories* v. *Carl A. Schroeder*, 284 F. 2d 445 (1960) and *U.S. Health Club* v. *Majer*, 292 F. 2d 665 (1961).

9. *United States* v. *Halseth*, 342 U.S. 277 (1952). This section in the code dealing with lotteries had just been amended to make it clear that it would not apply to "any fishing contest not conducted for profit wherein prizes are awarded for the specie, size, weight, or quality of fish caught by contestants in any bona fide fishing or recreational event" (see 64 *Stat.* 451). Bookmaking in horse-racing was also declared not to constitute a lottery (see *United States* v. *Rich*, 90 Fed. Supp. 624 (1950).

10. 75 *Stat.* 492, 498.

11. House Report 1874, 82nd Cong., 2nd sess.

12. *Congressional Record*, 82nd Cong., 1st sess., H.R. 5850; Senate Report 1850, 82nd Cong., 2nd sess.; House Report 850, 83rd Cong., 1st sess.; *Congressional Record*, 83rd Cong., 2nd sess., H.R. 569; Senate Report 2499.

13. See Alvin Shuster, ". . . Nor Gloom of Censorship," *New York Times Magazine*, Aug. 2, 1959.

14. "Postmaster General Penalizes 'Esquire,'" *Christian Century* 61 (Jan. 12, 1944): 37, criticized Walker's action as being directed by the Catholic League of Decency; *Newsweek* 23, no. 2 (Jan. 10, 1944), noted that *Esquire* would have to pay over $500,000 a year in postage, which would probably mean the magazine would have to go out of business. See also *Congressional Record*, 78th Cong., 1st sess., pp. 3820–24, for criticism by Senator Langer; he introduced a resolution that Postmaster General Walker be divested of his power of censorship and that it be given to a qualified committee.

15. *Hannegan* v. *Esquire*, 327 U.S. 146 (1946).

16. 64 *Stat.* 451; *Congressional Record,* 81st Cong., 2nd sess., H.R. 8767; House Report 2335. Edward H. Rees of Kansas wanted blasphemous matter to be declared nonmailable also (see 81st Cong., 1st sess., H.R. 6467; 82nd Cong., 1st. sess., H.R. 1319; 83rd Cong., 1st sess., H.R. 571.

17. 69 *Stat.* 699; *Congressional Record,* 81st Cong., 2nd sess., S. 3800; Senate Report 2099, 81st Cong., 2nd sess.; *Congressional Record,* 82nd Cong., 1st sess., S. 34; *Congressional Record,* 83rd Cong., 1st sess., S. 11; Senate Report 39, 83rd Cong., 1st sess.; *Congressional Record,* 84th Cong., 1st sess., S. 600; H.R. 3333, Senate Report 113, 84th Cong., 1st sess.; House Report 690, 84th Cong., 1st sess.

18. 70 *Stat.* 699; *Congressional Record,* 84th Cong., 2nd sess., pp. 12288–89; *New York Times,* July 12, 1956.

19. Kilpatrick, *Smut Peddlers,* pp. 67–68.

20. 72 *Stat.* 940; *Congressional Record,* 85th Cong., 2nd sess., S. 4287, H.R. 4283.

21. *Congressional Record,* 85th Cong., 2nd sess. (S. 3667, H.R. 6239), pp. 6865, 15227–28, 15611, 17831–32; House Report 1614; 72 *Stat.* 962.

22. *New York Times,* Nov. 21, 1957.

23. Ibid., May 3, 1958; Jan. 20, 1959.

24. Edward de Grazia, "Obscenity, Censorship and the Mails," *New Republic* 134, no. 5 (Jan. 30, 1956): 17–19. He was counsel for the rare book dealer whose copy of Aristophenes' *Lysistrata* was seized by the Post Office. He obtained a preliminary injunction, but Summerfield had the book returned after being assured it was not for general distribution.

25. *Roth* v. *Goldman,* 172 F. 2d 788 (1949). Roth had been one of the few witnesses who had testified before the Kefauver subcommittee on juvenile delinquency not pleading the Fifth Amendment (see Senate Report 2381, 84th Cong., 2nd sess., pp. 55–56.

26. *United States* v. *Roth,* 237 F. 2d 796 (1956).

27. *Publishers' Weekly* 171, (May 6, 1957).

28. *Roth* v. *United States,* 354 U.S. 476 (1957). Kilpatrick, *Smut Peddlers,* pp. 81–168 gives a detailed analysis of the Roth case. He comments (p. 81), "all roads lead up to it [Roth decision]; now fresh paths descend from it."

29. *New York Times,* March 8, June 7, 1957.

30. Ibid., Oct. 29, 31, 1958.

31. Ibid., April 9, 28, May 6, June 16, Oct. 7, 1959.

32. Ibid., May 7, June 12, 16, 1959. Ablard was dismissed from office March, 1960 (see ibid., March 7, 1960). For comments on the case see *New Republic* 140, no. 21 (May 25, 1959): 13–15; *Time* 73

(June 22, 1959): 84; *Saturday Review of Literature* 42 (Aug. 29, 1959): 5–6. Grove Press sent 135,000 copies out by Railway Express trucks and United Parcel. Macy's ran an advertisement without mentioning the name of the book but merely starring the number two book on the best-seller list, which was left blank.

33. *New York Times*, July 22, 23, 1959. *The Saturday Review*, Aug. 29, 1959, said the trial had been described as a "cross between a lively literary tea and a Grade-B movie."

34. *Grove Press, Inc.* v. *Robert K. Christenberry*, 276 F. 2d 433 (1960); *New York Times*, Dec. 3, 1959.

35. *Summerfield* v. *Sunshine Book Co.*, 221 F. 2d 42 (1954). See editorial in *New Republic* 134, no. 25 (June 18, 1956): 5.

36. *Sunshine Book Co.* v. *Summerfield*, 249 F. 2d 114 (1957); *New York Times*, Oct. 4, 1957.

37. *Sunshine Book Co.* v. *Summerfield*, 355 U.S. 372 (1958); *New York Times*, Jan. 14, 1958.

38. *One, Inc.* v. *Otto K. Oleson*, 241 F. 2d 772 (1957); 355 U.S. 371 (1958); *New York Times*, Jan. 19, 1958.

39. *United States News and World Report*, Sept. 7, 1959.

40. *Congressional Record*, 86th Cong., 1st sess., p. 16451. For the bills see S. 354, S. 2123, S. 2562, H.R. 1154, H.R. 1877, H.R. 2234, H.R. 3967, H.R. 6818, H.R. 7048, H.R. 7247, H.R. 7753, H.R. 7379; 2nd sess., S. 3654, H.R. 10173, H.R. 10957, H.R. 11051, H.R. 11280, H.R. 11317, H.R. 11454, H.R. 12772, H.R. 12931, H.R. 13150, H.R. 13177.

41. Ibid., 86th Cong., 1st sess. (H.R. 7379), pp. 9167, 10189–92, 16446, 17573–84, 17697; *New York Times*, Sept. 2, 1959.

42. *Congressional Record*, 86th Cong., 2nd sess., pp. 15063, 15427, 15756; 74 *Stat.* 553.

43. *Frank L. Collier* v. *United States*, 283 F. 2d 780 (1960), 365 U.S. 833 (1961); *United States* v. *Roy A. Oakley*, 290 F. 2d 517 (1961), 368 U.S. 888 (1961); *Kahm* v. *United States*, 300 F. 2d 79 (1962), 369 U.S. 859 (1962).

44. *Manuel Enterprises, Inc.* v. *Day, Postmaster General*, 370 U.S. 478 (1962); *New York Times*, Aug. 16, 1960, June 26, 1962. The dealer involved in this decision (Herman Womack) has had many controversies with the Post Office Department and with the courts since 1962. In August, 1971, he was sentenced to seven and a half years in prison for mailing obscene matter (see *New York Times*, Aug. 29, 1971).

45. *Congressional Record*, 87th Cong., 2nd sess., p. 3763.

46. *New York Times*, June 10, 1963, Nov. 7, 1964, Oct. 18, 1965.

47. *Ralph Ginzburg* v. *United States*, 383 U.S. 463 (1966); *New York Times*, March 22, 1966.

48. *New York Times*, June 22, 1966. For article sympathetic to Ginzburg see Merle Miller, "Ralph Ginzburg, Middlesex, N.J. and the First Amendment," *New York Times Magazine*, April 30, 1972.

49. *United States News and World Report*, June 20, 1966, p. 51. The Supreme Court handed down another decision concerning the obscenity statute in May, 1966. A husband and wife had been convicted of violating the statute by mailing to each other nude self-portraits. The conviction was reversed on basis that prosecution for mailing private correspondence allegedly obscene should be confined to repeating offenders. See *Redmond* v. *United States*, 384 U.S. 264 (1966).

50. 76 *Stat.* 841, sec. 307. For attempts of industry to purify the mails, see John B. Halper, "The Mail Industry Fights Back. Legitimate Mail Advertisers Try to Halt the Flow of Obscenity through the Mail," *America* 108, no. 8 (Feb. 23, 1963): 260–61.

51. *Congressional Record*, 88th Cong., 2nd sess. (H.R. 319), p. 16575; 89th Cong., 1st sess., H.R. 9880. See *New York Times*, June 5, July 22, 1964.

52. *New York Times*, Feb. 11, 1967.

53. 81 *Stat.* 645; *New York Times*, April 4, 1968.

54. Letter from Glen Co., Los Angeles, postmarked July 22, 1969.

55. *New York Times*, Oct. 28, 1968; *United States News and World Report*, July 21, 1969.

56. *Daniel Rowan, dba American Book Service et al.*, v. *United States Post Office Department*, 397 U.S. 728 (1970).

57. 84 *Stat.* 749–50, 781; *New York Times*, Oct. 2, 1969.

58. *New York Times*, Aug. 28, 1970; *Wall Street Journal*, Aug. 19, 1970.

# Chapter 11

1. *Congressional Record*, 90th Cong., 1st sess., pp. 8100–8107.

2. *New York Times*, June 30, 1968; *United States News and World Report*, July 29, 1968.

3. *Congressional Record*, 91st Cong., 2nd sess., p. 19106.

4. Ibid., 91st Cong., 1st sess. (S. 492), pp. 1447–68, 2662–63.

5. Ibid. (H.R. 4), pp. 176–78, 10748.

6. Ibid. (H.R. 1382), pp. 14035, 14170–76. Glenn Cunningham of Nebraska, and others, introduced a bill (H.R. 11750) for total reform; see p. 14234.

# Notes for Chapter Eleven

7. Fuller, *The American Mail*, p. 340; *New York Times*, Sept. 3, 1969.

8. *Congressional Record*, 91st Cong., 1st sess., pp. 15062–69, 21827–28; *New York Times*, Aug. 23, 1969.

9. *New York Times*, Sept. 3, 1969; *Congressional Record*, 91st Cong., 1st sess., pp. 23359–68, 25106–107, 25514, 34482; 2nd sess., pp. 6051, 6274. See Gerald Cullinan, *The United States Postal Service*, pp. 5–12.

10. *Congressional Record*, 91st Cong., 2nd sess., pp. 12957, 13368, 14781, 15751, 19852; *Wall Street Journal*, April 8, 1971.

11. *Congressional Record*, 91st Cong., 2nd sess. (H.R. 17070), pp. 19837, 19844–59, 20200–225, 20432–53.

12. *Congressional Record*, 91st Cong., 2nd sess. (S. 3842), pp. 19106, 21509–27, 21708–14, 22279–300, 22313–33.

13. Ibid., pp. 23523–26, 23876, 26953–66, 27057–80, 27595–610.

14. Ibid., pp. 19848, 26943.

15. Cullinan, *United States Postal Service*, pp. 1–2; *New York Times*, Aug. 13, 30, 1970.

16. 84 *Stat.* 719–86.

17. 84 *Stat.* 745–46, 748; 81 *Stat.* 623; *Congressional Record*, 90th Cong., 1st sess. (H.R. 7977), pp. 28414, 28659–60.

18. 84 *Stat.* 746; 82 *Stat.* 997; *Congressional Record*, 90th Cong., 2nd sess. (H.R. 14935), pp. 3276–82, 20914–15, 28864–68, 28314.

19. *New York Times*, June 15, 23, 1968; 82 *Stat.* 228, 1213.

20. 84 *Stat.* 746–47; 82 *Stat.* 1153; *Congressional Record*, 90th Cong., 1st sess. (H.R. 1411), pp. 27686, 27738–45, 35736, 36529; 2nd sess., p. 29633.

21. 84 *Stat.* 749. See *United States News and World Report*, Feb. 8, 1971, p. 67.

22. *Congressional Record*, 91st Cong., 2nd sess., pp. 7834–35, 13862–71, 20482, 20499; *Wall Street Journal*, Aug. 28, 1973; *New York Times*, Jan. 8, April 24, July 18, 22, Aug. 4, 6, 1975.

23. Cullinan, *United States Postal Service*, pp. 190–94, 239–41; 84 *Stat.* 783; *Congressional Record*, 91st Cong., 2nd sess., pp. 20851–52. In subsequent Congresses several bills to permit private carriage of letters have been introduced.

24. Cullinan, *United States Postal Service*, pp. 176–77; *United States News and World Report*, May 4, 1970, pp. 46–51.

25. There have been three postmasters general since 1971. Elmer T. Klassen, former president of American Can Company, replaced Winton M. Blount on Oct. 30, 1971, and then Benjamin K. Bailar followed Klassen on Feb. 16, 1975. Both Klassen and Bailar had been the deputy postmaster general.

# Notes for Chapter Eleven

26. Cullinan, *United States Postal Service*, pp. 228–33. For examples of the criticism see *Congressional Record*, 92nd Cong., 1st sess., p. 36152; 93rd Cong., 1st sess., Jan. 26, 1973 (Rep. Gross); 94th Cong., 1st sess., Feb. 18, 1975 (Sen. Hollings), March 6, 1975 (Rep. Hanley); see Robert J. Myers, *The Coming Collapse of the Post Office*.

27. *Publishers' Weekly*, 181, no. 1 (Jan. 1, 1962): 41–42.

28. *Congressional Record*, 90th Cong., 1st sess., H.R. 7461, H.R. 8947; 91st Cong., 1st sess., H.R. 4605; 84 *Stat.* 1973: *United States Code, Annotated*, June, 1974, p. 1184.

29. *New York Times*, Aug. 12, 1962, June 11, 1967, Sept. 7, Nov. 28, 1974; *United States Code, Annotated*, Feb., 1975, p. 797.

30. *Wall Street Journal*, April 10, 1972; *New York Times*, Aug. 24, 1975.

31. *Congressional Record*, 91st Cong., 2nd sess., p. 14777–79; two bills passed the House but failed in the Senate, H.R. 11032, H.R. 15693; 92nd Cong., 1st sess., H.R. 8805 also passed House.

32. *Daniel Rowan*, dba *American Book Service* v. *U.S. Post Office Department*, 397 U.S. 728 (1970). American Express is giving card holders the choice of whether they wish to receive "junk mail" advertising by enclosing a card on which they can indicate their preference (see *New York Times*, July 27, 1975).

# Bibliography

## I. PRIMARY SOURCES

### A. Manuscripts

Manuscripts were of little value for this study. The Samuel Gouverneur Papers, in the New York Public Library, contained letters between Alfred Huger, postmaster at Charleston, S.C., and the postmaster in New York City and correspondence between the latter and the American Anti-Slavery Society during the controversy over the mailing of incendiary pamphlets. The Postmaster General Letterbooks, now in the National Archives, Washington, D.C., also had some letters dealing with the incendiary publications, but most of the letters dealt with more routine matters, patronage, and politics. Presidential Papers in the Library of Congress were of some use, especially those of Andrew Jackson, Martin Van Buren, and Theodore Roosevelt.

### B. Government Documents

*1. Pre-Constitutional Era*

Force, Peter, ed. *American Archives.* 4th series (1774–1776), 6 vols. 5th series (1776), 3 vols., Washington, D.C.: M. St. Clair Clarke and Peter Force, 1837–1853.

Ford, Worthington C., and Gaillard Hunt, eds. *Journals of the Continental Congress.* 34 vols. Washington, D.C.: Government Printing Office, 1904–1937.

*2. The Constitution*

Elliot, Jonathan, ed. *The Debates in the Several State Conventions on*

245

*the Adoption of the Federal Constitution.* 5 vols. Philadelphia: J. B. Lippincott, 1836.

Farrand, Max, ed. *Records of the Federal Convention.* 4 vols., rev. ed. New Haven: Yale University Press, 1966.

## 3. *Congressional*

Since this is a study of Congress's delegation of authority to the Post Office Department to declare matter unmailable, the most important sources are the Congressional debates.

*American State Papers: Documents, Legislative and Executive of the Congress of the United States,* 1789–1833. 38 vols. in 10 classes. Washington, D.C.: Gales and Seaton, 1832–1861.

United States Congress. *Annals of Congress,* 1789–1833. Washington, D.C.: Gales and Seaton, 1834.

United States Congress. *Register of Debates,* 1825–1837. Washington, D.C.: Gales and Seaton, 1825–1837.

United States Congress. *Congressional Globe,* 1834–1873. Washington, D.C.: The Globe Office, 1834–1873.

United States Congress. *The Congressional Record,* 1873–1975. Washington, D.C.: Government Printing Office, 1873–1975.

Closely related to the record of proceedings and debates in Congress are the House and Senate Reports and Documents. These vary in length from a few pages to several hundred pages and contain committee reports, communications from the postmasters general and other executive officers, text of some court decisions, and annual reports of the postmasters general.

For text of the acts:

*United States Statutes at Large,* 1789–1974.

*United States Code. Annotated.* Title 18 (Criminal) and Title 39 (The Postal Service). St. Paul, Minn.: West Publishing, 1962.

*United States Code. Annotated.* 1974, 1975. St. Paul, Minn.: West Publishing, 1974–1975.

## 4. *Executive*

Department of Justice. *Official Opinions of the Attorneys General of the United States Advising the President and Heads of Department in Relation to their Official Duties.* VIII, comp. Caleb Cushing. Washington, D.C.: Government Printing Office, 1858. XII, ed. J. Hubley Ashton. Washington, D.C.: Government Printing Office, 1870. XIX, ed. A. J. Bentley. Washington, D.C.: Government Printing Office, 1891. XXVI, ed. James A. Finch and John L. Lott. Washington, D.C.: Government Printing Office, 1908.

# Bibliography

Department of State. *Bulletin*, XLIV, no. 1136 (April 3, 1961). Washington, D.C.: Government Printing Office, 1961.

Department of War. *The War of Rebellion Records. A Compilation of the Official Records of the Union and Confederate Army.* 70 vols. Washington, D.C.: Government Printing Office, 1897.

Post Office Department. *Reports of the Postmasters General, 1909–1965.* Washington, D.C.: Government Printing Office, 1909–1965.

Richardson, James D., comp. *A Compilation of the Messages and Papers of the Presidents.* 10 vols. Washington, D.C.: Bureau of National Literature and Art, 1904.

## 5. *Judiciary*

*The Federal Reporter.* Cases argued and Determined in the Circuit Court of Appeals and District Courts of the United States, 1880–1925. St. Paul: West Publishing, 1880–1925.

*The Federal Reporter. Supplement.* Cases argued and Determined in the Circuit Courts of Appeals and District Courts of the United States and the Court of Appeals of the District of Columbia. St. Paul: West Publishing, 1925–1971.

*United States Supreme Court Reports*, 1789–1974. Washington, D.C.: Government Printing Office, 1789–1975.

## 6. *State Documents*

Alabama. *Acts of the General Assembly, 1836.* Tuscaloosa, 1937.

Georgia. *Acts and Resolutions of the General Assembly of the State of Georgia, 1835.* Atlanta, 1836.

Kentucky. *Acts Passed at the First Session of the Forty-Fourth General Assembly of the Commonwealth of Kentucky, 1836.* Frankfort, 1937.

Maryland. *Laws Made and Passed by the General Assembly of the State of Maryland, 1835.* Annapolis, 1836.

Massachusetts. *Resolves of the General Court of the Commonwealth of Massachusetts, 1836.* Boston, 1837.

Mississippi. *Laws, 1836.* Jackson, 1837.

Missouri. *Laws, 1836.* Jefferson City, 1836.

New York. *Laws of the State of New York, 1836.* Albany, 1837.

North Carolina. *Journal of the House of Representatives, 1835.* Edenton, 1835.

North Carolina. *Journal of the Senate, 1835.* Edenton, 1836.

North Carolina. *Session Laws, 1835.* Raleigh, 1836.

Ohio. *Acts of a General Nature, 1835.* Columbus, 1836.

South Carolina. *Acts and Joint Resolutions of the General Assembly, 1835.* Columbia, 1836.

# Bibliography

Tennessee. *Public Acts, 1835–1836.* Nashville, 1837.

Vermont. *Acts and Resolves Passed by the Legislature, 1833–1836.* Windsor, 1837.

Virginia. *Acts of the General Assembly of Virginia, 1835–1836.* Richmond, 1836.

## C. Memoirs and Published Correspondence

Barry, William T. "Letters to his daughter," *William and Mary Historical Magazine* 14 (1905–1906).

Bassett, John Spencer, ed. *Correspondence of Andrew Jackson.* 7 vols. Washington, D.C.: Carnegie Institution, 1926–1935.

Beale, Howard K., ed. "The Diary of Edward Bates," American Historical Association, *Annual Report, 1930* 4. Washington, D.C.: Government Printing Office, 1930.

Boyd, Julian P. ed. *The Papers of Thomas Jefferson.* 17 vols. Princeton, N.J.: Princeton University Press, 1950–1965.

Brown, Everett Somerville, ed. *William Plumer's Memorandum of Proceedings in the United States Senate.* New York: Macmillan, 1923.

Burnett, Edmund Cody, ed. *Letters of Members of the Continental Congress.* 8 vols. Washington, D.C.: Carnegie Institution, 1921–1936.

Butler, Harriet Allen, ed. *William Allen Butler: A Retrospect of Forty Years.* New York: Charles Scribner's Sons, 1911.

Cushing, Harry Alonzo, ed. *The Writings of Samuel Adams.* 4 vols. New York: G. P. Putnam's Sons, 1907.

Dix, Morgan, comp. *Memoirs of John Adams Dix.* 2 vols. New York: Harper and Brothers, 1883.

Dumond, Dwight, ed. *Letters of James Gillespie Birney.* 2 vols. New York: D. Appleton-Century, 1938.

Fitzpatrick, John C., ed. *The Diaries of George Washington.* 4 vols. Boston: Houghton Mifflin, 1925.

———, ed. *The Writings of George Washington.* 39 vols. Washington, D.C.: Government Printing Office, 1939–1944.

Ford, Paul Leicester, ed. *The Writings of Thomas Jefferson.* 12 vols. New York: G. P. Putnam's Sons, 1904.

Ford, Worthington Chauncey. *Some Letters of Elbridge Gerry of Massachusetts.* Brooklyn: New York Historical Printing Club, 1896.

———, ed. *The Writings of George Washington.* 14 vols. New York: G. P. Putnam's Sons, 1889–1893.

Jameson, J. F., ed. "Correspondence of John C. Calhoun," American

# Bibliography

Historical Association, *Annual Report, 1899* 2. Washington, D.C.: Government Printing Office, 1900.

Lodge, Henry Cabot, ed. *Works of Alexander Hamilton.* 12 vols. New York: G. P. Putnam's Sons, 1903.

Maclay, William, ed. *The Journal of William Maclay.* New York: Albert and Charles Boni, 1927.

Morison, Elting E., et al., eds. *Letters of Theodore Roosevelt.* 8 vols. Cambridge: Harvard University Press, 1951–1954.

Pease, Theodore, and James G. Randall. *The Diary of Orville Hickman Browning.* 2 vols. Springfield: Illinois State Historical Library, 1925.

Rowland, Dunbar. *Jefferson Davis. Constitutionalist: His Letters, Papers, and Speeches.* 10 vols. Jackson: Mississippi Department of Archives and History, 1923.

Russell, William Howard. *Diary North and South.* Boston: T. O. H. Burnham, 1863.

Sparks, Jared, ed. *Works of Benjamin Franklin.* 10 vols. Boston: Whittimore, Niles and Hall, 1856.

————, ed. *The Writings of George Washington.* 12 vols. Boston: F. Andrews, 1833–1839.

Syrett, Harold C., ed. *The Papers of Alexander Hamilton.* 15 vols. New York: Columbia University Press, 1961–1969.

Webster, Fletcher, ed. *The Writings and Speeches of Daniel Webster.* 18 vols. Boston: Little, Brown, 1903.

Williams, T. Harry, ed. *Hayes: The Diary of a President, 1875–1881.* New York: David McKay, 1964.

## D. Contemporary Newspapers and Magazines

*American Annual Cyclopaedia and Register of Important Events of the Year.* 1861, 1862, 1863, 1864. New York: D. Appleton.

*Aurora.* 1800. Philadelphia.

*Federalist*, ed. by Jacob Cooke. Middletown, Conn.: Wesleyan University Press, 1961.

*Gazette of the United States.* 1788–1789. Philadelphia.

*Harper's Weekly* 55 (June 10, 1911). New York.

*Journal of Commerce.* 1861–1865. New York.

*Life.* Sept. 12, 1960. New York.

*Massachusetts Mercury.* 1800. Boston.

*Nation* 93 (Oct. 5, 1911), 107 (Sept. 28, 1918), 131 (Aug. 6, 1930), 188 (May 30, 1959), 189 (Oct. 10, 1959). New York.

*National Intelligencer.* 1860–1865. Washington, D.C.

*New Republic* 19 (May 10, 17, 1919), 21 (Jan. 7, 1920), 26 (March

# Bibliography

30, 1921), 59 (June 19, 1929), 134 (Jan. 23, 30, 1956), 160 (May 11, 25, 1959). New York.

*Newsweek* 23 (Jan. 10, 1944), 24 (July 24, 1944), 25 (June 11, 1945), 55 (June 27, 1960).

*New York Evening Post.* 1905.

*New York Journal.* 1788.

*New York Times.* 1860–1975.

*New York Tribune.* 1861–1865.

*Niles' Weekly Register.* 1825–1836. Baltimore.

*North American Review* 155 (1892), 184 (April 19, 1907). New York.

*Publishers' Weekly* 144 (Sept. 11, 1943), 145 (Jan. 8, 15, May 20, 1944), 147 (June 9, 1945), 162 (Dec. 13, 1952), 170 (Dec. 31, 1956), 171 (May 6, 1957), 176 (Jan. 1, 1962). New York.

*Saturday Review of Literature* 27 (May 20, June 3, 10, 1944), 28 (June 16, 1945), 38 (April 23, 1955), 42 (Aug. 29, 1956). New York.

*Time* 43 (Jan. 10, 1944), 73 (June 22, 1959), 74 (Oct. 19, 1959). New York.

*United States News and World Report.* 1959–1975. Washington, D.C.

*Wall Street Journal.* 1969–1975. New York.

*World.* 1861–1865. New York.

# II. SECONDARY WORKS

## A. Post Office Department

Cullinan, Gerald. *The United States Postal Service.* New York: Praeger, 1973.

Cushing, Marshall. *Story of Our Post Office: The Greatest Government Department in all its Phases.* Boston: A. J. Thayer, 1893.

Fowler, Dorothy Ganfield. *The Cabinet Politician: The Postmasters General, 1829–1909.* New York: Columbia University Press, 1943.

Fuller, Wayne E. *The American Mail: Enlarger of the Common Life.* Chicago: University of Chicago Press, 1972.

Goldman, Albert. *The New York, N.Y. Post Office during the War Years, 1941–1945.* New York: Judicial Printing, 1949.

Kelly, Clyde Melville. *The United States Postal Policy.* New York: D. Appleton, 1931.

# Bibliography

Makris, John N. *The Silent Investigators*. New York: E. P. Dutton, 1959.

Myers, Robert J. *The Coming Collapse of the Post Office*. New York: Prentice-Hall, 1975.

Paul, James C. N., and Murray L. Schwartz. *Federal Censorship: Obscenity in the Mail*. New York: Free Press of Glencoe, 1961.

Rich, Wesley Everett. *The History of the United States Post Office to the Year 1829*. Cambridge: Harvard University Press, 1924.

Rogers, Lindsay. *The Postal Power of Congress*. Baltimore: Johns Hopkins Press, 1916.

Roper, Daniel C. *The United States Post Office: Its Past Record, Present Condition, and Potential Relation to the New World Era*. New York: Funk and Wagnalls, 1917.

# B. Biographies

Baker, Ray Stannard. *Woodrow Wilson: Life and Letters*. 8 vols. New York: Doubleday, Doran, 1939.

Beveridge, Albert J. *The Life of John Marshall*. 4 vols. Boston: Houghton Mifflin, 1916.

Bowers, Claude. *Beveridge and the Progressive Era*. New York: Literary Guild, 1932.

Broun, Heywood, and Margaret Leech. *Anthony Comstock: Roundsman of the Law*. New York: Albert and Charles Boni, 1927.

Cramer, C. H. *Royal Bob: The Life of Robert G. Ingersoll*. Indianapolis: Bobbs, Merrill, 1952.

Curtis, George Tichnor. *Life of James Buchanan*. 2 vols. New York: Harper, 1883.

Fuess, Claude M. *Daniel Webster*. 2 vols. Boston: Little, Brown, 1930.
———. *Life of Caleb Cushing*. 2 vols. New York: Harcourt, Brace, 1923.

Gibbons, Herbert Adams. *John Wanamaker*. 2 vols. New York: Harper, 1926.

Gresham, Matilda. *Life of Walter Quintin Gresham, 1832–1895*. 2 vols. Chicago: Rand McNally, 1919.

Harper, Robert S. *Lincoln and the Press*. New York: McGraw Hill, 1951.

Jervey, Theodore. *Robert Y. Hayne and His Times*. New York: Macmillan, 1909.

Johnson, Allen, and Dumas Malone, eds. *Dictionary of American Biography*. 20 vols. New York: Charles Scribner's Sons, 1928–1936.

# Bibliography

La Follette, Belle and Fola. *Robert M. La Follette.* 2 vols. New York: Macmillan, 1953.

Lynch, Dennis Tilden. *An Epoch and a Man: Martin Van Buren and His Times.* New York: Horace Liveright, 1929.

McMaster, John Bach. *Benjamin Franklin as a Man of Letters.* Boston: Houghton Mifflin, 1887.

Meigs, William M. *Life of Thomas Hart Benton.* Philadelphia: J. B. Lippincott, 1904.

Parks, Joseph Howard. *Felix Grundy: Champion of Democracy.* Baton Rouge: Louisiana State University Press, 1940.

Parton, James. *Life and Times of Benjamin Franklin.* 2 vols. Boston: James R. Osgood, 1953.

Pratt, Fletcher. *Stanton, Lincoln's Secretary of War.* New York: W. W. Norton, 1953.

Pusey, Merlo. *Charles Evans Hughes.* 2 vols. New York: Macmillan, 1951.

Rovere, Richard. *Senator Joe McCarthy.* New York: Harcourt, Brace, 1959.

Schurz, Carl. *Life of Henry Clay.* 2 vols. Boston: Houghton Mifflin, 1894.

Smith, William Ernest. *The Blair Family.* 2 vols. New York: Macmillan, 1933.

Summers, Festus P. *William L. Wilson and Tariff Reform.* New Brunswick, N.J.: Rutgers University Press, 1953.

Thomas, Benjamin P., and Harold M. Hyman. *Stanton, The Life and Times of Lincoln's Secretary of War.* New York: Alfred A. Knopf, 1962.

Trumbull, Charles Gallaudet. *Anthony Comstock, Fighter.* New York: Fleming H. Revell, 1913.

Upham, Charles. *Life of Timothy Pickering.* 4 vols. Boston: Little, Brown, 1873.

Van Deusen, Glyndon. *The Life of Henry Clay.* Boston: Little, Brown, 1937.

Weisenburger, Francis P. *The Life of John McLean: A Politician on the United States Supreme Court.* Columbus: Ohio State University Press, 1937.

Wiltse, Charles M. *John C. Calhoun: Nullifier.* Indianapolis: Bobbs-Merrill, 1949.

Woodward, C. Vann. *Tom Watson: Agrarian Rebel.* New York: Macmillian, 1938.

Younger, Edward. *John A. Kasson: Politics and Diplomacy from Lincoln to McKinley.* Iowa City: State Historical Society of Iowa, 1955.

# Bibliography

## C. Books on Background Topics

Baral, Robert. *Turn West on 23rd Street*. New York: Fleet Publishing, 1965.

Bowers, Claude. *The Party Battles of the Jacksonian Period*. Boston: Houghton Mifflin, 1922.

Burnett, Edmund Cody. *The Continental Congress*. New York: Macmillan, 1941.

Chafee, Zechariah. *Government and Mass Communications*. 2 vols. Chicago: University of Chicago Press, 1947.

Fraenkel, Osmond Kessler. *Our Civil Liberties*. New York: Viking Press, 1944.

Hamilton, John C. *History of the Republic of the United States of America as Traced in the Writings of Alexander Hamilton*. 6 vols. Philadelphia: J. B. Lippincott, 1864.

Kelly, Alfred H., and Winfred A. Harbison. *The American Constitution*. New York: W. W. Norton, 1963.

Kilpatrick, James Jackson. *The Smut Peddlers*. New York: Doubleday, 1960.

Miller, John C. *Crisis in Freedom*. Boston: Little, Brown, 1951.

Mock, James R. *Censorship, 1917*. Princeton, N.J.: Princeton University Press, 1941.

Murray, Robert K. *Red Scare: A Study in National Hysteria, 1919–1920*. Minneapolis: Minnesota University Press, 1955.

Nye, Russel B. *Fettered Freedom*. East Lansing: Michigan State University Press, 1949.

Patterson, Giles J. *Free Speech and a Free Press*. Boston: Little, Brown, 1939.

Paxson, Frederic L. *America at War*. Boston: Houghton Mifflin, 1939.

Peterson, H. C., and Gilbert C. Fite. *Opponents of War, 1917–1918*. Madison: University of Wisconsin Press, 1957.

Randall, James G. *Constitutional Problems under Lincoln*. New York: D. Appleton, 1926.

Sanders, Jennings B. *Evolution of Executive Departments of the Continental Congress*. Chapel Hill: University of North Carolina Press, 1935.

Savage, W. Sherman. *The Controversy over the Distribution of Abolition Literature, 1830–1860*. Washington, D.C.: Association for the Study of Negro Life and History, 1938.

Short, Lloyd Milton. *The Development of National Administrative Organization in the United States*. Baltimore: Johns Hopkins Press, 1923.

# Bibliography

Swisher, Carl Brent. *American Constitutional Development.* Boston: Houghton Mifflin, 1954.

Taylor, Hannis. *Origin and Growth of the American Constitution.* Boston: Houghton Mifflin, 1911.

White, Leonard D. *The Federalists: A Study in Administrative History.* New York: Macmillan, 1948.

―――. *The Jacksonians.* New York: Macmillan, 1954.

―――. *The Jeffersonians.* New York: Macmillan, 1951.

―――. *The Republican Era.* New York: Macmillan, 1958.

## III. Magazine Articles

Abrams, Ray H. "The Jeffersonian Copperhead Newspaper, *Pennsylvania Magazine of History and Biography* 57 (July, 1933): 260–88.

Eaton, Clement. "Censorship of Southern Mails," *American Historical Review* 48 (Jan., 1943): 266–81.

Randall, James G. "The Newspaper Problem in its Bearing upon Military Secrecy during the Civil War," *American Historical Review* 23 (Jan., 1918): 303–23.

Sanger, Donald Bridgmen. "The Chicago Times and the Civil War," *Mississippi Valley Historical Review* 17 (March, 1931): 557–81.

Schwartz, Murray L., and James C. N. Paul. "Foreign Communist Propaganda in the Mails: A Report on Some Problems of Federal Censorship," *University of Pennsylvania Law Review* 107 (March, 1959): 621–66.

―――. "Obscenity in the Mails: A Comment on Some Problems of Federal Censorship," *University of Pennsylvania Law Review* 106 (Dec., 1957): 214–53.

―――. "Propaganda in the Mails: A Proscript," *University of Pennsylvania Law Review* 107 (April, 1959): 796–801.

Smith, William. "The Colonial Post Office," *American Historical Review* 21 (Jan., 1916): 258–76.

# Index

# Index

# Index

# Index

Dixon, James, 57

Donaldson, Jesse M.: mail identification bill, 149; power to impound, 167; definition of obscene matter, 170

*Donaldson, Postmaster General v. Read Magazine*, 164–65

Douglas, William O.: *San Francisco v. Leif Heilberg*, 159; Read Magazine case, 164; *United States v. Halseth*, 166; *Esquire* case, 169; Roth case, 174; Ginzburg case, 182

Duell, R. Holland, 39–40

Dulski, Thaddeus, 189–90

*Dunlop v. United States*, 78

Eastman, Max, 114

Eighth Amendment, 107, 165

Ellenbogen, Henry, 141

Emerson, Henry L., 124

Enloe, Benjamin A., 80

Espionage: act of June 1917, 109–13; Trading with the Enemy Act, 116–17; amendment in 1918, 118–19; sedition bills, 1919–1921, 124; repeal of act of 1918, 125; amended in 1940, 144

Evarts, William M., 58–59, 218n12

Ewing, Thomas, 23

*Ex parte John L. Rapier*, 85–86

Farley, James, 140, 143

Farnsworth, John F., 59

Federal Commission on Obscenity and Pornography, 186, 201

Field, Stephen J., 65

Fifth Amendment, 165, 174

Firearms: subject to state law, 129–30; act of 1927, 130; Second Amendment, 130; switchblade knives nonmailable, 195; concealed weapons, 195; gun control law, 195; officers exempt, 232n10

First Amendment: 66; obscenity law, 69; newspaper advertisements of lotteries, 81–86; Thaw trial, 100; Espionage Act, 113, 119–20; violations, 115; *Mil-*

*waukee Leader* case, 121; act of Congress unconstitutional, 159; fraud orders, 165; obscenity, 174; dissenters in Ginzburg case, 182

Fitzsimmons, Thomas, 11

Fong, Hiram, 191

Ford, Gerald R., 189

Foreign Affairs Department, 6

Foreign divorces, 139–40, 140

Forsyth, John, 26

Fortas, Abe, 182

Fourth Amendment, 66, 165

Fowler, H. Robert, 104

Frankfurter, Felix, 163

Franking privilege: members of Congress, 6, 10; postmasters, 18, 207n51

Franklin, Benjamin: deputy postmaster general for American colonies, 1–2; postmaster general, 1775–1776, 3, 203n3,5, 204 n11, 205n24

Fraud: protest of mayor of New York, 27; green goods swindle, 79–80; act of March 2, 1889, 80; bond investment houses, 90; section broadened in 1909, 103; Hitchcock's attack, 106; land and mining deals, 106, 108; grain futures, 134–36; sale of securities, 138; after World War II, 162–68; freedom of religion, 162–63; mail essential part of fraud, 163; newspapers' advertising stock speculation, 221n23; incorrect stamping of metal, 227n33; falsified statements, 228n41; land frauds, 228n44; false advertisements of seeds, 234n36; mailing of check, 237n4

Fraud Orders: lottery cases, 60, 66–67; Louisiana State Lottery, 67–68; obscenity cases, 79; regular letters, 87; judicial safeguards, 94; number issued, 94; bill to limit defeated, 95–96; use by Hitchcock, 106–07; power to is-

258

# Index

# Index

# Index

# Index

# Index

265

# Index